Distributed Learning

This Reader forms part of the Open University course *Understanding Distributed and Flexible Learning* (H805), which, together with two other courses, *Applications of Information Technology in Open and Distance Education* (H802) and *Implementation of Open and Distance Learning* (H804), comprises the Postgraduate Programme in Open and Distance Education.

This programme of courses can lead to professionally recognised qualifications at Certificate, Diploma and Masters levels. It offers a unique opportunity to study the theory and practice of open and distance education in the company of Institute of Educational Technology experts who are now using information technology to re-invent open and distance learning. Working with them you will be at the forefront of the latest developments as they happen. *Applications of Information Technology in Open and Distance Education* has recently won a teaching fellowship, which awards outstanding practice in teaching and learning.

Open and distance learning is increasingly the first choice of adult learners and various kinds of distributed learning are making campus learning more flexible. Many kinds of professionals contribute to this success – teachers, trainers, support staff, educational technologists, media specialists, learning systems managers, librarians, learning centre advisory staff – and these courses have something to offer them all.

For further information about the Open University or details of these or other study options, please contact the Call Centre, the Open University, Walton Hall, Milton Keynes, MK7 6AA. Telephone: +44 (0)1908 653231. Fax: +44 (0)1908 654806. Email: Ces-Gen@open.ac.uk Website: www.open.ac.uk

Distributed Learning

Social and cultural approaches
to practice

Edited by Mary R. Lea and
Kathy Nicoll

London and New York

First published 2002 by RoutledgeFalmer
11 New Fetter Lane, London EC4P 4EE

Simultaneously published in the USA and Canada
by RoutledgeFalmer
29 West 35th Street, New York, NY 10001

RoutledgeFalmer is an imprint of the Taylor & Francis Group

Typeset in Goudy by RefineCatch Limited, Bungay, Suffolk
Printed and bound in Great Britain by
TJ International, Padstow, Cornwall

British Library Cataloguing in Publication Data
A catalogue record for this book is available from the British Library

Library of Congress Cataloging in Publication Data
Distributed learning: social and cultural approaches to practice/edited
by Mary R. Lea and Kathy Nicoll.
    p. cm.
  Includes bibliographical references and index.
  1. Distance education—Social aspects. 2. Open learning—Social
aspects. 3. Information technology—Social aspects. I. Lea, Mary R.
(Mary Rosalind), 1950– II. Nicoll, Kathy, 1954–

LC5803.L43 D56 2002
378.1'75—dc21
                                                              2001048106

ISBN 0-415-26808-7 (hbk)
ISBN 0-415-26809-5 (pbk)

Contents

Contributors

Stephen Billett is a Senior Lecturer in the School of Vocational, Technology and Arts Education, Faculty of Education, Griffith University, Australia. He has worked as an educator, educational administrator, teacher educator and professional development practitioner within vocational education. He was, until recently, Director of the Centre for Learning and Work Research, which focuses on learning in and for the workplace.

James Cornford is a Principal Research Associate in the Centre for Urban and Regional Development Studies (CURDS) at the University of Newcastle, UK. His research is concerned with the implications of information and communications technologies for organisations and the economic and social development of cities and regions.

Charles Crook received a PhD from Cambridge University and developed a research and teaching career in developmental psychology, with a special interest in educational practice and sociocultural theories of cognitive development. He is currently Reader in Psychology at Loughborough University, UK. His recent research has concerned collaborative learning in primary school settings and the cultural context of undergraduate learning.

Richard Edwards is Professor of Education at the University of Stirling, UK. He has written and researched extensively on post-modernism, globalisation and lifelong learning. His most recent book, with Robin Usher, is *Globalisation and Pedagogy: Space, Place and Identity* (Routledge, 2000).

Gill Kirkup is a Senior Lecturer in the Institute of Educational Technology, the Open University. She has worked for many years on equal opportunities and gender issues, in particular in the use of ICTs in post-school education, and has written extensively in this area. She is an active member of a number of networks concerned with EO and ICTs.

Michele Knobel is an Adjunct Associate Professor in the Faculty of Education and Creative Arts at Central Queensland University and an Investigardora Titular in the Universidad Nacional Autónoma de México (UNAM). She researches and writes mainly in the areas of literacy, new technologies and youth culture. When offline she enjoys cycling through the Mexican countryside.

Colin Lankshear is Adjunct Professor in the Faculty of Education and Creative Arts at Central Queensland University and Heritage Fellow of the Mexican Council of Science and Technology, based in the Universidad Nacional Autónoma de México (UNAM). He has written widely in the areas of literacy, critical pedagogy and educational appropriations of new technologies. He has a passion for classic British motorcycles.

Jean Lave is an anthropologist whose work is informed by theories of social-practice. She has done ethnographic research on apprenticeship among Vai and Gola tailors in Liberia, on everyday maths practices in Orange County and on how elite British port wine merchant families in Portugal continue to 'get to be British'. All of these studies are linked to her continuing interest in the politics of everyday life.

Mary R. Lea is a Lecturer in the Institute of Educational Technology, the Open University. She has wide experience of research and practice in student writing and academic literacies, recently co-editing with Barry Stierer, *Student Writing in Higher Education: New Contexts* (SRHE/Open University Press, 2000). Her present research is in cultural and linguistic issues in electronic global course delivery.

Alison Lee is Associate Professor in the Faculty of Education, University of Technology, Sydney, Australia. She has researched extensively in the areas of curriculum and literacy. Her most recent research project focused on the experiences of research students in doctoral programmes.

Barbara Mayor is a Lecturer in the Faculty of Education and Language Studies at the Open University. Her teaching and research interests include bilingualism and code switching, cultural diversity and the role of English as a global language. She has recently worked on two projects, to be published by the British Council, investigating aspects of the IELTS test.

Wendy Morgan is a Senior Lecturer in the School of Cultural and Language Studies in Education at Queensland University of Technology and Deputy Director, Research Centre for Language, Literacy and Diversity. Her current research includes novices' hypertextual reading and writing, relationships between ICTs and teachers' theories-in-action, critical literacy and aesthetic theories and practices.

Kathy Nicoll is a Lecturer in Education at the University of Stirling, UK. She has worked extensively in open and distance learning and adult education in Australia and the UK. Her research interests are in the areas of post-structuralism, policy studies and professional development.

Michael Peters is Research Professor of Education at the University of Glasgow and holds a personal chair at the University of Auckland. He is also Adjunct Professor of Communications Studies at the Auckland University of Technology. He has research interests in educational theory and policy and in contemporary philosophy. He has published some twenty books and over 100 articles in international journals in these areas.

Neil Pollock is a Research Associate in the Centre for Urban and Regional Development Studies (CURDS) at the University of Newcastle, UK. He is currently undertaking research, funded by the ESRC, into the development and implementation of a new student management system.

Anne L. Russell lectures at the Queensland University of Technology, Brisbane, Australia in the School of Cultural and Language Studies in Education. In the open learning Graduate Diploma in Education (Teacher-Librarianship) Course, she explores innovative interactive strategies and focuses on how personality preferences influence communications within information environments.

David R. Russell is Professor of Rhetoric and Professional Communication at Iowa State University. His book *Writing in the Academic Disciplines, 1870–1990* examines the history of writing instruction in the USA. He has published widely on writing across the curriculum, drawing on activity theory and genre theory.

Michael Ryan is a Senior Lecturer in the Faculty of Education at Queensland University of Technology, Australia. He researches the development of network-based learning environments, particularly those where the focus lies in academic discourses. He teaches undergraduate and postgraduate students who learn about conceptualising and designing effective technological learning environments.

Joan Swann is a Senior Lecturer in the Faculty of Education and Language Studies at the Open University. Her teaching and research interests include the English language and various aspects of sociolinguistics. Recent publications include *Introducing Sociolinguistics* (with Raj Mesthrie, Ana Deumert and William Leap, Edinburgh University Press, 2000).

Mary Thorpe is a Professor and Director of the Institute of Educational Technology at the Open University. Since joining the University in 1975, she has evaluated course materials, tuition and learner support systems, and authored courses in Third World Studies, Adult Learning, and Open and Distance Learning. She has contributed to the development of courses for the professional accreditation of teachers in Higher Education.

Etienne Wenger is a globally recognised leader in the field of communities of practice and their application to the design of organisations. Author of *Communities of Practice: Learning, Meaning, and Identity* (Cambridge University Press, 1998), he helps organisations apply these ideas through consulting, workshops, online teaching and public speaking.

Editors' introduction

This edited volume sets out to explore what it means to think about distributed learning from a social and cultural, practice-based approach. We hope that the book will serve as a useful introduction to those working across the spectrum of post-compulsory education who are finding themselves having to explore the use of new information technologies for teaching and learning in both face-to-face and open and distance learning settings. In the first section of this Introduction, we explore what we mean by the term 'distributed learning'. We then contextualise these approaches against the backdrop of the changing context of post-compulsory education, including the breaking down of the historical distinction between distance and face-to-face teaching, and moves towards the globalisation of course delivery. Finally, we introduce you to the different chapters in this volume.

Exploring distributed learning

We recognise that the audience for this volume will be diverse and that as practitioners you will be coming from a range of different contexts. Our aim has been to create a book that is able to address and acknowledge this diversity and that has something of value to say to all our potential readers; at the same time, we recognise that some chapters will resonate with readers more than others depending on their background and experience. The chapters themselves also indicate diversity, not only in terms of the theoretical perspectives they draw upon, but also because they embrace many different writing styles ranging from personal accounts of practice to more traditional academic texts. We see this as a strength of the volume, and believe that it both represents and mirrors what is happening in many practice contexts where practitioners now find themselves working together with others who are informed by very different disciplinary and vocational contexts. This can result in an eclectic mix of ideas and perspectives, which, at the end of the day, need to be translated into real grounded practices. We hope that this volume will help practitioners to think about the ways in which those coming from very different academic traditions and backgrounds can draw on the perspectives of others to inform their own practice.

The idea for this volume developed during the preparation of a new course for the Open University's Masters in Open and Distance Education. The MA programme is delivered globally and attracts students from many different areas of post-compulsory education: for example, higher education; the health service; the voluntary sector and language teaching. Students are situated across the world, and therefore bring very different experiences of education, work, culture and language to the course. In itself, this diversity has become a strength of the course; it indicates the variety of practices that are being engaged in by students as they undertake their studies and communicate with each other, their tutors and the course team with the aid of computer conferencing, e-mail and web resources. Although the use of new information technologies plays a substantial part in course delivery and creating a supportive learning environment, we have learned to reaffirm and recognise the value and importance of the use of more traditional technologies, for example, the use of printed course material in global course delivery.

We know from our own experience that the use of the term 'distributed learning' is in many senses a confusing one. As with other terms used in today's post-compulsory education – 'open', 'distance', 'flexible' – there is no clear definition of this term. In some cases, particularly in the USA, distributed learning has become synonymous with distance education and embraces all that is not face-to-face teaching. It is also being used to denote the shift of open and distance education towards the use of new information technologies, commonly called information and communication technologies (ICTs), for course delivery, in preference to print-based courses. In other contexts, where the focus is more broadly upon learners and learning, it is being used to mirror and build upon work in distributed cognition (Salomon 1993), which views learning as distributed among individuals. In still other contexts, it is a descriptor for a body of work in Human Computer Interaction (HCI). In this volume, our main concern is with the relationship between learning and technologies (both new and old), and therefore we take a very broad definition for our use of the term 'distributed learning'. As it is being taken up and explored in this volume, we suggest that distributed learning is concerned with:

- the breaking down of traditional boundaries between face-to-face and open and distance education;
- the growth of new information technologies as mediational means in distributed learning settings;
- changes in our conception of the ways in which learning and teaching are distributed across space and time;
- learning as a shared enterprise distributed between individuals in several different contexts;
- learning as distributed between diverse contexts and not tied to formal institutional settings;
- the relationship between the global and local contexts of learning.

A quick review of the literature in the different contexts in which this term is used indicates that one overarching feature of distributed learning is of an often unproblematic relationship between the learner and the use of new technologies. For example, there is a belief that, as long as we focus upon teaching students the requisite skills of using a computer – what is sometimes referred to as 'computer literacy' – learning will be enhanced. There is rarely any suggestion that the use of ICT might, at best, merely serve to reinforce the existing practices of teaching and learning in tertiary education, or, at worst, actually result in less effective practices. As Crook indicates in Chapter 9, educational developers often seem confident about the way harnessing ICT results in better learning. In contrast, the authors in this volume challenge the idea of a simple and uncomplicated relationship between learning and technologies and, in doing so, draw upon examples of practice in a wide range of post-compulsory settings. Most recognise the value of ICT in post-compulsory settings but are cautious of adopting a position which suggests that the use of new information technologies in education has already changed – or has the capacity in the future to radically change – the nature of education.

The sociologist Castells, in his explorations of the 'networked' society (Castells 1996), makes a strong case against technological determinism, which would see changes in society as being a direct result of the introduction of technology, with no other elements at play. His work is concerned with the broader economic and social structures, and processes, of the global capitalist economy and not with education specifically; but we believe that we, too, need to be mindful of this position – the challenge to technological determinism – in our explorations of distributed learning.

The chapters in this volume, then, indicate the need to move away from a technologically driven view of changes in post-compulsory education and training and to recognise the use of ICTs for what they are: part of a range of media used in specific social and cultural contexts of learning and teaching. One of the contributors to this volume reminded us recently that 'the problem with technology is not a technological one' (J. Cornford, personal communication, informed by Heidegger 1977), reaffirming our focus upon the social and cultural aspects of distributed learning. We see developments in new information technologies taking place alongside broader structural changes in education linked to both global and local policy changes; we explore these in more depth later in this Introduction, when we consider these changes and the historical perspective in more detail.

One of the purposes of this book is to introduce readers to several different theoretical perspectives that we hope they will find useful when thinking about and conceptualising their own practices of teaching and learning. These are informed by several different disciplinary traditions: anthropology, psychology, sociology, philosophy, economics, linguistics, geography and education itself. There are inevitably both overlaps and sometimes possibly contradictions between the ways in which different theoretical frames are being developed and used by authors in this book. However, what characterises all the chapters is an overriding focus upon social and cultural theoretical frames in understanding learning as practice. Adopting such an approach, we are acknowledging the ways in which the last 20 years of the twentieth century were characterised by what has been referred to as the 'social turn', as many disciplines began to move their focus away from the individual towards social and cultural considerations of human behaviour. Gee, for example, suggests that such developments were a reaction both to the behaviourism of the early twentieth century and the cognitive revolution that took place in the 1960s and 1970s, both of which concentrated upon the individual mind (Gee 2000). These directions can be found across disciplines and fields of study within the social sciences, humanities and even the natural sciences, in explorations of the social and cultural practices inherent in knowledge formation. Although in some senses these could be seen, primarily, as intellectual movements, such debates have been influential in education, where people are often more pragmatically interested in teaching and learning. Approaches that adopt a social and cultural approach to teaching and learning recognise that learning cannot be reduced to a set of cognitive skills, played out by an individual in a context-free environment. Increasingly, researchers from several different disciplinary perspectives have begun to explore the importance of context in understanding how people learn (Chaiklin and Lave 1993; Cole *et al.* 1997). They have concentrated their attention upon the social dimensions of learning and the cultural and social practices that learners participate in within different contexts. For many, learning is seen as situated social activity, and many of the chapters in this volume adopt such an approach to learning with their focus upon meaning and identity.

As we have indicated, there has recently been a burgeoning of interest in the harnessing of new information technologies in learning contexts and a dominant rhetoric in the post-compulsory education sector championing the marvels of ICT and the vision that it can hold out for the future, in particular for dramatic changes in post-compulsory education and the development of global virtual universities. However, those who are already adopting social and cultural approaches to teaching and learning have begun to take a more tempered approach towards developments in the use of new information technologies and, in so doing, have attempted to move away from a simple position of technological determinism. We believe that the chapters in this book add constructively to these debates by considering the contextualisation of both new and old technologies in specific learning settings and that they are neither used in isolation nor predictable. They are always associated with different sets of practices depending upon the part they play for the learner in any context. Neither the technological hardware nor software results in particular ways of learning. The different ways in which technologies are taken up in social contexts through diverse practices illustrate why, if we are concerned with learning, we need to be concerned with the social and cultural practices that surround technologies in different learning environments.

Changing contexts

In the preceding section, we suggested that distributed learning acknowledges the breaking down of the distinction between face-to-face and distance education. There is now an expectation that learners who study at a distance are able to communicate with students and tutors within electronic tutorial groups online, wherever they are based. Physical distance is conceptualised in different ways when we are able to send an e-mail to a fellow student thousands of miles away and expect to get a response within minutes. At the same time, changes in face-to-face institutions, the traditional bastions of higher education and training, with large student numbers, vast lectures and the lack of individual tutorial support, mean that, here too, new information technologies are being used for both course delivery and tutorial support. Students may find themselves instructed to download lecture notes from the web or engage in a computer conference online in place of a face-to-face seminar or tutorial. In this sense, distribution of learning is taking place in many different contexts.

Another dimension of distribution lies in the increased understanding of learning being a shared enterprise, and moves away from conceptualising learning as an individual cognitive activity concerned with the acquisition of a set of skills that can be transferred with ease from context to context. Lave and Wenger's seminal work on communities of practice (see Chapter 3) explores situated learning and the role of legitimate peripheral participation in helping novice members of a community engage in a particular community's situated practices, and thus learn to participate as full members of that community. Learning then becomes both a joint enterprise and a situated enterprise, something one does with others in a particular learning context and not only confined to formal educational institutions.

This leads us on to a further dimension of distributed learning: that of the recognition that learning is distributed across contexts and does not only exist in formal settings of post-compulsory education. With policy directions in many countries embracing the concept of lifelong learning, there is an increasing recognition that adults are always learners in their work, home and community context, even when they are not engaged in what we might describe as formal education. Debates around lifelong learning and the breaking down of a binary divide between formal educational institutions and the workplace as sites of learning are just some of the important changes that have taken place in the context of post-compulsory teaching and learning during the past decade. In many countries, there has been a shift from elite to mass post-compulsory education systems; simultaneously, previous boundaries between education and work have been opened up for more diverse cohorts of learners. Many post-compulsory education institutions have been pressured by governments to find ways of diversifying and extending their course offerings. Education policies have increased access and participation in learning but this has gone hand in hand with the setting up of quasi-market conditions, which have encouraged the integration of post-compulsory education systems into national economies. This is one of the mechanisms for the building of, and response to, the 'information age' or 'knowledge society' with its focus upon the commodification of knowledge, as knowledge is bought and sold like any other commodity. Here the production and global exchange of information and knowledge are taken as critical factors in the success of current and future economies, and lifelong learning is required for individuals and workers if they are to contribute to success in a world of increasing uncertainty and change. The 'information age', 'knowledge society' and 'lifelong learning' are thus heralded in many quarters as learning has gained emphasis and importance. The emphasis on learning and massification of systems is occurring within many countries, although its extent and features differ from context to context (Perraton 2000). Its occurrence can be placed in the context of a more general and gradual expansion of post-compulsory education over the past 40 years or so.

Hand in hand with such change has been a proliferation of forms of 'distributed', 'open', 'distance', 'flexible' and 'off-campus' learning. All are concerned in some way with the mediation of learning at a distance through various forms of technology, which facilitate expansion and massification, through overcoming constraints of space and time in learning. The physical proximity of teachers and learners within institutional spaces or sites of learning and at specific times is no longer necessary. There is no need for bodies to be physically gathered together for formal learning to take place. In a sense, this is nothing new, since correspondence and distance education have been overcoming the barriers of distance for many decades. What is new is the plethora of different technologies that are available to bring people together – telephone, radio, video, the web – all of which allow teachers and learners synchronous communication with one another, even though they may be distributed as individuals across geographical space. Text-based course materials, audio tapes, radio and television programmes, and computer-based course materials enable interaction to occur at a time and place of the learner's own choosing, at work or in the home, and without the immediate or physical presence of a teacher. Computer conferencing enables asynchronous communication between students and students as well as between students and tutors. Course designers have always had a range of technologies at their disposal but the variety of technologies available today surpasses what was available in the past and allows a convergence of appropriate media for distributed learning.

As learning has become increasingly distributed across space and time, distinctions that have traditionally been held between on- and off-campus education have become increasingly blurred. It is less common now to find an institution where teaching occurs solely through face-to-face interaction at a physical site. Many institutions draw on a range of technologies (both new and old) to make their courses more accessible, enriched and enhanced, and offer greater choice in the times and places of study. Whereas previously institutions identified themselves in part through their dominant mode of offering – as on- or off-campus (correspondence, external, open or distance learning colleges and universities) – such distinctions are now increasingly difficult to maintain, requiring those who teach, design, develop and administer courses to think about their work anew. The emergence of new communication and information technologies produces new demands and expectations of learning and a requirement to assess not merely their potentials but also their limitations for learning; in Chapter 10, Cornford and Pollock caution us to be mindful of the value of the physical campus as a site of learning.

ICT is commonly promoted through governments and the media as mere 'technical' improvement to the learning systems: enhancing the efficiency of systems, competition within them, and increasing access and choice for the learner. Technology can thus be viewed unproblematically as a mere vehicle for the same kinds of communications that have always taken place between teacher and learner, where pedagogy and the organisation of learning remain unaffected. However, this view masks the extent and complexity of the changes taking place, of the requirements for substantial institutional change and of reconfigured practices and understandings of pedagogy (cf. Lankshear *et al.* 2000), all of which are explored by authors in this volume. New information technologies do not simply support and make more efficient existing learning and teaching practices; rather they reconfigure them and require new ones.

Subtleties of learning, and the social and cultural systems and practices upon which they rely, and to which they contribute, may become more or less visible. The influence of new information technologies on learning and on understandings of learning and teaching may therefore be far-reaching and the broader effects profound. A view of technologised learning as technical improvement thus elides the extent and complexities of the reconfigurations required. In this, there are issues and questions, relevant to managers, administrators and policymakers and members of the public, as well as to learners and teachers, that may be important to recognise.

The changing context within which this volume is set also includes the context of globalisation (see Edwards, Chapter 6), which has become a key area of debate in recent years, and has particular implications as institutions of tertiary education look ever further afield for students and for markets for their courses (Mason 1998). The idea of globalisation can suggest an increasing uniformity or 'homogenisation' of economic, social and cultural worlds, in which the advancing influence of economic exchange through multinational corporations takes hold and displaces local differences. There are increasing senses of interconnectedness around a world that feels smaller than before. Globalisation and the commodification of education have gone hand in hand, and the tertiary sector is increasingly looking to offer global course delivery, harnessing the use of new information technologies to do this in apparently uncomplicated ways. The complex relationship between the global and the local context is nowhere more evident than in global courses using ICT for course delivery. Increased attention is being paid to the ways in which powerful educational institutions, normally in the developed world, are now able to offer globally delivered courses to students situated anywhere in the world. Increasingly, there are challenges to the way in which the view that globalisation leads to homogenisation has been presented as unproblematic. Gayol and Schied (1997) and Goodfellow et al. (2001) indicate the need to be mindful of the relationship between the global delivery of courses and the local contexts within which the learner is situated. Students may be studying a global course, but their place and context of study is in many respects a very local one, and they may be unfamiliar with the 'academic ground rules' of the institution delivering the course, from, for example, the UK, USA or Australia.

Developments in new information technologies have followed swiftly upon the global spread of English, which accelerated at an incredible speed during the last decades of the twentieth century. In this sense, globalisation and the dominance of English as a global language have gone hand in hand. In Chapter 7, Mayor and Swann explore what it means for non-native speakers of English to study at a distance with a traditional print-based technology, and draw our attention to the complex relationship between the local context and the implications this has for learners studying what was designed as a globally delivered course. They illustrate with clarity the importance of understanding the local in global contexts.

As education has been reconfigured as an element of the market, previous ideals and values of education are put aside in a new focus on the criterion of efficiency. There has been an emphasis on the skills required to optimise the functioning of the economy. This raises issues and questions as to the knowledge and skills to be taught and the role of the teacher. What becomes important is not knowledge as 'truth' but knowledge as a commodity to be sold. The added value of learning to the economy and society may be in the ability of individuals and groups to reconfigure information in new ways, and in ways that can contribute to added 'performativity', rather than in the production of knowledge, as it has been previously understood. The very certainty of the status of our knowledge, learning, teaching and researching is undermined and currently undergoing profound questioning, in part through the influence of changing understandings of epistemology and the use of web-based technologies. These technologies help blur traditional distinctions between disciplinary and other knowledges, and between information and knowledge. These implications are explored in Chapter 1 by Lankshear, Peters and Knobel, who argue that 'educationists who avoid asking questions of the epistemological significance and implications of their practices involving the new information and communications technologies do so at their peril'.

Finally, we turn to the issue of literacies and the way features associated with distributed forms of learning raise crucial questions about literacy. Not least questions about the multi-modal nature of texts, which, unlike traditional printed text, now require 'readers' to make sense of visual and written information at the same time (cf. Goodman and Graddol 1996), for example, in web documents. Several of the contributors to this volume explore issues concerned with changing literacies in relation to changing technologies. In Chapter 12, Edwards, Nicoll and Lee suggest that, with the changing demands of learning, the question of literacy ought to loom large.

They explore the idea of 'flexible literacies' and the literacy demands on the learner and teacher within contexts of distributed learning. Changing forms and modes of textual and electronically mediated literate practices are often in play in curriculum and pedagogy without any explicit intention or attention. Literacies cannot be adequately separated out as skills from the contexts of their use; they are social meaning-making processes through which media, meanings, identities and communities are transformed. This raises questions about the complexities of the literacy demands upon students within distributed learning environments, and the kinds of media, meanings, identities and communities with which teachers and learners are working. The increased emphasis on computer-mediated learning creates considerable pressures for curriculum and pedagogy with attendant new and diverse forms of textual contexts and practices and, with that, arguably, changing literacies. In Chapter 2, Morgan, Russell and Ryan explore the ways in which literacy, technology and learning are intertwined and suggest that there is nothing new about a relationship between literacy practices and technologies. Literacies are not a set of decontextualised cognitive skills but a set of social practices with an intricate relationship to the technologies of which they are a part; that is, they are both shaped by and shape one another.

It is against this background of the changing context of tertiary education – including the breaking down of distinctions between traditional higher education contexts and distance education, between formal and informal sites of learning, a focus on 'lifelong learning', globalisation, the increased commodification of knowledge, the inexorable spread of English, the complex relationship between technologies and learning and the concomitant practices that accompany such changes – that the chapters in this volume are set, each contributing a particular perspective concerned with social and cultural approaches to distributed learning.

The chapters in this volume

In Chapter 1, Colin Lankshear, Michael Peters and Michele Knobel explore the ways in which the status of knowledge is being challenged in what they call 'the digital age'. They suggest that traditional educational practices are being challenged by the use of ICTs in educational contexts and that we may well need to rethink how we conceptualise knowledge in the future. Although they direct their argument towards the use of ICTs in schools and the need for teachers and other professionals to be aware of changes in epistemological assumptions and beliefs, their argument is as valid for those of us working in post-compulsory settings. They illustrate how we need to look closely at what we count as knowledge and truth within new contexts of learning, and to be careful not to assume that these will remain stable, but rather to find ways to help learners to operate successfully in increasingly changing contexts. Their primary focus is upon the use of the internet and its implications for our understanding of the relationship between knowledge construction and information. Drawing upon the work of Lyotard (1984), they suggest that we need to be aware of the ways in which the status of knowledge in relation to ICTs is less concerned with truth and more with its possible usefulness.

In Chapter 2, Wendy Morgan, Anne Russell and Michael Ryan explore the nature of changed educational practices in terms of a complex relationship between literacy, learning and technology. They suggest that this is not a tidy relationship and that it will never be possible to predict in any particular context the kinds of implications that using new technologies will have for learning. They develop their argument through discussion of a specific case study concerned with the use of a communal hypertext space on a fiction and poetry course. They explore how literacies, technologies and ways of learning always need to be understood as sets of practices rather than as merely 'things'. Introducing new technologies to the tertiary classroom will not result in particular ways of student learning, and we need to move away from conceptualising instructional design as a stable technology with stable structures. The authors also remind us that all learning and all forms of literacy are mediated by technology but that over time older and more familiar technologies, for example, print, become invisible. They examine the ways in which information becomes knowledge through particular forms of literacies, technologies, learning and teaching, drawing upon actor network theory which sees technologies as far more than inert objects and which is concerned with both human and non-human elements interplay in any given situation.

We are aware of the seminal nature of the work on 'communities of practice' by Jean Lave and Etienne Wenger (1991) and the way in which this has been taken up by practitioners in educational settings. Indeed, many of the chapters in this volume refer to this work and build upon it in different ways. It is for this reason that we wanted to include some of the original writings on situated learning, and chose for this volume a reading concerned with Lave and Wenger's notion of legitimate peripheral participation. Chapter 3 demonstrates how the concept of legitimate peripheral participation sits within broader debates around situated learning. The authors develop a historical perspective on their use of the concept and how newcomers become part of a community of practice. They focus not upon formal educational settings but on the ways in which learning is part of all social practice and not confined to formal settings. They propose, therefore, a social theory of learning. Lave and Wenger make the point that the notion of legitimate peripheral participation is not in itself an educational form or pedagogical strategy but a way of understanding learning. We wish to emphasise this since Lave has recently expressed concern at how the broader concept of 'communities of practice', of which legitimate peripheral participation is a part, has been taken up and imposed in a top-down way in educational settings as a sort of model of 'good pedagogy' (J. Lave, personal communication). Lave and Wenger indicate the ways in which being a newcomer and participating in a community of practice involves complex relationships of power involving both powerfulness and powerlessness within a community of practice.

Chapter 4 by David Russell is the first of two chapters that draw upon activity theory (AT) and point to its value and relevance for exploring distributed learning environments. He suggests that AT is useful for instructional designers and educational researchers because it goes beyond the individual learner and the interface to look at how learning is mediated by a range of material and symbolic tools. He argues that distributed learning needs to take into account all the tools people use and the ways in which they mediate activity. Computers are just one of a range of mediational means, which enable things to happen and learning to take place within activity systems. For Russell, the value of AT is that it looks beyond the 'student with computer' by looking at how humans learn together within activity systems. He also illustrates how AT can help us to understand the contradictions among activity systems and why using technologies may result in all sorts of unexpected consequences, which is resonant of Morgan, Russell and Ryan's findings in Chapter 2. AT can be a way of understanding about the relationships between the participants in a learning environment and the tools they use in the learning context. Russell stresses that any number of different things can act as mediating cultural tools, including symbolic tools such as language, illustrating that he is not merely concerned with the interface between a learner and the computer.

Chapter 5 takes us away from formal educational institutions to explore work-based learning. Stephen Billett uses theoretical perspectives from AT and 'communities of practice' to support his argument that it is not possible to separate learning at work from participation in work-based practices. He explores how knowledge is distributed across work practices and suggests that knowledge is mediated through both the workplace and the agency of individuals within that workplace. Billett investigates a number of 'categories of interdependencies' as an illustration of how workplaces afford individuals differing learning opportunities through their particular participation at work. In other words, participating in a community of work practice is key to understanding both learning at work and the development of an identity in the workplace. At the same time, AT comes into play as Billett examines how learning in workplace settings is always structured by the kinds of activities being engaged in within any given context. He also suggests that the pedagogic principles that arise from his explorations of learning in the workplace are not dissimilar from those concerned with learning in formal educational institutions, echoing Wenger (1998), who suggests that learning is fundamentally concerned with participation in practice whatever the context. Billett argues that, to understand learning in the workplace, we need to go beyond the day-to-day activities of work and explore how individuals engage with these activities. In his analysis, Billett also points to workplaces as contested terrain where opportunities for participation and guidance on that participation are unevenly distributed.

In Chapter 6, we move towards a rather different theoretical framing from earlier chapters with an exploration of the economic, social and cultural considerations of globalisation and their relevance to distributed learning. Richard Edwards suggests that it is important to consider distributed learning in relation to broader processes of globalisation. He provides a useful overview of globalisation debates, in particular those concerned with the relationship between local and global contexts; these have particular relevance for practitioners involved in course design who want to think about the ways in which their courses may be taken up by those in cultural settings, which are different from those of the institution responsible for course design and delivery. Edwards cautions us against viewing global processes as being primarily a result of ICTs; technology alone is not enough to account for the complex processes of globalisation. Edwards also suggests that there is a complex interplay between the economic, political and cultural in globalising processes and suggests that we need to consider all these in terms of our assessment of the significance of distributed learning. Drawing on work concerned with the hidden curriculum, Edwards explores the ways in which a different, and in a sense looser, organisation of time and space has unpredictable consequences for the distributed learning curriculum.

In Chapter 7, Barbara Mayor and Joan Swann explain in detail some of the questions raised in the previous chapter concerning global course delivery and global contexts. They come from a very different theoretical perspective however – that of sociolinguistics – and are concerned with both traditional technology and a traditional mode of distance education: a print-based course. Mayor and Swann suggest that one of the problems with the use of English for global course delivery is how English is often presented as a neutral international language detached from any cultural contexts. Using case study material from an undergraduate distance learning course delivered globally, they illustrate how the use of English embeds all sorts of cultural assumptions, which has wide-ranging implications for teaching and learning strategies. Students from different educational traditions may have little knowledge of the educational 'ground rules' embedded in course delivery. For example, they may be used to different rhetorical strategies in essay writing or have a different understanding of the pedagogic relationship between tutor and student embedded in the course materials, and particularly in the assessment strategy. At worst, such misunderstandings can lead to confusion about what counts as plagiarism. The authors also raise the question of whose voices are dominant in globally delivered courses, and the inherent difficulties in trying to balance up alternative voices and perspectives when the course is delivered from a UK higher education institution in the dominant English language. Although the research material they draw on comes from a traditional print-based course, they raise important issues which are as relevant – if not more so – for courses delivered using ICT.

The starting point for Chapter 8 is also the more traditional context of distance education and learning. Mary Thorpe explores these against a backdrop of what she sees as changed communities of practice in open and distance learning. These involve changes in how teachers interact with learners and also changes in terms of the kinds of research and theory practitioners have been drawing on during the past 30 years. She steers a middle way between using the concept of communities of practice to explore changing practices towards teaching and learning – for example, in an increased emphasis upon collaboration – and supporting the imposition of a top-down model through the artificial creation of communities of practice in learning environments. She argues that there are some changes for practitioners in the communities in which they participate today, not least that these now embrace a broader range of people, including library staff and software designers, who increasingly play a part in course design, delivery and support. Nevertheless, despite these changes, she concludes that many of the challenges posed of access for learners have still not been overcome through the use of ICT, and therefore, as practitioners, we would do well to look back and learn from where we have come as we look forward to the future.

In Chapter 9, Charles Crook takes us away from the history of open and distance education and towards the face-to-face learning environment of the traditional entrant to undergraduate higher education, the 18-year-old school leaver. He reports upon the findings of some of his own research, which indicate that such students are sceptical that virtual learning will offer the lived experiences of university study. Crook is concerned that moves towards the virtualisation of higher education do not take account of how learning needs to be conceptualised as a cultural practice. He suggests that we need to get away from thinking that learning is about individuals and towards exploring the variety of settings within which learning is organised. To explore this further, he examines some of the differences between formal and informal learning and, with his focus upon the former, suggests that this is most usefully understood as a cultural practice. He questions whether virtual universities will be able to provide the organisation and design that motivates learners to engage in formal learning. For Crook, it is that learning is embedded within institutional organisation and design which helps us to conceptualise learning as a cultural practice. Moves towards virtualisation suggest a disembedding of learning from these structures, and therefore from the cultual settings that support formal learning. He argues that the traditional entrant to higher education may find such disembedding more difficult to deal with than other groups of students, for example, older adult learners. He suggests, therefore, that to be successful, virtualisation will need to take account of learning as a cultural practice and recognise the importance of the different cultural settings in which tertiary education has traditionally taken place.

In Chapter 10, James Cornford and Neil Pollock develop a related theme in their exploration of the campus as a 'resourceful constraint'. They suggest that those who are developing distributed education through the use of ICTs need to be mindful of the kinds of support offered by the physical setting of the traditional university campus and provide equivalent support in these new contexts. They argue that the notion of the virtual university seems to be based upon a view of education as an informational process; the virtual environment facilitating the movement of information from one place to another. They use concepts from actor-network theory to get away from this informational view of education and learning and to consider the lateral links brought into play on the campus between objects, people, texts, machines, and so on. They indicate that this has enabled them to consider more closely both the forms of the informational content and the work done by the different physical structures of the campus. For example, they illustrate how an examination hall does more than provide a physical space for sitting exams; it also acts to minimise falsifying identity in the examination process. Without this physical setting, virtual universities are forced to go to great lengths to verify the identities of their examination candidates and to put procedures in place to prevent plagiarism. Cornford and Pollock suggest that the campus supports lateral relationships between learners and teachers, whereas there is a danger in virtual learning environments of a focus upon the processes – for example, the flows between teachers and students. They suggest that, to be successful, distributed learning environments using ICTs need to support the lateral relationships found on physical university campuses.

In Chapter 11, Gill Kirkup explores the issue of identity in distributed learning settings and asks how far explorations of meaning and identity in communities of practice might have relevance in virtual environments. She draws upon the social model of learning developed by Wenger (1998) and in particular upon how identity is produced through participation and non-participation in educational online communities. Kirkup is concerned to explore how far Wenger's theoretical perspective can be usefully applied to virtual environments that do not have an embodied location for their practices. She asks whether communities need a spatial location and, if so, what is the nature of the knowledge created through participation in virtual communities in educational settings? She examines how the concepts of 'network' and 'community' have been taken up and the ways in which they embed different understandings and meanings, with network being the more pejorative term in virtual educational settings associated with 'e' learning. For example, in some instances, students might be encouraged to put together their own choices of curriculum rather than engage actively in a virtual learning community. Kirkup raises an issue considered in the previous chapter concerning students' real and embodied identities, and the implications of using 'false' identities in online environments in terms of issues of authenticity and authority, which in turn may be linked to plagiarism. She draws some similar conclusions to the two preceding chapters in suggesting that an understanding of the relationship between community, meaning and identity might help course designers in distributed learning environments to focus upon the most appropriate media, rather than regarding internet-based education as always the preferred option.

The final chapter raises some broader policy issues concerned with the notion of 'flexibility' in higher education. Richard Edwards, Kathy Nicoll and Alison Lee suggest that the issue of literacies has been largely ignored in debates about the flexibility of provision of learning opportunities. They suggest that both flexibility and literacies are central to any understanding of distributed learning and explore what it might mean to talk about flexible literacies. Flexible learning has been a response to what they see as a number of changes in higher education: increased access, customisation of products, increased efficiency of delivery, the use of ICTs. Responses to such changes have gone hand in hand with more attention to efficiency, competitition and choice for lifelong learners. They situate their argument in terms of broader debates in the social sciences around flexibility and reflexivity. Central to the changes taking place in the tertiary sector have been changes in the practices of teaching and learning; the authors argue that this has resulted in diverse literacy practices, which they refer to as 'flexible literacies'. New contexts of learning require students to be flexible and to engage with and master a wide range of literacy practices in the changing contexts of higher education delivery. The authors suggest that bringing together the terms 'flexible' and 'literacies' enables an exploration of these new contexts in productive ways, not merely in terms of the kinds of texts that are being created but also the power relations that are embedded in the new contexts of post-compulsory education.

We believe this is the first time that the different social and cultural perspectives explored in this volume have been brought together in this particular way to help us to think more critically about our practices of teaching and learning in distributed learning environments. We hope that the directions being examined by the contributors will be taken up productively and built upon to the benefit of both teachers and learners.

Mary R. Lea and Kathy Nicoll

References

Castells, M. (1996) *The Information Age: Economy, Society and Culture. Vol. 1. The Rise of the Network Society*. Oxford: Blackwell.

Chaiklin, S. and Lave, J. (eds) (1993) *Understanding Practice: Perspectives on Activity and Context*. Cambridge: Cambridge University Press.

Cole, M., Engestrom, Y. and Vasquez, O. (eds) (1997) *Mind, Culture and Activity*. Seminal Papers from the Laboratory of Comparative Human Cognition. Cambridge: Cambridge University Press.

Gayol, Y. and Schied, F. (1997) Cultural imperialism in virtual classroom: critical pedagogy in transnational distance education, in *The New Learning Environment: A Global Perspective*, Proceedings to the ICDE Conference, 2–6 June 1997, Pennsylvania State University.

Gee, J. (2000) The new literacy studies: from 'socially situated' to the work of the social, in D. Barton, M. Hamilton and R. Ivanic (eds) *Situated Literacies: Reading and Writing in Context*. London: Routledge.

Goodfellow, R., Lea, M., Gonzalez, F. and Mason, R. (2001) Oppportunity and equality: intercultural and linguistic issues in global online learning', *Distance Education*, 22 (1).

Goodman, S. and Graddol, S. (1996) *Redesigning English: New Texts, New Identities*. London: Routledge.

Heidegger, M. (1977) *Question Concerning Technology and Other Essays* (translated by M. Lovitt). New York and London: Garland.

Lankshear, C., Snyder, I. and Green, B. (2000) *Teachers and Techno-literacy: Managing Literacy, Technology and Learning in Schools*. St Leonards, NSW: Allen & Unwin.

Lave, J. and Wenger, E. (1991) *Situated Learning: Legitimate Peripheral Participation*. Cambridge: Cambridge University Press.

Lyotard, J.-F. (1984) *The Postmodern Condition: A Report on Knowledge* (translated by G. Bennington and B. Massumi; Foreword by F. Jameson). Minneapolis, MN: University of Minnesota Press.

Mason, R. (1998) *Globalising Education: Trends and Applications*. London: Routledge.

Perraton, H. (2000) *Open and Distance Learning in the Developing World*. London: Routledge.

Salomon, G. (1993) *Distributed Cognitions: Psychological and Educational Considerations*. Cambridge: Cambridge University Press.

Wenger, E. (1998) *Communities of Practice: Learning, Meaning and Identity*. Cambridge: Cambridge University Press.

Chapter 1

Information, knowledge and learning*

Some issues facing epistemology and education in a digital age

Colin Lankshear, Michael Peters and Michele Knobel

Introduction

Philosophers of education have always been interested in epistemological issues. In their efforts to help inform educational theory and practice they have dealt extensively with concepts like knowledge, teaching, learning, thinking, understanding, belief, justification, theory, the disciplines, rationality and the like. Their inquiries have addressed issues about what kinds of knowledge are most important and worthwhile, and how knowledge and information might best be organised as curricular activity. They have also investigated the relationships between teaching and learning, belief and opinion, knowledge and belief, and data and information. For some a key issue has been how students can become autonomous knowers. This issue has often been bound up with questions about what count as appropriate standards for reasonableness or rationality, and the conditions under which we can properly regard understanding as having occurred. During the past decade renewed interest has been shown in what is involved in becoming an authority, expert or competent performer in a given area of knowledge, as well as in how we evaluate and critique different or competing beliefs, theories, points of view or paradigms.

Until recently, such activity was conducted under relatively stable conditions. We could assume that the printed word/book comprised the paradigm medium for knowledge production and transmission; that propositional knowledge and denotation comprised the principal mode and space of knowledge work; that educational activity was underwritten by ideals of progress, liberal enlightenment, and personal and collective enhancement made possible through knowledge; and that scientific pursuit of knowledge was based on secure foundations.

We are presently living through a period in which such assumptions have been undermined to the point where they are no longer tenable. The circumstances, conditions and the very *status* of knowledge, learning, teaching and researching are currently in a state of profound upheaval under the double impact of rapid and far-reaching technological change and the massive assault on longstanding narratives of foundation and legitimation.

In this context new work in epistemology for education assumes great urgency, and should be given very high priority by philosophers of education. Indeed, many of the very questions about knowledge that in the past have been fundamental to epistemological work no longer seem relevant. In an age which *fetishises* information (Poster 1993), knowledge may seem either to be passé or in need of a serious reframing. What follows is an attempt to identify some areas and concerns we believe need close attention in the context of the burgeoning use of new communications and information technologies, including their rapid incorporation into school-based teaching and learning. One important dimension of this, although by no means the only one, is the exponential growth of public and professional participation in the Internet.

Life online: social epistemology and practices in spaces on the Internet

One of the most difficult challenges facing attempts to think about epistemology in relation to 'the Internet' has to do with what we might call the Internet's spatial 'ontology'.

For some people, the Internet can seemingly be understood as an elaborate infrastructure for transmitting, receiving and manipulating information. As such, it may be thought of in terms of a number of more or less discrete but linkable 'technologies' including email, pre-print archives and the World Wide Web. From this perspective, Paul Thagard (1997) talks of such Internet technologies as now being 'ubiquitous parts of scientific practice'. He describes a range of these technologies and then offers what he calls 'an epistemological appraisal of their contributions to scientific research'. This involves working from the assumption that 'science aims at and sometimes achieves truth understood as correspondence between beliefs and the external world'. Scientists increasingly use Internet technologies in their efforts to achieve 'truth', and Thagard provides typical everyday examples of such uses. He then takes Alvin Goldman's (1986, 1992) five 'epistemic criteria' – reliability, power, fecundity, speed and efficiency – and uses them as a framework for evaluating 'the largely positive impact of Internet technologies on the development of scientific knowledge'. So, for example, the criterion of power is treated in terms of measured ability to help people find true answers to their chosen questions. Thagard looks at various ways in which the World Wide Web (WWW) is 'powerful in helping scientists find answers to the questions that interest them'. He identifies the availability of video simulations, the hypertextual organisation of material, the availability of digital databases and their capacity 'to be searched quickly and thoroughly', the use of email and news groups 'to solicit answers to interesting questions', the ready availability of software on the Web which scientists can use 'to generate answers to statistical or other questions that would be unanswerable otherwise', the availability of electronic pre-print archives as sources of answers to questions and the fact that scientists with common interests can find each other and work collaboratively on the Internet. Thagard then works through the remaining criteria in the same way, typically beginning his accounts by showing how the printing press previously helped scientists in their pursuit of truth, and how the Internet now builds on and amplifies the power, fecundity, speed, efficiency and reliability enabled by print.

For Thagard the Internet seems to be just another facility for conducting business as usual. Scientists continue to practise the pursuit of truth much as they always have done, but now they have new technologies to help them in their efforts. Thagard calls this 'Internet epistemology', understood as the contributions of new information technologies to scientific research (which he understands in scientific realist and objectivist terms).

In many ways Thagard's conception of the Internet illustrates what Weston (1994) refers to as 'Phase II of the old boys' operation . . . [of] remodelling the modern apparatus' – an operation codenamed the 'Information Superhighway'. Following a well-established line of argument within the analysis and critique of mass media, Weston claims that 'all social institutions have their relative certainties made possible by the centralizing power of the technologies of mass communication'. In other words, the operating logic of public media throughout history and exemplified in the broadcast mass media of late modernity has followed a familiar pattern, in which:

> successive public communication technologies either began as, or very quickly were made to conform to, the extreme send:receive imbalances that, somewhere along the line, we started calling the mass media, or simply the media . . . Public access to these media is simply not problematical. On the one hand, there are the media and, on the other, there are their audiences, consumers, constituents, and publics.
>
> (Weston 1994)

Weston notes that the development of what is now known as the Internet was intended by those with the power to oversee such things to follow the same media operating logic. He says that by 'the information revolution' they only meant 'to digitize the modern industrial state'. The so-called 'information superhighway' was 'supposed to be about a five hundred, not a one hundred million channel universe'. And it was certainly *not* 'supposed to be about a technological adventure that would reconfigure social relations [of communication and media] or blur the well-constructed boundaries between the public and the private ground'. The intended 'model' would fit well with the picture of state and corporate scientific endeavour made more efficient by Internet technologies painted by Thagard.

However, as is now obvious, the Internet has to date evolved rather differently. It has so far defied centralisation and the restriction of channels that are controlled by a few. It is a truly distributed public medium. It is certainly inadequate to view 'it' (simply) in terms of an information infrastructure involving multiple discrete but connectable 'technologies'. Neither is it appropriate to think of the Internet in terms solely of information and data except, perhaps, in some trivial sense in which *anything* that is communicated can sooner or later be called data or information. Instead, we can envisage the Internet as a range of technologically mediated spaces of communicative practice that are amazingly diverse – a multiplicity of language games that are by no means confined to informing, and that are not best understood solely in terms of content.

Weston notes that the exponential growth in participation within diverse spaces of practice on the Internet has occurred *despite* a range of well-known constraints – initially including difficulty of access, frustratingly narrow bandwidth, and continuing observations that much of what is to be found there is banal or otherwise offensive, and often disorganised. For perhaps a majority of people who actively participate in online activities the Internet, unlike conventional mass media, is 'less about information or content, and more about relations'. Weston argues that practices in the Internet are mainly about 'people finding their voice' and about 'speaking for themselves in a public way'. From this perspective the matter of the content carrying this new relationship 'is of separate, even secondary, importance'. It remains important, however, because people usually want to '[re]present themselves as well as they can' (Weston 1994). Hence, if we are to understand the Internet in more than merely infrastructural and technicist terms, or as a massive conduit for information transmission, retrieval and manipulation – which we must – we need to understand the ways in which the relational aspects of the diverse kinds of practices and purposes played out there 'qualify and define what gets transmitted as content'.

At the same time, if we are seriously to address issues of epistemology in relation to the development of the Internet we need to sort out how the complex range of practices engaged in on the Internet relate to epistemology – what, if any, the epistemological implications of particular practices are; and within this field of possible epistemological implications, we have to work out which ones are (most) educationally relevant (which will involve difficult questions about the extent to which education should be about preparing people for lives and futures that will seemingly be increasingly lived out in cyberspace). This means at least three things. First, we have to recognise that the way academics understand and approach the Internet is only one way, and that it may differ greatly from the way non-academic publics understand and use the spaces and technologies in question. Second, to make plausible judgements about social practices on the Internet we need to know a lot more about what people actually do there than we know at present, and we need to look for patterns of practice and purpose and 'production' that go far beyond our current knowledge. Third, we must problematise our limited and often mystified understandings of the Internet which, to use an analogy from Chris Bigum (personal communication), may be more like a chameleon than an elephant. If, to continue the analogy, we are like blind persons trying to discover the nature of the beast by fumbling for parts of it, the fact is that it will be even more difficult to do this if the beast is a chameleon than if it is an elephant! And this makes epistemological work especially difficult.

Nonetheless, as educationists we neglect investigating the possible epistemological significance and implications of practices involving new Information and Communications Technologies (ICTs) at our peril. This would be to hand the game over completely to the 'visions' of neo-liberal policymakers, technoscientists and corporations who stand to gain from technologising educational provision in the image of computing hardware and software. What follows is a tentative preliminary exercise in considering some 'patterns', features and issues of social practices that have been associated with the rapid growth of electronic ICTs generally and Internet-based practices more specifically, and how these might call for rethinking epistemology in a digital age. This rethinking might conceive of epistemology in social terms as practices of knowing that reflect a range of strategies for 'assembling', 'editing', 'processing', 'receiving', 'sending', and 'working on' information and data to transform 'data' into 'knowledge'. We might think here of Ludwig Wittgenstein's (1953) 'performative' epistemology, an epistemology of performance – 'Now I know how to go on!' (Wittgenstein 1953: 105) – that conceives knowing as making, doing and acting. This account is based on the relation of knowing to the 'mastery of a technique'. Such a view of performance epistemology might be usefully applied to a range of emergent practices. These include 'bricolage', understood as assemblage of elements, and 'collage', understood as the practice of transferring materials from one context to another. They also include 'montage', construed as the practice of disseminating borrowings in a new setting (Ulmer 1985).

Patterns and practices of the new communications and information technologies

Knowledge in the postmodern condition

In *The Postmodern Condition* Jean-François Lyotard (1984) advances what has proved to be a highly prescient and compelling account of scientific (as distinct from narrative) knowledge in so-called 'advanced' societies (Peters 1995). His analysis resonates powerfully with the experiences of knowledge workers in modern neo-liberal states over the past 10–15 years. Lyotard's working hypothesis is that 'the status of knowledge is altered as societies enter what is known as the postindustrial age and cultures enter what is known as the postmodern age' (Lyotard 1984: 3). Lyotard's analysis of the postmodern condition is a report on the status of knowledge under the impact of technological transformation within the context of the crisis of narratives – especially Enlightenment meta-narratives concerning meaning, truth and emancipation, which have been used to legitimate both the rules of knowledge in the sciences and the foundations of modern institutions. His concept of the postmodern condition describes the state of knowledge and the problem of its legitimation in the most 'highly developed' countries, in the wake of 'transformations which, since the end of the nineteenth century, have altered the game rules for science, literature and the arts' (Lyotard 1984: 3).

By 'transformations' Lyotard means particularly the effects of new technologies since the 1940s and their combined impact on the two main *functions* of knowledge: namely, research and the transmission of acquired learning. He argues that the leading sciences and technologies are all grounded in *language-based* developments – in theories of linguistics, cybernetics, informatics, computer languages, telematics, theories of algebra – and on principles of miniaturisation and commercialisation. This is a context in which: 'knowledge is and will be produced in order to be sold, and it is and will be consumed in order to be valorized in a new production: in both cases, the goal is exchange' (Lyotard 1984: 4). Knowledge, in other words, 'ceases to become an end in itself'; it loses its use value and becomes, to all intents and purposes, an exchange value alone. The changed status of knowledge comprises at least the following additional aspects:

- Availability of knowledge as an international commodity becomes the basis for national and commercial advantage within the emerging global economy.
- Computerised uses of knowledge become the basis for enhanced state security and international monitoring.
- Anything in the constituted body of knowledge that is not translatable into quantities of information will be abandoned.
- Knowledge is exteriorised with respect to the knower, and the status of the learner and the teacher is transformed into a commodity relationship of 'supplier' and 'user'.

Lyotard sees some important implications and corollaries associated with this changed status of knowledge. In particular:

- As the principal force in economic production, knowledge 'effects' include radically changing the composition of the workforce.
- Mercantilisation of knowledge widens the gap between 'developed' and 'developing' countries.
- Commercialisation of knowledge and emerging new forms of media circulation – including, par excellence, the Internet – raise new ethico-legal issues including intellectual property rights, the state's role in promoting and providing learning, issues of decency, offence and censorship and issues concerning the relationship between the state and information-rich multinationals.

Lyotard's critique frames the central question of legitimation of scientific knowledge in terms of its functions of research and transmission of learning within computerised societies where meta-narratives meet with 'incredulity' (Lyotard 1984: xxiv). In his critique of capitalism Lyotard argues that the state and company/corporation have found their only credible goal in power. Science (research) and education (transmission of acquired learning) as institutionalised activities of state and corporation are/become legitimated, in *de facto* terms, through the principle of *performativity*: of optimising the overall performance of social institutions according to the criterion of efficiency or, as Lyotard puts it, 'the endless optimization of the cost/benefit (input/output) ratio' (Lyotard 1993: 25). They are legitimated by their contribution to maximising the system's performance, a logic which becomes self-legitimating – that is, enhanced measurable and demonstrable performance as its own end.

The implications for the education function of knowledge are especially pertinent here. In terms of status, education – until recently regarded as a universal welfare right under a social democratic model – has been reconstituted in instrumental and commodified terms as a leading contributor to and sub-sector of the economy; indeed, one of the main *enterprises* of the post-industrial economy. The focus of educational work and provision is no longer based on questions of educational aims and ideals in the old sense that drew on language games involving values, aspirations, conceptions of and beliefs about humanity, potential, personal worth and autonomy, emancipation and dignity and the like. Rather, attention has moved from aims, values and ideals to a new focus on 'means and techniques for obtaining [optimally] efficient outcomes' (Marshall 1998: 8). That is to say, the education language game has been forced into commensurability with the varieties of technicist language games, and is required to play – to perform – according to the technological criterion of efficiency. The problem of legitimation, which is ever a problem of rationalising *power*, is addressed by making efficiency the basis of legitimation and then extending this logic across *all* the language games of the public–social institutional domain.

At the level of daily practice, performativity in education at all levels calls for our schools and universities to make 'the optimal contribution . . . to the best performativity of the social system' (Lyotard 1984: 48). This involves creating the sorts of *skills* among learners that are indispensable to maximum efficiency of the social system. For societies like our own, this is a system of increasing diversity and is seen as being composed of players competing in the market-place of global capitalism. Accordingly, two kinds of skills predominate: first, skills 'specifically designed to tackle world [economic] competition', which will vary 'according to which "specialities" the nation-states or educational institutions can sell on the world market', and second, skills which fulfil the society's 'own needs'. These have to do with maintaining the society's 'internal cohesion'. Under postmodern conditions, says Lyotard, these cohesion skills displace the old educational concern for *ideals*. Education is now about supplying 'the system with players capable of acceptably filling their roles at the pragmatic posts required by its institutions' (see Lyotard 1984: 48). As Marshall notes:

> educational institutions . . . will be used to change people away from the former liberal humanist *ideals* (of knowledge as good in itself, of emancipation, of social progress) to people who through an organised stock of professional knowledge will pursue performativity through increasingly technological devices and scientific managerial theories.
>
> (Marshall 1998: 12)

What are the implications for the content and processes of education so far as knowledge is concerned? Lyotard identifies several with specific reference to higher education. We will look at five of these implications which are especially relevant to our topic.

First, transmitting the 'organised stock of established knowledge' required for professional training may increasingly be left to new technologies. That is:

> to the extent that learning is translatable into computer language and the traditional teacher is replaceable by memory banks, didactics can be entrusted to machines linking traditional memory banks (libraries, etc.) and computer data banks to intelligent terminals placed at the students' disposal.
>
> (Lyotard 1984: 50)

Second, from a pedagogical perspective, didactic instruction by teachers would be directed to teaching students 'how to use the terminals'. Lyotard identifies two aspects here: (a) teaching new languages (e.g. informatics, telematics), and (b) developing refined abilities to handle 'the language game of interrogation' – particularly, to what information source should the question be addressed, and how should the question be framed in order to get the required information most efficiently?

A third implication noted by Lyotard is of particular concern here. He suggests that a primary concern of professionally oriented students, the state and education institutions will be with whether the learning of information is of any use – typically in the sense of 'Is it saleable?' or 'Is it efficient?' – not with whether it is *true*.

A fourth implication that runs parallel to the third is that competence according to criteria like true/false, just/unjust has been displaced by competence according to the criterion of high performativity.

Finally, under conditions of less than perfect information the learner–student–graduate–expert who has knowledge (can use the terminals effectively in terms of computing language competence and interrogation) and can access information has an advantage. However, the more closely conditions approximate to conditions of perfect information (where data are in principle accessible to any expert), the greater the advantage that accrues to the ability to arrange data 'in a new way'. This involves using imagination to connect together 'series of data that were previously held to be independent' (Lyotard 1984: 52). That is, in the final analysis, imagination becomes the basis of extra performativity.

We need to emphasise two important points here with respect to Lyotard's analysis. First, his working hypothesis and the exploration based on it were not intended to have predictive value but, instead, strategic value in relation to the question of the status of knowledge in advanced societies. Nonetheless, Lyotard's account is very close to what has emerged in developed neo-liberal states. Second, we do not see Lyotard as advocating or endorsing the values and orientation emerging from his analysis. Instead, we see him as reporting the direction in which exploration of his hypothesis points.

Our own view is that Lyotard's investigation of his working hypothesis has, in the event, proved to be disturbingly accurate. His account of the changed status of knowledge corresponds closely to the lived experience of many teachers and researchers working in reconstituted and increasingly professionalised universities. Moreover, with the current strong push to technologise school classrooms, we can already see at least the second, third and fourth of the implications described above applying increasingly to school learning contexts (cf. Lankshear *et al.* 1997; Lankshear and Snyder 2000).

We would argue that Lyotard's investigation of the implications for the status of knowledge of computerisation occurring under conditions of incredulity towards meta-narratives is massively important. At the same time, it is at most a part of a much larger story so far as epistemology and education in a digital age are concerned. Lyotard's work predated the dramatic developments in and uptake of new ICTs during the 1990s. Practices involving new ICTs – and, notably, the Internet – occurring within non-formal and non-educational sites have crucial significance for how we think about knowledge and truth, and about their relationship to educational work. It is high time that educationists tried to 'tell the larger story as it is', and to face square on its implications for established epistemological positions, and for educational practices and emphases predicated on these. At the same time, it is important in the context of what are confused and confusing times not to give too much away too easily so far as epistemological principles are concerned. The rapid and far-reaching changes in which we are embroiled may have thrown into serious doubt some substantive epistemological theories, and various educational priorities, values, assumptions and practices associated with them. This, however, is *not* to argue against the importance of trying to get clear about the nature of knowledge, the significance of truth and the distinctions between and relationships among knowledge, truth, belief, information and the like, under changed and changing conditions. Our argument is not so much with the principles and concerns of conventional epistemologies as with some substantive theories that have been dominant throughout modernity.

It seems to us very likely that the relationship between education and knowledge needs to be rethought in profound ways within the mode of information (Poster 1993). There are at least two important aspects to this inquiry. One will involve considering the extent to which education will henceforth be concerned with knowledge under foreseeable conditions. The other will involve asking the question: 'to the extent that education will still be concerned with knowledge, what kind or kinds of knowledge will be most important for schools to address, and what substantive changes in educational emphasis will this entail?'

We are aware that in much of what we have to say it may appear we believe that there is no longer any truth or any knowledge beyond what circulates as information. This is *not* our position. Rather, we think three things here. One is that new conditions require us to look again and, perhaps, in different ways from those we are used to, at what counts as knowledge and truth. The second is that we need carefully to consider the extent to which everyday practices – including many on the Internet – simply are not concerned with knowledge and truth as we have often understood them, but instead 'play' on quite different terrain. Third, we need to consider the extent to which education must help prepare learners for successful participation in such practices.

The superabundance of information

The Internet marks the current high point of what Mark Poster (1995) calls the second media age, or the second age of mass communications to emerge in the twentieth century. The first age, comprising film, radio and television, was based on the logic of broadcast. Here 'a small number of producers sent information to a large number of consumers', transcending earlier constraints of time and space by initially electrifying analogue information and, later, by digitising it. The integration of satellite technology with telephone, television and computer media has brought the emergence of a many-to-many logic of communication, which is Poster's second media age. This is a logic in which boundaries between producers, distributors and consumers of information break down, and where social relations of communication are radically reconfigured under conditions of infinitely greater scope for interactive communication than in the broadcast model (Poster 1995: 3).

There is more to matters here than simply an analytic distinction between operating logics: one-to-one versus many-to-many. In addition, there are important contingencies associated with the development of the Internet that are relevant to our purposes. Three in particular are worth noting briefly here. These will already be familiar to readers and are rehearsed here for subsequent analytic purposes.

First, there is the now notorious issue of the sheer volume of available information. While the phenomenon known as 'info-glut' (Postman 1993; Gilster 1997: 6) or 'data smog' (Shenk 1998) is by no means confined to the Internet, it certainly reaches an apex here. In part the superabundance of information can be seen simply in gross quantitative terms. There is a mountain of the stuff in the ether, so to speak, which presents serious challenges to negotiating this mass to find what one wants or needs. In addition, however, the information resources of the Internet are readily *customisable*. Services and software are available that enable users to have gigabytes of data on identified topics 'dumped' direct onto their hard drives on an ongoing basis. Once the parameters of interest have been set the data dumping operation is automatic (until one decides to end it).

Second, the Net is a radically 'democratic' inclusive medium where information is to a large extent unfiltered. Paul Gilster (1997: 38–9) notes that, even with the introduction of cable television, conventional mass media are nonetheless exclusive. Certain categories of content are excluded through the filtering decisions and actions of programming executives and the like. While many information sources on the Internet (especially on the WWW) filter and otherwise moderate content in accordance with their perceived interests and purposes, this is in no way the norm.

Third, a great deal of information on the Internet is *presented*. Two aspects must suffice here. First, Gilster (1997: 2–3) notes that with the tools of electronic publication being dispersed practically on a global scale, 'the Net is a study in the myriad uses of rhetoric'. In this context, says Gilster, the ability to distinguish between content and presentation in order to achieve a balanced assessment is crucial. The importance of presentation and the incentives to present information in maximally compelling ways should not be underestimated in the context of what Goldhaber (1997) calls 'the attention economy' (see below). Second, on the WWW much information is hyperlinked in ways that reflect conceptions of interrelatedness, relevance, emphasis, significance and values of the presenters. The information texts available on the Web are intensely mediated/interpreted, and this is further iterated through the operating logics and assumptions of search engines. As Standish observes:

> the links we encounter are ready made. As such they are the products of the author or designer of the hypertext and so reflect in some degree that person's biases and preoccupations. The facility one easily acquires in clicking on icons enhances the appearance of naturalness that the links so quickly come to have and so covers over the more or less idiosyncratic nature of the connections they supply.
>
> (Standish 2000; see also Burbules 1998)

Of course, we find similarities in other media – for instance, author choices of key sources and references in print texts. But on the Internet the hypertextual, hypermediated nature of information sources is more complex and profound than in other media. This is largely a function of the ease of creating hyperlinks and the speed and facility with which linkable resources can be mobilised online. It is also partly a function of the logic of the attention economy and the desires of web publishers to create (potential) associations with other presences on the web. Other matters related to image and identity also operate to generate information presentation effects that are much more complex and ambiguous than typically occur in, say, print texts.

Writers have identified numerous issues associated with the potential constraints to sound information retrieval and processing practices resulting from the logic of many-to-many communication and contingencies like those we have raised here. One such issue is that of *credibility in cyberspace*. Nicholas Burbules and Thomas Callister (1997), for example, address the issue of how Internet users can assess the credibility of particular items of information and of information providers, and how they can acquire credibility in their own right as informers. They argue that the Internet poses important challenges to our more traditional ideas of how to assess and gain credibility in relation to information and knowledge. Traditionally, they say, our criteria for credibility have emphasised qualifications and characteristics of identifiable knowledge and information agents (and for all the fallibility this may entail). On the Internet, however, it may be impossible to identify original sources of information – seemingly much more so than in the more finite world of print-based information. In such cases we (may) have to rely on a range of commonplace proxies. Judgements must rely on such indicators as 'the avenues through which that information was gained' – drawing on the idea of the Internet and, particularly, the WWW as 'a vast network of credibility relations' within which 'the people who establish active links to reliable information, and whose information or viewpoints are in turn identified as and recommended by others, gain credibility as both users of information and providers'; the links that 'others who are better known' have made to the information; how frequently the information has been accessed (e.g. page visitor counters) and so on.

Burbules and Callister emphasise that these are indirect and imperfect measures of credibility, yet they may be all that Internet users can draw on to evaluate information that is beyond their experience and expertise in a field. Clearly, traditional epistemological concepts, criteria and practices – particularly those adhered to by knowledge 'professionals' like academics – are put under considerable strain here.

A second issue concerns *the quest for perspective and balance*. Paul Gilster (1997, Chapter 7) describes a practice he calls 'knowledge assembly' which he sees as a necessary new literacy in and for the information age. He asks how one builds knowledge out of online searching and catching, and how specific items of information are to be evaluated. He seeks open, non-prejudiced inquiry, which strives for balance, goes where the evidence leads, and aims to get at the heart of the themes or issues in question. For Gilster, knowledge assembly is 'all about building perspective'. It proceeds by way of 'the accretion of unexpected insights' (Glister 1997: 195, 219). When it is used properly, says Gilster:

[n]etworked information possesses unique advantages. It is searchable, so that a given issue can be dissected with a scalpel's precision, laid open to reveal its inner workings. It can be customized to reflect our particular needs. Moreover, its hypertextual nature connects with other information sources, allowing us to listen to opposing points of view, and make informed decisions about their validity.

(Gilster 1997: 196)

Knowledge assembly is about targeting issues and stories using customised newsfeeds and evaluating the outcomes. It is the:

ability to collect and evaluate both fact and opinion, ideally without bias. Knowledge assembly draws evidence from multiple sources, not just the World Wide Web; it mixes and distinguishes between hard journalism, editorial opinion, and personal viewpoints. [It] accepts the assumption that the Internet will become one of the major players in news delivery . . . but it also recognizes the continuing power of the traditional media.

(Gilster 1997: 199)

Gilster describes the tools and procedures of knowledge assembly using the Internet in terms of a five-step process. The first step involves developing a customised, personalised electronic news service – a personal newsfeed. Subscribing to an online news service and entering keywords that define the topics or issues you want to receive breaking stories about does this. The service – often fee-charging, depending on the range of information sources it culls – then sends you by email or via a Web page which can be tailored for personal use stories on topics of interest as they break. (For more detailed descriptions of the kinds of services available, see Gilster 1997: 201–8.)

The second step augments the first (which draws on formal 'published' information or 'hard news'). In the second step one subscribes to online newsgroups and mailing lists that deal with the subject(s) of interest. These offer the personal viewpoints and opinions of participants on the issues in question, providing access to what (other) 'netizens' make of the topic. Some newsgroups make their own newsfeeds available, which helps with focused searching by subtopics and the like among the myriad postings that occur across a range of lists on daily and even hourly bases.

In Gilster's third step one searches the Internet for background information – e.g. by going to the archives of online newspapers to get a history of the buildup of the story or issue thus far. Gilster also mentions using search engines to find Internet links to sites covering key players in the story or issue. These may provide related stories or other information that helps contextualise the issue or topic, providing additional breadth, variables and angles.

The fourth step involves drawing together other helpful Internet news sources, such as radio archives accessed by software like RealAudio, interactive chat sessions, video archives and so on. Although the facility should not be abused, direct email links might also be used to verify or disconfirm information.

The final step in the assembly process takes us beyond Internet sources of information and involves relating the information obtained from networked sources to non-networked sources such as television, conventional newspapers, library resources and so on. This is indispensable to seeking balance and perspective, since it puts the issue or story being worked on into a wider context of news and information – including prioritised contexts (e.g. where newspapers consistently run the story on page 1, or on page 12).

These steps towards 'filling the information cache' entail diverse understandings, skills and procedures – many of which are only acquired through regular use and 'practice'. For example, learning to find one's way around the innumerable mailing lists, news groups and discussion lists; identifying the 'predilections' of different search engines, and which one to use (and with which other ones) for particular areas or topics; how to narrow searches down by refining keyword checks; how to use Boolean logic, and which search engines employ which Boolean commands and protocols, and so on. Gilster also mentions specific 'tools' of content evaluation that one uses along the way to filling one's information cache, item by item; for instance, the credentials of the sources, the probable audience a source pitches at, the likely reliability of the source, distinctions such as those between 'filtered, edited news', personal opinion and propaganda (Gilster 1997: 217).

Constitutive effects of how we interrogate the world

In a chapter called 'Logic and intuition', Michael Heim (1993) explores some constraining influences on how we interrogate the world of information – and, indeed, the world itself – that can be seen as associated with normalised practices of a digital regime. He focuses on Boolean search logic, since nowadays to a large and growing extent we 'interrogate the world through the computer interface' and 'most computer searches use Boolean logic' (Heim 1993: 14–15).

Heim's underlying point is that to live within the digital regime means that using Boolean search logic and similar computing strategies rapidly becomes 'second nature' – something we take for granted (Heim 1993: 14). He is interested in how this will 'affect our thought processes and mental life and, to that extent, how we will be constituted as searchers, thinkers, and knowers'. He builds on two key ideas: the types of questions we ask shape the possible answers we get, and the ways we search limit what we find in our searching.

Looking at Heim's account of the relationships between question types and answers, and between search modes and what our searches turn up, we arrive at the operating mode of the search engine. On the surface it may appear that search engines have already moved beyond using Boole's tools: the use of AND, NOT, OR, NEAR, and so on, in conjunction with 'key words, buzz words and thought bits to scan the vast store of knowledge' (Heim 1993: 22). Some search engines now invite us simply to ask them a question or enter a few words. But beneath the surface of our natural language questions or phrases the software is still operating on largely Boolean lines. The point is that *all* such searching makes use of logics that presume pre-set, channelled, tunnelled searching: *pointed* rather than *open* searching. Invitations from the machine to refine our search (as when too many data sources are identified) are invitations to further sharpen focus 'an already determined will to find something definite'; to 'construct a narrower and more efficient thought tunnel; to create still finer funnels to sift and channel "the onrush of data"' (Heim 1993: 22–3).

Heim contrasts this kind of information scan with what he calls 'meditative perusal'. He distinguishes his notion of meditative work from that recommended by numerous advocates of online searching. For the latter, 'meditating' means no more than engaging in reflective efforts to find sharper and more discriminating key words. From this perspective, information scanning is preconceived, focused, highly goal-directed and treats texts as data. The key values of information scanning are speed, functionality, efficiency and control. The answers we get from scanning are bounded and defined, comprising data which falls within overlapping circles in Venn diagrams. We can then use what we get in accordance with our knowledge purposes.

In contrast to this, Heim describes 'meditative perusal' as the kind of 'contemplative, meditative meander along a line of thinking' that we might engage in by slowly reading a book and keeping 'the peripheral vision of the mind's eye' open. Here the reader is open to unexpected connections, meaning and interpretation, options that were taken and others that were not, authorial hunches, tensions and contradictions and so on. This is an approach to knowledge/getting to know (about) something which privileges intuition, the unexpected, openness to 'discoveries that overturn the questions we originally came to ask' and to 'turning up something more important than the discovery we had originally hoped to make' (Heim 1993: 25–6). Insofar as spaces on the Internet can, like books, be browsed in this mode, doing so will require us to resist the wider web of values and purposes to which search logics are recruited or, at the very least, to be and remain aware of wider options that may exist.

Economies of information and attention

The superabundance of information has been linked to the hypothesis of an emerging attention economy in ways that have important epistemological implications. The fact that information is in over-saturated supply is seen as fatal to the coherence of the idea of an information economy, since 'economics are governed by what is scarce' (Goldhaber 1997). Yet, if people in post-industrial societies will increasingly live their lives in the spaces of the Internet, these lives will fall more and more under economic laws organic to this new space. Numerous writers (e.g. Thorngate 1988, 1990; Lanham 1994) have argued that the basis of the coming new economy will be attention and *not* information. Attention, unlike information, is inherently scarce. But like information it moves through the Net.

The idea of an attention economy is premised on the fact that the human capacity to produce material things outstrips the Net capacity to consume the things that are produced – such are the irrational contingencies of distribution. In this context, 'material needs at the level of creature comfort are fairly well satisfied for those in a position to demand them' (Goldhaber 1997) – the great *minority*, it should be noted, of people at present. Nonetheless, for this powerful minority, the need for attention becomes increasingly important, and increasingly the focus of their productive activity. Hence, the attention economy:

[T]he energies set free by the successes of . . . the money-industrial econ-omy go more and more in the direction of obtaining attention. And that leads to growing competition for what is increasingly scarce, which is of course attention. It sets up an unending scramble, a scramble that also increases the demands on each of us to pay what scarce attention we can.

(Goldhaber 1997)

Within an attention economy, individuals seek stages – performing spaces – from which they can perform for the widest possible audiences. Goldhaber observes that the various spaces of the Internet lend themselves perfectly to this model. He makes two points of particular relevance to our concerns here. First, gaining attention is indexical to originality. It is difficult, says Goldhaber, to get new attention 'by repeating exactly what you or someone else has done before'. Consequently, the attention economy is based on 'endless originality, or at least attempts at originality'.

Second, Goldhaber argues that in a full-fledged attention economy the goal is simply to get enough attention or to get as much as possible. (In part this argument is predicated on the idea that having someone's full attention is a means for having them meet one's material needs and desires.) This becomes the primary motivation for and criterion of successful performance in cyber-space. Generating information will principally be concerned either with gaining attention directly, or with paying what Goldhaber calls 'illusory attention' to others in order to maintain the degree of interest in the exchange on their part necessary for gaining their attention.

Multimodal truth

Since the invention of the printing press the printed word has been the main carrier of (what is presented as) truth. Mass schooling has evolved under the regime of print, and print has more generally 'facilitated the literate foundation of culture' (Heim 1999). Of course various kinds of images or graphics have been used in printed texts to help carry truth (such as tables, charts, graphs, photographic plates, illustrations). However, Web technology merges pictures and print (not to mention sound) much more intricately and easily than has ever been possible before. As Heim puts it:

The word now shares Web space with the image, and text appears inextric-ably tied to pictures. The pictures are dynamic, animated, and continually updated. The unprecedented speed and ease of digital production mounts photographs, movies, and video on the Web. Cyberspace becomes visual-ized data, and meaning arrives in spatial as well as in verbal expressions.

(Heim 1999)

This situation now confronts the primary focus within classroom-based edu-cation on the linguistic–verbal–textual resources of reading, writing and talk. Teaching and learning have been seen throughout the history of mass education as principally linguistic accomplishments (G. Kress, personal communication). Recently, however, teachers and educationists have become increasingly interested in the role of visual representations in relation to teaching and learning. 'The importance of images as an educational medium is beginning to be realised, as text books, CD ROM, and other educational resources become increasingly reliant on visual communication as a medium for dealing with large amounts of complex information' (Heim 1999).

Some implications for epistemology and education

The patterns, features and issues associated with social practices involving new ICTs sketched here are by no means the only ones we could address. They are, however, quite diverse and well-subscribed, and they provide a reasonably broad-based 'catalyst' for considering how much and in what ways we may need to rethink epistemological matters in relation to educational theory and practice. This final section will identify some of the issues and challenges we believe should be taken up as priorities by educational philosophers (among others).

We can begin by identifying in a broad sweep some of the key elements of the epistemological model that has underpinned education throughout the modern-industrial era. We can then go on to consider how far these elements may be under question in a digital age where more and more of our time, purposes and energies are invested in activities involving new communications and information technologies.

Throughout the modern-industrial era of print, learning has been based on curriculum *subjects* organised as bodies of content which are in turn based on work done in the disciplines (history, mathematics, natural science and so on). The primary object of learning was the content of subjects. This was based on the premise that what we need to know about the world in order to function effectively in it, and that is to be taught in formal education, is discovered through (natural and social) scientific inquiry. Even the very 'practical' or 'manual' subjects (such as cooking, woodwork) contained a considerable 'theory' component.

School learning has also been based on the idea that by participating in curriculum subjects derived from the disciplines learners could come to see how this content gets discovered and justified by experts, in addition to learning (about) the content itself. To use a once-common formulation from Anglo-American educational philosophy, knowledge has both its literatures (content) and its languages (disciplined procedures), and successful learning initiates learners into both (cf. Hirst 1974). Of course, it is another matter as to how far this ever actually occurred in practice within schools. The fact remains, however, that for educational philosophers as otherwise different as John Dewey, Israel Scheffler, Maxine Greene, Paul Hirst and Kevin Harris, the epistemological ideal for education has always been to promote the development of *knowers* as well as to transmit *knowledge*.

The broad epistemological model which has dominated school education since its inception has been the standard view of knowledge which has dominated Western thought since the time of Plato. This is widely known as the 'justified true belief' model. According to this epistemology, for A (a person, knower) to know that *p* (a proposition), A must *believe* that *p*, *p* must be *true*, and A must be *justified* in believing that *p* (see, for example, Scheffler 1965).

This general model allowed for many variations, for instance in theories of truth (correspondence, coherence, pragmatist), in theories of reality (realism, idealism) and so on. But beneath all such variations, justified true belief has been the epistemological standard for two millennia, and has been applied (in a more or less particular way) to school curricular learning. The ideas canvassed in the body of this chapter pose a range of issues for this epistemology and for established educational practices based on it. We will identify and comment briefly on five points here, aware that what we have to say is at most a tenuous beginning to a pressing area of inquiry.

First, the standard epistemology constructs knowledge as something that is carried linguistically and expressed in sentences/propositions and theories. This is hardly surprising considering that for two millennia the modes for producing and expressing knowledge have been oral language and static print. To the extent that images and graphics of various kinds have been employed in texts their role has been, literally, to illustrate, summarise or convey propositional content.

The multimedia realm of digital ICTs makes possible – indeed, makes normal – the radical convergence of text, image and sound in ways that break down the primacy of propositional linguistic forms of 'truth bearing'. While many images and sounds that are transmitted and received digitally still stand in for propositional information (cf. Kress' notion of images carrying complex information mentioned above), many do not. They can behave in epistemologically very different ways from talk and text – for example, evoking, attacking us sensually, shifting and evolving constantly, and so on. Meaning and truth arrive in spatial as well as textual expressions (Heim 1999), and the rhetorical and normative modes displace the scientific-propositional on a major scale.

Michael Heim (1999) offers an interesting perspective on this in his account of what he calls 'the new mode of truth' that will be realised in the twenty-first century. He claims that as new digital media displace older forms of typed and printed word, questions about how truth is 'made present' through processes that are closer to rituals and iconographies than propositions and text re-emerge in similar forms to those discussed by theologians since medieval times. Heim argues that incarnate truth as the sacred Word is transmitted through a complex of rituals and images integrated with text-words. In the case of the Catholic church, for instance:

> communal art is deemed essential to the transmission of the Word as conceived primarily through spoken and written scriptures. The word on the page is passed along in a vessel of images, fragrances, songs, and kinesthetic pressed flesh. Elements like water, salt, and wine contribute to the communication. Truth is transmitted not only through spoken and written words but also through a participatory community that re-enacts its truths through ritual.
>
> (Heim 1999)

The issue of how truth is made present in and through the rituals of the community of believers/practitioners has been an abiding concern of theologians for centuries. Is the presence of incarnate truth granted to the community through ritualised enactment of the sacred word real, or should it be seen as symbolic or, perhaps, as a kind of virtual presence? Heim suggests that this and similar questions take on new significance with the full flowering of digital media. If truth 'becomes finite and accessible to humans primarily through the word', he asks, 'what implications do the new media hold for the living word as it shifts into spatial imagery?' (ibid.).

Heim casts his larger discussion of these issues in the context of avatar worlds being constructed by online users of virtual reality (VR) software to express their visions of virtual reality as a form of enacted truth. (Avatars are graphic images or icons adopted by users to represent themselves in three dimensional worlds which are inhabited and co-constructed by other participants represented by avatars. As such, avatars are graphic extensions of the textual descriptors for online identities adopted by participants in earlier text-based MOOs, MUDs and MUSHs.) Heim speaks of participants realising and transmitting their 'visions' of virtual reality – the worlds they construct online – through what he calls the 'new mode of truth'.

A second challenge facing much established epistemological thinking concerns the fact that knowing has generally been seen as an act we carry out on, and truth has been seen as pertaining to, something that already exists. In various ways, however, the kind of knowing involved in social practices within the diverse spaces of new ICTs is very different from this. More than propositional knowledge of what already exists, much of the knowing that is involved in the new spaces might better be understood in terms of a performance epistemology – knowing as an ability to perform.

At one level we can understand this in terms of procedures like knowing how to make and follow links when creating and reading Web documents. At another level it is reflected in Lyotard's observation that under conditions of the changed status of knowledge the kinds of knowledge most needed by knowledge workers include procedural knowledge of languages like telematics and informatics, and knowledge of how to interrogate information sources. Of particular importance to 'higher order work' and other forms of performance under current and foreseeable conditions – including performances that gain attention – is knowledge of how to make new moves in a game and how to change the very rules of the game. This directly confronts some dominant assumptions in conventional epistemological thought, such as those concretised in normal science which presuppose stability in the rules of the game as the norm and paradigm shifts as the exception. While the sorts of shifts involved in changing game rules cannot all be on the scale of paradigm shifts, they nonetheless subvert stability as the norm.

Once again, it is important to note here that Lyotard does not endorse the state of affairs he describes any more than we endorse the features and patterns of practice described earlier. Rather, the operating logic is: 'If this is how things are, this is what follows from them.' Accepting the way things are and accommodating to them educationally and epistemologically is one option. Problematising them, however, is a different option. And it is the option we favour. But in order to problematise them they need first to be *named*. Lyotard names some of them and we have tried to name others – as a basis for problematising them and working towards developing considered epistemological and educational responses.

Third, practices involving new media help to identify weaknesses in trad-itional individualistic epistemologies which, following Descartes, have always existed. Problems with the notion that knowing, thinking, believing, being jus-tified and so on are located within the individual person (the 'cogitating' sub-ject) have become readily apparent in postmodernity. Theories of distributed cognition, for example, have grown in conjunction with the emergence of 'fast capitalism' and networked technologies (Gee *et al.* 1997; Castells 1998). A fur-ther aspect is apparent in the role and significance of multi-disciplinary teams in 'imaging new moves or new games' in the quest for extra performance. The model of multi-disciplinary teams supersedes that of the expert individual as the efficient means to making new moves (Lyotard 1984). In addition, we have seen that in the information-abundant world of the Internet and other search-able data sources it is often impossible for individuals to manage their own information needs, maintain an eye to the credibility of information items and so on. Practices of information gathering and organising are often highly cus-tomised and dispersed, with 'the individual' depending on roles being played by various services and technologies. Hence, a particular 'assemblage' of know-ledge that is brought together – however momentarily – in the product of an individual may more properly be understood as a *collective* assemblage involving many minds (and machines).

Fourth, it is important to recognise that the role and significance of know-ledge in the social conditions of postmodernity have changed in ways that should not be ignored by epistemologists and educationists. For a start, none of the three logical conditions of justified true belief is necessary for information. All that is required for information is that data be sent from sender to receivers, or that data be received by receivers who are not even necessarily targeted by senders. Information is used and acted on. Belief *may* follow from using infor-mation, although it may not, and belief certainly need not precede the use of information or acting on it.

Furthermore, the 'new status' knowledge of the postmodern condition as described by Lyotard – knowledge that is produced to be sold or valorised in a new production – does not necessarily require that the conditions of justified true belief be met. This follows from the shift in the status of knowledge from being a use value to becoming an exchange value. For example, in the new game of 'hired gun' research where deadlines are often 'the day before yesterday' and the 'answer' to the problem may already be presupposed in the larger policies and performativity needs of the funders, the efficacy of the knowledge pro-duced may begin and end with cashing the cheque (in the case of the producer) and in being able to file a report on time (in the case of the consumer). Belief, justification and truth need not come near the entire operation.

Even Gilster's account of assembling knowledge from news feeds stops short of truth, for all his emphasis on critical thinking, seeking to avoid bias, dis-tinguishing hard and soft journalism and so on. The objectives are perspective and balance, and the knowledge assembly process as described by Gilster is much more obviously a matter of a production performance than some unveil-ing of what already exists. We assemble a point of view, a perspective, an angle on an issue or story. This takes the form of a *further* production, not a capturing or mirroring of some original state of affairs.

Once again, we are not endorsing, advocating or passively accepting the direction of these changes. We are identifying them as matters educationists have not to date taken sufficiently seriously. They prompt many questions. For example, if the accounts of features, patterns and growing significance of social practices involving new ICTs provided here are reasonably accurate, how are we to interpret and enact epistemological principles like commitment to truth, knowledge as a use value, the importance of following arguments and evidence where they lead and so on? What place is left for such principles in educational practices and everyday life, and do we need to shore up space for them? How should educationists respond to the fact that many teachers currently have no clear idea of what to do with the information new ICTs make available to learners? To what extent and in what ways should schools be seeking different operating conceptions of knowledge from those inherent in subject-based learning, and how do we decide what these are? What kind of mix and balance should we be seeking among propositional kinds of knowledge, procedural and performance knowledge, and how can curricula take account of this? What is the proper relationship between how learning is organised in school and 'insider' versions of social practices involving new ICTs occurring in the world beyond school?

Finally, so far as performances and productions within the spaces of the Internet are concerned, it is questionable how far 'knowledge' and 'information' are even the right metaphors for characterising much of what we find there. In many spaces where users are seeking some kind of critical assent to what they produce, it seems likely that constructs and metaphors from traditional rhetoric or literary theory – for example, composition – may serve better than traditional approaches to knowledge and information.

Conclusion

The digital age is throwing many of our educational practices and emphases and their underlying epistemological assumptions, beliefs, concepts and substantive theories into doubt. The relationship between what students learn in school and the ways in which they learn it and what people actually do and how they do it in the world beyond school in contexts increasingly mediated by new ICTs has become increasingly tenuous. There are many aspects of this which we have barely taken up here, including the extent to which mindsets associated with physical-industrial space and those associated with cyber-information space may be inherently different and, indeed, incompatible (Tunbridge 1995; Bigum and Lankshear 1998). Those aspects we have addressed here suggest that our capacity to understand what will be involved in making informed and principled responses to the conditions of postmodern life in computerised societies will depend greatly on our willingness to problematise and rethink *both* the role and significance of knowledge and truth within existing and emerging social practices and social relations *and* some of our longstanding epistemological investments. We need to rethink these each in relation to the other, and in relation to postmodern means of producing and enacting power. If this chapter does no more than encourage us to explore these claims further, it will have done its job.

* Chapter 1 first appeared in *The Journal of the Philosophy of Education Society of Great Britain*, Vol. 34, No. 1, 2000, published by Blackwell Publishers.

References

Bigum, C. and Lankshear, C. (1998) Literacies and technologies in school settings: findings from the field. Keynote Address to 1998 ALEA/ATEA National Conference, 7 July, Canberra. http:// www.schools.ash.org.au/litweb/bigum.html.

Burbules, N. (1998) Questions of content and questions of access to the Internet, *Access: Critical Perspectives on Cultural and Policy Studies In Education*, 17(1): 79–89.

Burbules, N. and Callister, T. (1997) Who lives here? Access to and credibility within cyberspace, in C. Lankshear *et al.* (eds) *Digital Rhetorics: Literacies and Technologies in Education – Current Practices and Future Directions.* Canberra: Department of Employment, Education, Training and Youth Affairs.

Castells, M. (1998) *End of Millennium*. Oxford: Blackwell.

Gee, J.P., Hull, G. and Lankshear, C. (1997) *The New Work Order: Behind the Language of the New Capitalism*. Boulder, CO: Westview Press.

Gilster, P. (1997) *Digital Literacy*. New York: John Wiley.

Goldhaber, M. (1997) The attention economy and the net. Online at: http://firstmonday.dk/issues/issue2_4/goldhaber/.

Goldman, A. (1986) *Epistemology and Cognition*. Cambridge, MA: Harvard University Press.

Goldman, A.I. (1992) *Liaisons: Philosophy Meets the Cognitive and Social Sciences.* Cambridge, MA: MIT Press.

Heim, M. (1993) *The Metaphysics of Virtual Reality.* New York: Oxford University Press.

Heim, M. (1999) Trainsmogrification. Online at http://www.mheim.com/transmog/.

Hirst, P. (1974) *Knowledge and the Curriculum.* London: Routledge & Kegan Paul.

Lanham, R. (1994) The economics of attention. Proceedings of the 124th Annual Meeting of the Association of Research Librarians, Austin, TX. Online at: http://sunsite.berkeley.edu/ARL/Proceedings/124/ps2econ.html.

Lankshear, C., Bigum, C. *et al.* (eds) (1997) *Digital Rhetorics: Literacies and Technologies in Classrooms – Current Practices and Future Directions.* Canberra: Department of Employment, Education, Training and Youth Affairs.

Lankshear, C. and Snyder, I., with B. Green (2000) *Teachers and Technoliteracies.* Sydney: Allen & Unwin.

Lyotard, J-F. (1984) *The Postmodern Condition: A Report on Knowledge* (translated by G. Bennington and B. Massumi; Foreword by F. Jameson). Minneapolis, MN: University of Minnesota Press.

Lyotard, J-F. (1993) A svelte appendix to the postmodern question, in *Political Writings* (translated by B. Readings and K.P. Geiman). Minneapolis, MN: University of Minnesota Press.

Marshall, J. (1998) Performativity: Lyotard, Foucault and Austin. Paper delivered to the *Annual Meeting of the American Educational Research Association*, 11–17 April, San Diego, CA.

Peters, M. A. (ed.) (1995) *Education and the Postmodern Condition.* Westport, CT: Bergin & Garvey.

Poster, M. (1993) *The Mode of Information: Poststructuralism and the Social Context.* Chicago, IL: University of Chicago Press.

Poster, M. *(1995) The Second Media Age.* Cambridge, MA: Polity Press.

Postman, N. (1993) *Technopoly: The Surrender of Culture to Technology*. New York: Vintage Books.

Scheffler, I. (1965) *Conditions of Knowledge*. Chicago, IL: Scott, Foresman.

Shenk, D. (1998) *Data Smog: Surviving the Information Glut*. New York: HarperCollins.

Standish, P. (2000) Only connect: computer literacy from Heidegger to Cyberfeminism, *Educational Theory*.

Thagard, P. (1997) Internet epistemology: contributions of new information technologies to scientific research. Online at: http://cogsci.uwaterloo.ca/Articles/Pages/Epistemplogy.html.

Thorngate, W. (1988) On paying attention, in W. Baker, L. Mos, H. Van Rappard and H. Stam (eds) *Recent Trends in Theoretical Psychology*. New York: Springer-Verlag.

Thorngate, W. (1990) The economy of attention and the development of psychology, *Canadian Psychology*, 31: 262–71.

Tunbridge, N. (1995) The cyberspace cowboy, *Australian Personal Computer*, September.

Ulmer, G.L. (1985) The object of post-criticism, in H. Foster (ed.) *Postmodern Culture*. London: Pluto Press.

Weston, J. (1994) Old freedoms and new technologies: the evolution of community networking. Paper presented at *Free Speech and Privacy in the Information Age*, 26 November, University of Waterloo, Canada.

Wittgenstein, L. (1953) *Philosophical Investigations*. Oxford: Blackwell.

Chapter 2

Informed opportunism

Teaching for learning in uncertain contexts of distributed education

Wendy Morgan, Anne L. Russell and Michael Ryan

Introduction

We begin with the story of a project undertaken by one of us in using information and communication technologies (ICTs) with tertiary students. We then draw out of it some points for our arguments about the complex mix of literacy, learning and technology practices that contribute to tertiary education. This story might not seem immediately relevant to discussions of distance education in two respects. First, the students were present on campus. However, we believe that all learning – on- or off-campus – occurs in a variety of contexts, which are spread or 'distributed' over time and space. Some kinds of learning occur in the company of others, present in the flesh or through their words; others when one is alone with one's thoughts and materials, even in a crowd. And all learning occurs by means of various 'technologies' (pens, blackboards, books, classrooms). Second, the events happened in 1997 – a very long time in computerised education! – although similar stories of opportunities and challenges created by uncertain contexts of distributed education could be told today or tomorrow.

A cautionary tale of a hypertext project

Wendy

I teach a 13-week undergraduate teacher-education elective subject called 'Literature in Teaching', which explores hypertext fiction and poetry. I had become dissatisfied that the students often came to class without having read and recorded their responses to the literary hypertexts or theoretical texts set for discussion. Thus they were unable to share these with one another in the tutorial and thereby learn from comparing the various responses, analysing them, undertaking further activities, reviewing their first readings and making links with relevant theories about texts and reading. And when they hadn't begun to draft hyperfictions of their own, which also formed part of the ongoing business of the class, they couldn't profit from feedback. Their unpreparedness made a mockery of the pieties current in education about students 'taking responsibility for their learning' and 'becoming independent learners'.

I therefore decided to divide my class of 35 into two: one group attended class in the first week, the other the following week. In their 'off' week, students were required to undertake certain hypertext reading and writing tasks independently and to bring reading responses and writing drafts to class for discussion the following week. This arrangement meant I could give feedback to the smaller number of students who were present each week. It also gave me the opportunity to set up a kind of teaching–learning experiment. I conceived the idea of getting the students to contribute to a communal 'hyperspace' (utilising the Storyspace program, in which our hyperfictions were read and written). I did not want to use an online forum, but rather the very space for reading and writing we were focusing on – since a hypertext that allows readers to follow any of many pathways according to their interest is very different in effect and outcome.

A backbone to this hypertext was a paper I had written that analysed the hypertext reading and writing of students from previous years (http://meno.open.ac.uk/morgan1.html). I intended that the students would enter this common space, add their reflections on their own reading and writing of hyperfictions, comment on their classmates' notes, add links to weave these contributions together, and respond to my analyses by taking issue with my argument, supplementing it with accounts of their responses or offering alternative explanations for their preferences in reading and writing. That is, instead of recording and analysing their responses to their reading and writing individually, for my eyes only, they would also offer them up for each other. This collective and gradually growing hypertext would, I hoped, paradoxically encourage conversations between us in this virtual space and make up for the more limited time spent together in class. I saw it as a space apart from the classroom, which is so often characterised by those patterns of interaction that allow the teacher's voice to dominate and her eye to single out certain students for attention and approval. Thus I hoped this would be a space for a new kind of collaborative learning and writing in which the students could 'answer back' my text about their peers' writing and so instate their views alongside mine and each other's.

But when I came to carry out this plan – having already written into the subject plan that participating in the communal hypertext was one of the required assessment tasks – I found that the Local Area Network server would not allow me to load the hypertext on to our subject's website and then permit the readers to contribute to it as writers. Instead, I would have to put the hypertext on to a disk that the students would need to collect from me and write to each week. I would then have to upload the new version on to the website each week, so that students could read online, where it looked very different from the way it did on a single, stand-alone computer. (For example, Storyspace provides a map view of all the nodes and their links.) So I was forced to intervene – to be more present as manager – which I had neither intended nor desired.

I have insufficient space to detail here the disconcerting story of the effects that various technologies, including classrooms, timetabling and administrative procedures as well as computers, had on my plans. I will just mention that the Macintosh computers (no longer supported by our faculty technicians) broke down; IBM disks turned Mac-made hypertexts into unconnected fragments; the program did not behave on the network exactly as it did on a stand-alone machine; one hour out of the weekly three for the class was scheduled in a classroom with no computer projection facilities installed and no transportable projectors readily accessible, and so on. These and other contingencies meant that I was forced to abandon the joint hypertext project part way through the semester and modify other requirements of the subject.

In theory, as a curriculum designer I had authority ('This is what I as a teacher have determined is best for you'), power ('This is what you must do, or fail') and expertise (in Macintosh computers and the Storyspace program), and I intended to control the teaching–learning discourse. But fragile or obstinate technologies forced me to renegotiate those relationships of power, authority and control. I had to jettison my more elaborate teaching strategies to salvage the essentials of the subject. I learned with the students what we could achieve through what we could not, and what worked through what did not. I had to listen and learn from the students what I might require of them, in the circumstances, and what they could do independently – without my constant attention, cajoling or insistence – when I was focused on dealing with technological disasters. And the students learned from one another. Pedagogical authority was therefore 'distributed' across the class, and contingent on the particulars of each session.

I should add that, apart from this foiled attempt at sharing online, the subject went almost according to plan: the students contributed in class, learned important poststructuralist concepts about text, reading and writing, and actually enjoyed creating their individual hyperfictions.

Some contentions about literacies, technologies and practices of learning

Since every tale has more than one meaning, we next tease out of this story various threads that we weave together into our argument later in this chapter. In particular, we base our analysis on several contentions. Before we introduce these, we need to sketch the frameworks of theory and research from which they have been derived.

The first framework is sociolinguistics or the 'new literacy studies'. (The former draws on various linguistic methods of analysis, the latter sometimes on broader social theories of language use; for an overview see Gee 2000.) The work of Brian Street (1984) has been influential in refuting the common 'myth' that literacy is 'autonomous', a skill people exercise independently of the contexts in which literacy occurs (cf. the ground-breaking ethnographic work of Heath 1983). Instead, 'new literacy' scholars commonly argue that literacy is to be understood as a social practice. That is, what it means to be literate involves 'ways of talking, acting, interacting, valuing, and believing, as well as spaces and material "props" [any] group uses to carry out its social practices' (Gee 1992: 107), and these practices differ in different situations.

Some literacy scholars (e.g. Fairclough 1989, 1992; Gee 1990, 1991; Lemke 1995) focus on how these social practices of literacy give people various degrees of access to their society's goods and services. Some of these practices are more private and intimately interpersonal; others more public and institutionally endorsed. Some literacies are current among sub-groups that have relatively little access to power and social advantages in their society; other practices of literacy mark out a dominant group. In one way or another, literacies are practised within various social institutions and power relations which give rise to them and which they help maintain. An explicitly political kind of sociolinguistics is critical discourse analysis, which involves 'showing how discourse is shaped by relations of power and ideologies, and the constructive effects discourse has upon social identities, social relations, and systems of knowledge and belief, neither of which is normally apparent to discourse participants' (Fairclough 1992: 12).

Closely associated with the new literacy studies, and part of a larger movement of studies of learning that focus on social and cultural interaction rather than the capacities of individuals, is work on situated cognition (Rogoff 1990; Lave and Wenger 1991; Lave 1996). These scholars argue that knowledge and intelligence are not the products of individual minds; rather, they are distributed across social practices (including practices of literacy) and involve various technologies (artefacts, tools, symbols, etc.) that members of any 'community of practice' use to carry out their characteristic activities. 'Knowing' means knowing how to behave and speak, how to use 'the tools of the trade' of that community; 'learning' means participating in such a community.

This idea of situated practice is also at the heart of actor network theory (ANT) (Callon 1980; Latour 1987, 1994; Law 1992, 1997; see also Cornford and Pollock, Chapter 10). This theory is affiliated with broad theoretical movements concerning the social construction of technology and the nature of technological change. Perhaps the most radical principle of ANT is that it does not generally distinguish between human and non-human actors or 'actants'. Instead, it argues that both human and non-human components of any situation are to some extent 'agents' that can make things happen. Central to this theory is the notion of a 'network', although this term does not mean networks that are merely physical (e.g. a computer network) or social (e.g. a group of people with a common interest). Rather, networks are autonomous collections of actants that are formed and re-formed through complex interaction. Among the different types of interaction is 'translation', where actors continually reinterpret and reconstruct other actors' interests in terms of their own.

Over time, successful technologies become 'black-boxed' (a process by which their workings become assumed and invisible) and embedded within stabilised networks. Stabilised technologies as diverse as door closers, bicycles, power-stations and Internet protocols have been analysed using ANT. This theory could, for example, be used to interpret the development and stabilisation of the familiar QWERTY keyboard. As a technology, the keyboard is interesting because the arrangement of keys is awkward and inefficient; yet this keyboard arrangement is ubiquitous and pervasive. An ANT analysis would define the QWERTY keyboard as a highly stable, black-boxed technology surrounded by a network of actors (e.g. keyboarding trainers, typists) and devices (e.g. manufacturing plants) and would describe its evolution in terms of struggle and interaction between these various actants.

Now, to return to our contentions. First, literacy, technology and learning are always *plural* (New London Group 1996; Cope and Kalantzis 2000). Technology is never (just) a piece of equipment; literacy isn't a competence that's always the same; learning isn't a matter of transferring information unchanged from teacher to learner. Rather, each takes various forms because it is involved in various kinds of practice. For instance, learning is conceived and managed as a practice in very different ways in different cultures and contexts. Literacy – sometimes taken to be a matter of decoding and encoding language on the page – is a very different matter if one is reading a religious text or an animated advertisement on screen, writing an academic essay or e-mailing a friend (Graff 1987; Hoskin 1993; Sosnoski 1999). Technologies take many forms – pens, computers, books, assessment tasks, and so on – but they can never be understood as 'stand-alones': they are various ways of generating, shaping and communicating information that humans use. That is, each of these – literacies, technologies, kinds of learning – is not a 'thing' but a set of practices.

Next – a connected point – those practices of literacy, technology and learning are plural precisely because they are *embedded* in particular contexts – of time and place, culture and society, occasion and interaction – all simultaneously affecting the nature of the practice (e.g. Cuban 1986; Fairclough 1989, 1992; Gee 1990, 1991; Rogoff 1990; Lave and Wenger 1991; Lemke 1995; Hodas 1996). No kind of literacy, technology or learning can exist outside of those contexts in which it is practised.

Moreover, these practices of literacy, technology and learning are always *entangled* with one another. Literacy practices always involve some forms of technology as actants (even as simple-seeming as a stick in the sand); learning always entails some form of literacy (oral cultures also have ways of encoding knowledge) and hence also involve forms of technology, and so on (Green and Bigum 1996; Bigum *et al.* 1997; Lankshear 1997). The plurality of practices of literacy, technology and learning, together with the entanglement of one with another in their various forms, means that it is impossible to separate out one from another and pin it down, like a beetle on a board, and think we have captured 'it'.

Therefore – another of our points – practices of literacy, technology and learning are *unpredictable*. They are dynamic in their forms and interactions, perhaps even unstable, any one of them always open to change, particularly under pressure from the others (Kress 2000). For instance, although we may think we know how the introduction of a particular form of technology into the classroom will affect students' learning, that cause and effect relationship will certainly not be so simple and direct.

Given this complexity, it might appear that any of us who use literacies and technologies for forms of learning will end up like the centipede in the old rhyme:

> The centipede was happy, quite,
> Until a toad in fun
> Said, 'Pray, which leg goes after which?'
> This worked his mind to such a pitch,
> He lay distracted in a ditch,
> Considering how to run.

How we manage not to get tripped up brings us to the last of our key points here: particular practices of literacy, technology and learning are so customary they have become *invisible*; we take them for granted. For instance, we draw diagrams on a blackboard without thinking about the ways this technology shapes our reading, writing and learning. So we get on with the job without being conscious of how we too are entangled in those forms and practices. By contrast, newer forms of literacy, technology and learning are still visible to us – sometimes taking up so much of our view that we can see very little else.

The tale: three readings

We now examine Wendy's story with the help of those concepts of plurality, embeddedness, entanglement, unpredictability and invisibility. All readers tend to interpret things in their own terms, and we are no exception: Anne has focused on learning practices, Michael on technologies and Wendy reread her story for its lessons about literacies. But there are also commonalities across these responses.

Anne

I see many different learning practices going on here, some intended and some unintended. In trying to involve the students in their learning through the use of software foreign to them, you wanted learning to occur through students' personal reflections, student–student interactions as well as student(s)–teacher interactions. But the students' learning practices were embedded in and entangled with other cultural, social, technological and literacy baggage that each brought to this situation. At the same time you were also learning how to engage new technologies and new literacies in creating innovative instructional strategies. Your technological and literacy baggage was different from the students' and so you set up doubly complex learning expectations.

Initially, you were apparently not keeping in mind the prior social and cultural educational experiences these students brought to your class. Your expectations that they would be independent and self-motivated learners may not have been congruent with these students' experiences, when previous dominant teachers wanted to manage rather than facilitate the learning environment. These students had probably been conditioned to be 'reproductive' learners in classrooms where instruction was delivered 'at' them through the central distribution system of the teacher. Many of these students had learned to learn in isolation from their peers. In fact, you also wanted to manage the learning environment, albeit you intended it to be a different technological and literate environment from any they had encountered previously. You were offering learning practices that were more complex than they had come across previously. Perhaps these different expectations and hopes needed to be articulated between you and the students rather than being unspoken.

The students were trying to learn how to incorporate the new technologies and literacies (of hypertext) as independent and collaborative learners who would achieve satisfactory grades. Unfortunately, you failed to realise that the change from stand-alone Macintosh to networked technology would create frustrating chaos. Both you and the students needed scaffolding, to provide support in learning these new technologies and literacies. For your own scaffolding, you could have approached several students from a previous class, where hypertext and poststructuralist concepts were part of the curriculum, and asked these students to trial your planned project using the networked technologies. You would already have a rapport with these students, so they would feel comfortable acting as your colleagues to provide critical feedback on the operation of the technologies and the value of the learning activities. The resulting outcomes of critical reflection and interactive hypertext could be put online as a resource or model to provide a scaffold for the novice students.

Your aim was to give students equal 'air-time', but they needed to learn a new role in a (not entirely) democratic environment – and this contributed more complexity. Collaborative learning can be conducted through interactive communications technologies or during classroom interactions. In the classroom face-to-face situation, some students have more 'air-time' and particularly more verbal interactions with their teacher than others. You were attempting to provide the opportunity for all students to have equal access to space through using Storyspace, but for this to happen both you and they needed to become enculturated into new ways of learning and being taught. You were expecting the students to understand the new roles you were giving yourself and them. One of the new understandings your students needed to come to grips with was feeling comfortable interacting with their teacher and critiquing their teacher's text. In attempting to create an environment conducive to sharing between students and students and their teacher, you set up another learning practice entangled with the multiliteracies of new technologies and hypertext interactions. I suspect that the visualisation of the final product you had in mind bore little resemblance to the expectations in the minds of the students.

There was little that was familiar in the learning context (e.g. prior experience with you as a teacher), technologies or literacies in which students could embed the new learning practices and tasks you expected for assessment. So many aspects were entangled here, as the students needed to be critically aware of the nature of authorship, technologies, content and concepts. As long as the technologies and multiliteracies were intrusively visible to the students, they would find it difficult to concentrate on new creative applications. If any of these had become invisible through familiarity (Russell 1995), the students could have focused better on knowledge and text creation and there would have been more potential for interactive learning to occur.

Instead, you and your students experienced other, unanticipated forms of learning. Some of these entangled learning practices were unexpected: you discovered that some unpredictable technologies transformed tasks into non-practice; students identified when and how to approach you with problematic technologies and literacy tasks; you discovered that ideal conditions for learning were not represented in the reality of contradictions; and changes in assessment and learning/teaching strategies had to occur 'on the run'.

Both teachers and students take risks in using technologies to extend learning experiences, and in this instance you and they achieved some valuable outcomes. This is one reason why we argue in this chapter that instructional design cannot be seen as a stable technology with stable structures that direct learning.

As a teacher, you showed your students how to cope with change and failure in ever-changing technological environments. You and your students learned together to transform and reconstruct this learning environment. Thus you created a modified sociocultural space where some forms of information were transformed into knowledge and some new practices of (hyper)text construction became skilled performance.

You approached the subject with new hope for options that might well be available to you when the technologies catch up with your progressive thinking. As an opportunist teacher, you are prepared to see potential usefulness in new technologies and take risks through experimentation, evaluation and 'tweaking' according to the current technologies. Although the literacies and technologies had been intrusively visible, their operation may not have been clearly explained to the students. Perhaps you should have offered more scaffolding in supporting the students to make these literacies and technologies more visible, so they would be able to recognise why they were frustrated in learning the subject concepts. They might then recognise that their learning practices are expanding in unexpected and unanticipated ways.

I congratulate you on attempting this project with the students. You had the vision to see the potential for the technologies, but at that time the software and hardware available to you were not able to support this vision. Another time you might consider setting an alternative assignment for students who are not comfortable using the unstable technologies. For example, I provide an optional 'snail mail' assignment for students who do not have access to the newer technologies and therefore may not be able to participate in the collaborative practices I embed in an interactive online assignment. An additional benefit of the optional assignment is to have a fall-back piece of assessment in case the technologies do not meet expectations.

Michael

A curriculum plan can seem like an engineer's blueprint for building a highway between stated objectives and measurable outcomes: pass rates, student grades, satisfaction ratings, performance indicators, demonstrated competencies. But your calculations for this subject did not include the ways in which various technologies, including computers, timetabling, administrative procedures and the like, would affect the teaching and the hypertext-on-hypertext you had planned.

At least you didn't start with a form of technology as a 'solution' to a 'problem' you then had to find. Yours was a pedagogical problem; you decided it had a technological solution of two kinds – the timetable and the shared hypertext space. You assumed that those aspects of the hypertext technology would 'naturally' predominate in shaping the pedagogical environment. Thus you gave in to a kind of technological determinism – that is, a propensity to allow the agenda to be set by technological imperatives rather than by other elements in the situation.

What you did not take into account was the entanglement of these technologies: there is almost never a simple technological 'fix' to a complex problem. Certainly the timetabling and the shared hypertext may have been part of your solution – but there was also the need to make other, consequent changes that weren't strictly technological in nature. Even the technologies themselves would need to be managed in particular ways – for example, to get the Storyspace application to work effectively on the network.

If I may say so, you were rather naive in overestimating your expertise and your ability to shape things according to your plans, and so you underestimated other factors and their power to upset your design. Notice how you tell your story: it's full of 'I's. Yet you're not really the prime mover, the originator of all activities: you are an actor in a crowd of actors or agents, including technologies (Latour 1994). You drew a boundary around yourself and one around the technology, keeping them distinct from each other, and you thought you could wield the ICTs as a tool to do your will. But when you compartmentalised the technologies, you forgot what they were embedded in – all the contexts they brought with them, such as the network and the technicians who were involved with them. This made it so much more difficult for you to manage, especially on your own. It might have been easier if you had enrolled others – technicians, experienced fellow academics – in your endeavour.

Instead, the technologies also had some agency, some capacity to affect things around them, including you. I would say that Storyspace also had its own agenda: after all, was it not designed originally for individual authors' writing of fiction (whatever other uses it might subsequently be put to)? So you were perversely working against its grain in using it for joint academic argumentation.

And even if the technologies had somehow apparently worked according to your plan, there would still have been surprises, what Sproul and Kiesler (1991) call 'second-order effects': changes in the environments of practice and in practices themselves that are perhaps more indirect, more various, impossible to anticipate in our planning. You spoke of being 'disconcerted' by all those unexpected events; I'm not surprised. Our teaching has largely been formed by the technologies available to us – books, blackboards, timetables, and so on – so that, if they cause us even slight worries, this is discomfiting. After all, we depend on the technologies to be invisible so that we can get on with the business of teaching. But even the smallest seismic tremors, so to speak, offer us opportunities if we are ready and able to seize them. This means that we too would need to be different: more flexible, more varied, more responsive to the pedagogical environments of which we are part.

You talked about setting up 'a space apart from the classroom' where virtually the same discussions would occur. Of course, a classroom is a finely tuned technology too, which sets up particular relations between teachers and learners. Move into a differently technologised environment (as you tried to do) and you will have to build those relationships anew. I suspect you forgot you would need to do that because the technologies of classrooms and the behaviours they instil in us are so stable they have become 'natural', invisible. You assumed those behaviours, those relationships, would occur unchanged in a changed environment, forgetting how *entangled* literacies, technologies and learning practices are with each other.

Wendy

The whole subject was intended to teach students about how our practices of reading and writing are bound up with our histories, our cultures, our learning. That still happened, but the outcomes were not exactly as I had anticipated. What I failed fully to take into account when I planned the communal hyper-text was that the students had been thoroughly inducted into particular forms of academic reading and into certain forms of academic writing. They were already cast as readers and writers of print, and they were not at all comfortable with the hypertextual mode of public reflection and analysis I was asking of them. In other words, among the plural forms of literacy, this form – of schol-arly hypertext writing – was alien to them. Moreover, embedded as they were within that context of tertiary education, the students were rather reluctant to experiment by taking flight in the space of this hypertext. Those familiar prac-tices of academic reading and writing have become normative for teachers and students alike: each knows what is to be produced in exchange for grades.

This literacy practice was made more complex because of its necessary entanglement with computer technologies. Many of the students were unfamiliar with the Macintosh platform, many were nervous novices even to word processing, and all were still learning the features of Storyspace through the semester. Yet I expected them to be confident readers and fluent writers in a form of text with many pathways through it, a form in which an argument can be distributed across many nodes, and which cannot exist apart from a computer.

I saw the space in which they were to write as 'rhizomatic' – that is, a form that spreads out in all directions with no single centre, like bamboo (Deleuze and Guattari 1983). Hypertext theorists have argued that such a space is demo-cratic in being a network with no 'top' or 'bottom' (Johnson-Eilola 1997). In keeping with these theories I wanted to open up the closed, finished form of the academic paper to permit the students to insert their own assertions and counter-assertions. I wanted the students to destabilise my text as an argument and as an instance of a genre. But I had not realised that new literacy practices also set up new power relations among those who are experienced and those who are novices, among those who are fluent and assured in their scholarship and argumentation and those who are necessarily more tentative.

Even if literary and scholarly hypertext (Kolb 1994) had not become exactly invisible to me – we are always looking at the structure as well as at the meaning (Landow 1997) – I had failed to understand how intrusively visible the program would be to my students. That was what they saw – that, and the looming 'technology' of assessment. Both of these precluded them from engaging with me and their peers in a hypertextual conversation about hypertext. The whole task was far too complex for them (or me, as it turned out) to manage, given the fragility of the computer systems: that instability was one last straw that broke my resolve and their capacity to attempt the assignment.

Developing those contentions

To develop our argument, we now need to tease out our points about the plurality, embeddedness, entanglement, unpredictability and (in)visibility of certain practices of literacy, technology and learning. We then suggest how teachers can work with those features to become 'informed opportunists'.

All literacies involve some form(s) of technology. These forms may be as invisible, as 'natural', as pen and paper have been in some societies over the last few hundred years, or as letters are to those whose literacy is alphabetic. Or those technologies may be as visible as computer-based multimedia programs are to some of us. Whatever the technology, it influences and shapes the very form and practice of literacy. Think of how hypertext programs pushed Wendy's students into reading and writing in new ways. (But remember, too, how other technologies – of assessment, of classrooms, of print itself – also nudged those students' literacy practice back towards safely familiar practices.) Conversely, aspects of print literacy are becoming embedded in and transformed by the technologies: think of fonts (equivalent to forms of handwriting), grammar and spell checkers; consider how the forms of address in a letter are different in e-mail, with its fields for addressee, subject, carbon copies. Or oral and written communication may converge – and be further transformed. For example, in a MOO or chat room used for educational purposes, the participants key in their conversation (which still maintains some of the features of speech). The program allows the script to be archived; the students may then re-compose their dialogue as narrative or more formal argument. Literacy practices are thus being transformed by ICTs.

Clearly, then, literacy practice takes many forms, which occur within particular cultural and textual contexts, within and for certain social and communicative situations. Such diverse forms of practice are now, as noted above, sometimes called 'multiliteracies' (New London Group 1996). For example, when students read course materials online, they need to be able to decode the various symbols (letters, underlining, icons, menu bars, buttons, etc.) to understand how to navigate a website constructed of linked pages, infer the functions of a web page (information and display, communication and entertainment, etc.), to determine what status and authority the text has in their learning context (to be memorised, to be worked with and applied in problem-solving, to be interrogated and argued with), and so on. These forms of literate knowledge and practice may be very different from those practised by learners in other cultural contexts.

That is, knowledge becomes knowledge within particular (sub)cultures. (Each of us participates in several such cultures: at home, at work, among friends, when practising religious rituals or following a sport.) Particular forms of information make sense and are valued and used – that is, become knowledge – in particular ways within particular subcultural contexts. Such information is produced – shaped and made knowable – through particular forms of language and literacy, technologies, and practices of teaching and learning (formal or informal). For instance, a student from a western culture may have learned to practise particular forms of reflective writing for self-disclosure, because this is valued by her teacher (Gilbert 1989) and more generally by the culture. In an online forum these 'confessions' may be distributed among widely separated peers. And where the learners understand how to read these texts – how to look for particular themes and emphases, how to find certain information significant – they come to know themselves and others in certain ways. It is, of course, much easier to do this if you are already an insider to the culture that values such self-exploration.

In such cultural contexts and social situations, technologies (visible or invisible) are to various degrees active participants or agents, and not merely tools or resources (as noted above, this understanding derives from actor network theory). In other words, technologies are more than inert objects: they exert an influence on patterns of interaction in learning contexts, and on the making and shaping of knowledge. One simple instance from Wendy's classroom was the way the size of the computer screen led students to compose their fictions in shorter chunks (for each hypertext node) that would fit on that screen without scrolling. That is, the screen was an agent, actively nudging them away from the continuous composition with which students were familiar from word processing.

All such technologies are themselves also culturally constructed. Not only are they invented by humans to achieve objectives within particular cultural contexts of meaning-making, they are also endowed with meaning, importance and value within those contexts. Many institutions of higher education are pushing teachers to use online means of communication, even when other channels (print, audio-conferencing) may be better (if not cheaper) for a particular communicative purpose. It is clear that, when institutions are competing for market share, ICTs come with an aura (fostered by advertising) of immediacy, currency, accessibility and interactivity – although many students experience frustration at their limited access to terminals, their inexperience with computers, the narrow bandwidth of Internet connections or the overwhelming amount of data available.

Since all practices of learning are embedded within cultural contexts and social situations, they develop particular forms within those contexts. What it means to learn, how learners act and interact, how learning is used and valued, these will be very diverse in different times and places, among different groups. Many of us who are older, or who come from tradition-oriented cultures, will remember the importance placed on rote learning and recitation of information imparted by a teacher or textbook. Our children and grandchildren may well be learning in contexts in which their teachers encourage them to locate information from a range of sources, including online, select and skim them for their relevance, copy them or make notes (often electronically), and transform the information according to their purpose and audience. Sometimes the manners learners have been taught to show towards their teachers and peers may be under pressure to change in new environments – such as in a MOO, where previous patterns of interaction very different from the students' and teachers' have become the norm.

Such learning practices are always structured by particular technologies and literacies. By structuring we mean organised, even given their very form. To take a simple instance: consider how a textbook (a particular form of literacy and a technology for presenting information and producing knowledge) displays information in lockstep linear form or moves from an overview of the whole to component parts, sequences the stages of learning, encourages learners to focus on certain matters and even to act in certain ways as learners. Consider how differently structured the learning may be when those same materials are online with many hyperlinks, and when students may move seamlessly between reading and writing and communicating via ICTs.

For all these reasons, any practices of learning entail something other than the pure and simple transmission of knowledge and skills. When newcomers in a particular situation of learning (whether on the job or in more formal educational settings) observe 'old hands' and learn to perform as more experienced practitioners do, they are being enculturated into particular forms of sociocultural practice ('This is the way we do things here.'). But when practices of (literacy) learning change under the pressure of new technologies, young learners may have the edge and have much to teach their teachers. However, if the learning, like the technologies, is not to become 'schooled' – that is, practised only in ways peculiar to formal educational sites – then that learning will need to occur, at least in part, within a 'package' or 'ensemble' of practices as these arise within the subculture. Thus, if students are to create a report on an industry's customer services, they need to understand how such reports are developed by a team with diverse forms of expertise, how they will be read (executive summary, supporting data, recommendations), how they will be distributed and what use may be made of them to inform decision-making. If those students have insider knowledge about such sociocultural practice, they will be better able to shape their text with bullet points, appropriate register, graphs and tables and the like, and act more appropriately around it – via PowerPoint presentation, for instance.

Thus learners must be inducted into the particular practices of a (sub)culture if, over time, they are to participate fully as experts. Such induction may encourage learners to conform to what is already known, to the way things have always been done; but learners may be able to appropriate forms of (literate, technologised) practice for their own purposes. In this way, they may in some measure transform those practices and their understanding of learning.

Examples of conformity or reproduction of known practice, enhancement and transformation may also be found in the educational uses of ICTs in distributed learning (and could no doubt be traced back to the educational subculture). For instance, the 'delivery' of print-based course materials unchanged via the World Wide Web is an instance of reproduction of older literacies and forms of teaching via newer technologies. This notion of delivery is one of a number of commonplace, apparently commonsense concepts and metaphors about learning at a distance. They include the notions that 'information' is mere data, to be transmitted with as little interference as possible from teacher to learner; that 'instructional design' is a stable technology for the stable structuring of learning; that 'distributed' learning is freighted in a container from a central depot to an outlying post; and that 'communities of practice' or learning are coherent, unified commonalities. Such terms bring with them assumptions about learning as transmission and reproduction, and if we use them mindlessly we invite them to 'colonise' our discussion and thinking about learning.

By contrast, ICTs might be used to enhance the literacies and learning practices available in face-to-face learning. An example of such enhancement would be the use of Web forums to provide a virtual space for new forms of textual and social engagement. These forums might be seen as the equivalent to the bulletin board, or letters, or the tutorial room, but they have distinct characteristics that extend the communicative capacities of each. Because they are asynchronous, students can be 'present' in different time zones across the globe and each participant's 'voice' can be represented; because they have subject threads, participants can follow any of several 'conversations' always available to them as archives; and, because they can be written offline, learners can shape their contributions more thoughtfully, even strategically, after the conversation has passed on to a new topic.

ICTs may also contribute to the transformation of educational practice. Had Wendy's shared hypertext worked as planned, this would have – in part at least – transformed students' academic writing as well as teacher–student relations. Or had a teacher taken those Web forum conversations and analysed with the students the nature of the arguments and used these as a springboard for further collaborative writing, this too would be to transform by merging two aspects of formal learning that are characteristically kept distinct – namely, the shared tutorial and the solitary assignment.

Such transformations are always shaped by the ways of thinking, knowing, acting, speaking, writing and being which are possible within the institutions that house learning; and transformative practices may not be equally available to everyone within or across such contexts. (Ill-paid sessional tutors, or students who are new to the educational game, or those who profit from the status quo, may be reluctant to invest in changing practice.) Transformations are not necessarily stable, of course – remember the points made earlier in the chapter about unpredictability. Because they are embedded in complex contexts, such new ICT-mediated practices are always susceptible to being taken up and transformed further – reappropriated – according to the various needs, inspirations and purposes of other teachers and learners. These causes and effects may also be unforeseeable, and they may also be retrograde. Hence such transformations always need to be open to critique and further negotiation.

This brings us to the concept captured in our title: as teachers we need *an opportunist disposition*. By this we mean being prepared to set up spaces for play and possibility, to take risks by experimenting, to respond to unanticipated changes, and to see the potential usefulness in unforeseen, second-order effects (Sproul and Kiesler 1991). Yet, as Wendy's case showed, that willingness to admit, see and use opportunities also needs to be *informed by understanding* of the plural, embedded, entangled, unstable and (in)visible characteristics of literacies, technologies and learning practices.

Of course, we teachers do not always consciously intend such transformations or appropriations of ICTs to our pedagogical purposes; nor can we always anticipate and plan for all the possible outcomes of any shifts in practice. Our learning may be retrospective, occurring after the event as we trace what happened, or it may be ongoing, immediately responsive to unpredictable contingencies resulting from the entanglement of literacies, technologies and forms of learning. Hindsight is a most powerful strategy if we listen to what our own monitoring is telling us, and to the insights, complaints, even (we hope) praise from our students and fellow teachers.

Towards some principles for informed opportunism

Tales such as Wendy's are both exemplary and cautionary. Nothing is ever as tidy as the instructional handbooks suggest. As any teacher or student knows, there are not only unevennesses, even contradictions across classrooms in formal educational sites, but even within the same teaching space and the same teacher's practice. First-level effects (that is, those that are intended) and second-level effects (consequences that are unforeseen, more indirect, because they follow from the context) may be detected in any aspects of our teaching. And, as noted earlier, these effects may often mean the domestication of ICTs to practices that belong to an age of print.

Those unevennesses may mean that what one teacher is familiar and comfortable with another teacher (even in the same institution) may find really unstable. The same may be true of students. For instance, as a teacher, Anne is familiar with audio-conferencing and brings that comfort to those sessions with her students. However, some of them may be uncertain about this use of telephone technology and the pedagogical approach that is shaped by it, including the language practices needed to negotiate interactions with a number of fellow students who seem merely disembodied voices. In such cases, Anne knows that all her students will have attended face-to-face tutorials at some time; that there will be some students who are familiar with this kind of tutorial by telephone and that everyone will at least have used the phone! She is alert to the various levels of comfort among her students, is explicit with the students about procedures that will foster orderly, comfortable interactions, and models appropriate patterns of interaction. Her students do catch on in the end.

Or, to take this example a little further, in some settings a computer conference might be stable in the sense that all the technical problems have been ironed out, and back-up organisational procedures and systems are in place in case of technical failure. In other words, the technology in this setting is 'robust' (like that old faithful stable educational technology, the blackboard). So too, the purposes and uses of this technology of the computer conference may have settled down (as with the blackboard – we all know what it is for, who can use it, to do what, and so on). Or such conferencing may still be relatively unstable, appropriated for different purposes in different contexts.

Of course, if we bring a particular pedagogical design in combination with a stable technology, that design does not necessarily inherit the stability of the technology. (If I ask 12-year-olds to participate in a blackboard-supported debate on the best football code – rugby league, rugby union, soccer, Australian rules or American gridiron – there might be chalk-fights if I'm not careful!)

Clearly, it is not a good idea to base an unstable pedagogical design on an unstable technology; better to take pedagogical risks in relation to a technology that is stable in context, or to choose a stable pedagogy and play with a less tried-and-true technology.

Recognising all this unevenness, this uncertainty, what can teachers do to maximise their chances of being wisely informed opportunists? The following are a few points our experiences have taught us:

- Start with those technologies, pedagogies and literacies that are relatively stable for you, in your context; be informed about them and make them visible to yourself and your students (recalling those concepts of plurality, instability and invisibility).
- Plan for manageable, incremental steps, allowing informal play and alternative activities (recognising that any dimension of the situation may change because of their instability, embeddedness and entanglement).
- Cultivate a disposition for opportunism in yourself and your students – allowing space for play and risk-taking, and seeing opportunity in complexity (and instability).
- Consult and, if possible, collaborate with experienced colleagues (or students), who may be able to anticipate possible traps and suggest alternatives (embeddedness).
- Transform practice through an opportunistic spiral of appropriation, transformation, reflection, reappropriation, without hoping to control everything neatly, because each element will pull in the rest (cf. embeddedness and entanglement).

And a final counter-point:

- Do not expect that you will be able to follow a tidy sequence as the points above suggest: be disposed to find and use your opportunities when and as you can.

References

Bigum, C., Lankshear, C., Durrant, C., Green, B., Morgan, W., Murray, J., Snyder, I. and Wild, M. (1997) *Digital Rhetorics: Literacies and Technologies in Education – Current Practices and Future Directions.* Canberra: Department of Employment, Education, Training and Youth Affairs.

Callon, M. (1980) Struggles and negotiations to define what is problematic and what is not: the sociology of translation, in K. Knorr, R. Krohn and R. Whitley (eds) *The Social Process of Scientific Investigation: Sociology of the Sciences Yearbook.* Boston, MA: Reidel.

Cope, B. and Kalantzis, M. (eds) (2000) *Multiliteracies: Literacy Learning and the Design of Social Futures.* Melbourne: Macmillan.

Cuban, L. (1986) *Teachers and Machines: The Classroom Use of Technology since 1920.* New York: Teachers College Press.

Deleuze, G. and Guattari, F. (1983) *Anti-Oedipus: Capitalism and Schizophrenia* (translated by R. Hurley, M. Seem and H. Lane). Minneapolis, MN: University of Minnesota Press.

Fairclough, N. (1989) *Language and Power.* London: Longman.

Fairclough, N. (1992) *Discourse and Social Change.* Cambridge: Polity Press.

Gee, J.P. (1990) *Social Linguistics and Literacies: Ideology in Discourses.* London: Falmer Press.

Gee, J.P. (1991) What is literacy?, in C. Mitchell and K. Weiler (eds) *Rewriting Literacy: Culture and the Discourse of the Other*. New York: Bergin & Garvey.

Gee, J.P. (1992) *The Social Mind: Language, Ideology, and Social Practice*. New York: Bergin & Garvey.

Gee, J.P. (2000) The new literacy studies: from 'socially situated' to the work of the social, in D. Barton, M. Hamilton and R. Ivanic (eds) *Situated Literacies: Reading and Writing in Context*. London: Routledge.

Gilbert, P. (1989) *Writing, Schooling and Deconstruction: From Voice to Text in the Classroom*. London: Routledge.

Graff, H. (1987) *The Labyrinths of Literacy: Reflections on Literacy Past and Present*. London: Falmer Press.

Green, B. and Bigum, C. (1996) Hypermedia or media hype? New technologies and the future of literacy education, in G. Bull and M. Anstey (eds) *The Literacy Lexicon*. Sydney: Prentice-Hall.

Heath, S. (1983) *Ways with Words: Language, Life and Work in Community and Classrooms*. Cambridge: Cambridge University Press.

Hodas, S. (1996) Technology refusal and the organisational culture for schools, in R. Ling (ed.) *Computerisation and Controversy: Value Conflicts and Social Choices*, 2nd edn. San Diego, CA: Academic Press.

Hoskin, K. (1993) Technologies of learning and alphabetic culture: the history of writing as the history of education, in B. Green (ed.) *The Insistence of the Letter: Literacy Studies and Curriculum Theorising*. London: Falmer Press.

Johnson-Eilola, J. (1997) *Nostalgic Angels: Rearticulating Hypertext Writing*. Norwood, NJ: Ablex.

Kolb, D. (1994) *Socrates in the Labyrinth* (computer disk). Cambridge, MA: Eastgate.

Kress, G. (2000) Design and transformation: new theories of meaning, in B. Cope and M. Kalantzis (eds) *Multiliteracies: Literacy Learning and the Design of Social Futures*. Melbourne: Macmillan.

Landow, G. (1997) *Hypertext 2.0: The Convergence of Contemporary Critical Theory and Technology*. Baltimore, MD: Johns Hopkins University Press.

Lankshear, C. (1997) *Changing Literacies*. Buckingham: Open University Press.

Latour, B. (1987) *Science in Action: How to Follow Scientists and Engineers Through Society*. Milton Keynes: Open University Press.

Latour, B. (1994) On technical mediation, *Common Knowledge*, 3(2): 29–64.

Lave, J. (1996) Teaching, as learning, in practice, *Mind, Culture, and Activity*, 3: 149–64.

Lave, J. and Wenger, E. (1991) *Situated Learning: Legitimate Peripheral Participation*. New York: Cambridge University Press.

Law, J. (1992) Notes on the Theory of the Actor Network: ordering, strategy and heterogeneity, Department of Sociology, Lancaster University. Online at: http://www.comp.lancs.ac.uk/sociology/soc054jl.html.

Law, J. (1997) Traduction/Trahison: notes on ANT, Department of Sociology, Lancaster University. Online at: http://www.lancaster.ac.uk/sociology/stslaw2.html.

Lemke, J. (1995) *Textual Politics: Discourse and Social Dynamics*. London: Taylor & Francis.

New London Group (1996) A pedagogy of multiliteracies: designing social futures, *Harvard Educational Review*, 66: 60–92.

Rogoff, B. (1990) *Apprenticeship in Thinking: Cognitive Development in a Social Context*. Cambridge: Cambridge University Press.

Russell, A.L. (1995) Stages in learning new technology: naive adult email users, *Computers and Education*, 24(4): 173–8.

Sosnoski, J. (1999) Hyper-readers and their reading engines, in G. Hawisher and C. Selfe (eds) *Passions, Pedagogies and Twenty-first Century Technologies*. Urbana, IL: National Council of Teachers of English.

Sproul, L. and Kiesler, S. (1991) *Connections: New Ways of Working in the Networked Organisation*. Cambridge, MA: MIT Press.

Street, B. (1984) *Literacy in Theory and Practice*. Cambridge: Cambridge University Press.

Chapter 3

Legitimate peripheral participation in communities of practice*

Jean Lave and Etienne Wenger

Introduction

Learning viewed as situated activity has as its central defining characteristic a process that we call *legitimate peripheral participation*. By this we mean to draw attention to the point that learners inevitably participate in communities of practitioners and that the mastery of knowledge and skill requires newcomers to move toward full participation in the sociocultural practices of a community. 'Legitimate peripheral participation' provides a way to speak about the relations between newcomers and old-timers, and about activities, identities, artifacts, and communities of knowledge and practice. It concerns the process by which newcomers become part of a community of practice. A person's intentions to learn are engaged and the meaning of learning is configured through the process of becoming a full participant in a sociocultural practice. This social process includes, indeed it subsumes, the learning of knowledgeable skills.

In order to explain our interest in the concept of legitimate peripheral participation, we will try to convey a sense of the perspectives that it opens and the kinds of questions that it raises. A good way to start is to outline the history of the concept as it has become increasingly central to our thinking about issues of learning. Our initial intention in writing what has gradually evolved into this book (Jean Lave and Etienne Wenger, 1991, *Situated Learning: Legitimate Peripheral Participation*. Cambridge: Cambridge University Press) was to rescue the idea of *apprenticeship*. In 1988, notions about apprenticeship were flying around the halls of the Institute for Research on Learning, acting as a token of solidarity and as a focus for discussions on the nature of learning. We and our colleagues had begun to talk about learners as apprentices, about teachers and computers as masters, and about cognitive apprenticeship, apprenticeship learning, and even life as apprenticeship. It was evident that no one was certain what the term meant. Furthermore, it was understood to be a synonym for *situated learning*, about which we were equally uncertain. Resort to one did not clarify the other. Apprenticeship had become yet another panacea for a broad spectrum of learning-research problems, and it was in danger of becoming meaningless.

Other considerations motivated this work as well. Our own earlier work on craft apprenticeship in West Africa, on intelligent tutoring systems, and on the cultural transparency of technology seemed relevant and at the same time insufficient for the development of an adequate theory of learning, giving us an urgent sense that we needed such a theory. Indeed, our central ideas took shape as we came to see that the most interesting features both of apprenticeship and of 'glass-box' approaches to the development and understanding of technology could be characterized – and analyzed – as legitimate peripheral participation in communities of practice.

The notion that learning through apprenticeship was a matter of legitimate peripheral participation arose first in research on craft apprenticeship among Vai and Gola tailors in Liberia (J. Lave, in preparation). In that context it was simply an observation about the tailors' apprentices within an analysis addressing questions of how apprentices might engage in a common, structured pattern of learning experiences without being taught, examined, or reduced to mechanical copiers of everyday tailoring tasks, and of how they become, with remarkably few exceptions, skilled and respected master tailors. It was difficult, however, to separate the historically and culturally specific circumstances that made Vai and Gola apprenticeship both effective and benign as a form of education from the critique of schooling and school practices that this inevitably suggested, or from a more general theory of situated learning. This added to the general confusion that encouraged us to undertake this project.

Over the past two years we have attempted to clarify the confusion. Two moments in that process were especially important. To begin with, the uses of 'apprenticeship' in cognitive and educational research were largely metaphorical, even though apprenticeship as an actual educational form clearly had a long and varied train of historically and culturally specific realizations. We gradually became convinced that we needed to reexamine the relationship between the 'apprenticeship' of speculation and historical forms of apprenticeship. This led us to insist on the distinction between our theoretical framework for analyzing educational forms and specific historical instances of apprenticeship. This in turn led us to explore learning as 'situated learning'.

Second, this conception of situated learning clearly was more encompassing in intent than conventional notions of 'learning *in situ*' or 'learning by doing' for which it was used as a rough equivalent. But, to articulate this intuition usefully, we needed a better characterization of 'situatedness' as a theoretical perspective. The attempt to clarify the concept of situated learning led to critical concerns about the theory and to further revisions that resulted in the move to our present view that learning is an integral and inseparable aspect of social practice. We have tried to capture this new view under the rubric of legitimate peripheral participation.

Discussing each shift in turn may help to clarify our reasons for coming to characterize learning as legitimate peripheral participation in communities of practice.

From apprenticeship to situated learning

Fashioning a firm distinction between historical *forms* of apprenticeship and situated learning as a historical–cultural *theory* required that we stop trying to use empirical cases of apprenticeship as a lens through which to view all forms of learning. On these grounds we started to reconsider the forms of apprenticeship with which we were most familiar as models of effective learning in the context of a broader theoretical goal. Nevertheless, specific cases of apprenticeship were of vital interest in the process of developing and exemplifying a theory of situated learning and we thus continued to use some of these studies as resources in working out our ideas. We might equally have turned to studies of socialization; children are, after all, quintessentially legitimate peripheral participants in adult social worlds. But various forms of apprenticeship seemed to capture very well our interest in learning in situated ways – in the transformative possibilities of being and becoming complex, full cultural–historical participants in the world – and it would be difficult to think of a more apt range of social practices for this purpose.

The distinction between historical cases of apprenticeship and a theory of situated learning was strengthened as we developed a more comprehensive view of different approaches to situatedness. Existing confusion over the meaning of situated learning and, more generally, situated activity resulted from differing interpretations of the concept. On some occasions 'situated' seemed to mean merely that some of people's thoughts and actions were located in space and time. On other occasions, it seemed to mean that thought and action were social only in the narrow sense that they involved other people, or that they were immediately dependent for meaning on the social setting that occasioned them. These types of interpretation, akin to naive views of indexicality, usually took some activities to be situated and some not.

In the concept of situated activity we were developing, however, the situatedness of activity appeared to be anything but a simple empirical attribute of everyday activity or a corrective to conventional pessimism about informal, experience-based learning. Instead, it took on the proportions of a general theoretical perspective, the basis of claims about the relational character of knowledge and learning, about the negotiated character of meaning, and about the concerned (engaged, dilemma-driven) nature of learning activity for the people involved. That perspective meant that there is no activity that is not situated. It implied emphasis on comprehensive understanding involving the whole person rather than 'receiving' a body of factual knowledge about the world; on activity in and with the world; and on the view that agent, activity, and the world mutually constitute each other.

We have discovered that this last conception of situated activity and situated learning, which has gradually emerged in our understanding, frequently generates resistance, for it seems to carry with it connotations of parochialism, particularity, and the limitations of a given time and task. This misinterpretation of situated learning requires comment. (Our own objections to theorizing in terms of situated learning are somewhat different. These will become clearer shortly.) The first point to consider is that even so-called general knowledge only has power in specific circumstances. Generality is often associated with abstract representations, with decontextualization. But abstract representations are meaningless unless they can be made specific to the situation at hand. Moreover, the formation or acquisition of an abstract principle is itself a specific event in specific circumstances. Knowing a general rule by itself in no way assures that any generality it may carry is enabled in the specific circumstances in which it is relevant. In this sense, any 'power of abstraction' is thoroughly situated, in the lives of persons and in the culture that makes it possible. On the other hand, the world carries its own structure so that speci-ficity always implies generality (and in this sense generality is not to be assimi-lated to abstractness). That is why stories can be so powerful in conveying ideas, often more so than an articulation of the idea itself. What is called general knowledge is not privileged with respect to other 'kinds' of knowledge. It, too, can be gained only in specific circumstances. And it too must be brought into play in specific circumstances. The generality of any form of knowledge always lies in the power to renegotiate the meaning of the past and future in construct-ing the meaning of present circumstances.

From situated learning to legitimate peripheral participation

This brings us to the second shift in perspective that led us to explore learning as legitimate peripheral participation. The notion of situated learning now appears to be a transitory concept, a bridge, between a view according to which cognitive processes (and thus learning) are primary and a view according to which social practice is the primary, generative phenomenon, and learning is one of its characteristics. There is a significant contrast between a theory of learning in which practice (in a narrow, replicative sense) is subsumed within processes of learning and one in which learning is taken to be an integral aspect of practice (in a historical, generative sense). In our view, learning is not merely situated in practice – as if it were some independently reifiable process that just happened to be located somewhere; learning is an integral part of generative social practice in the lived-in world. The problem – and the central preoccupation of this monograph – is to translate this into a specific analytic approach to learning. Legitimate peripheral participation is proposed as a descriptor of engagement in social practice that entails learning as an integral constituent.

Before proceeding with a discussion of the analytic questions involved in a social practice theory of learning, we need to discuss our choices of terms and the issues that they reflect, in order to clarify our conception of legitimate peripheral participation. Its composite character, and the fact that it is not difficult to propose a contrary for each of its components, may be misleading. It seems all too natural to decompose it into a set of three contrasting pairs: legitimate versus illegitimate, peripheral versus central, participation versus nonparticipation. But we intend for the concept to be taken as a whole. Each of its aspects is indispensable in defining the others and cannot be considered in isolation. Its constituents contribute inseparable aspects whose combinations create a landscape – shapes, degrees, textures – of community membership.

Thus, in the terms proposed here there may very well be no such thing as an 'illegitimate peripheral participant'. The form that the legitimacy of participa-tion takes is a defining characteristic of ways of belonging, and is therefore not only a crucial condition for learning, but a constitutive element of its content. Similarly, with regard to 'peripherality' there may well be no such simple thing as 'central participation' in a community of practice. Peripherality suggests that there are multiple, varied, more- or less-engaged and -inclusive ways of being located in the fields of participation defined by a community. Peripheral participation is about being located in the social world. *Changing* locations and perspectives are part of actors' learning trajectories, developing identities, and forms of membership.

Furthermore, legitimate peripherality is a complex notion, implicated in social structures involving relations of power. As a place in which one moves toward more-intensive participation, peripherality is an empowering position. As a place in which one is kept from participating more fully – often legitimately, from the broader perspective of society at large – it is a disempowering position. Beyond that, legitimate peripherality can be a position at the articulation of related communities. In this sense, it can itself be a source of power or powerlessness, in affording or preventing articulation and interchange among communities of practice. The ambiguous potentialities of legitimate peripherality reflect the concept's pivotal role in providing access to a nexus of relations otherwise not perceived as connected.

Given the complex, differentiated nature of communities, it seems important not to reduce the end point of centripetal participation in a community of practice to a uniform or univocal 'centre', or to a linear notion of skill acquisition. There is no place in a community of practice designated 'the periphery', and, most emphatically, it has no single core or centre. *Central participation* would imply that there is a centre (physical, political, or metaphorical) to a community with respect to an individual's 'place' in it. *Complete participation* would suggest a closed domain of knowledge or collective practice for which there might be measurable degrees of 'acquisition' by newcomers. We have chosen to call that to which peripheral participation leads, *full participation*. Full participation is intended to do justice to the diversity of relations involved in varying forms of community membership.

Full participation, however, stands in contrast to only one aspect of the concept of peripherality as we see it: It places the emphasis on what partial participation is not, or not yet. In our usage, *peripherality* is also *a positive* term, whose most salient conceptual antonyms are *unrelatedness* or *irrelevance* to ongoing activity. The partial participation of newcomers is by no means 'disconnected' from the practice of interest. Furthermore, it is also a dynamic concept. In this sense, peripherality, when it is enabled, suggests an opening, a way of gaining access to sources for understanding through growing involvement. The ambiguity inherent in peripheral participation must then be connected to issues of legitimacy, of the social organization of and control over resources, if it is to gain its full analytical potential.

An analytic perspective on learning

With the first shift in the development of this project we have tried to establish that our historical–cultural theory of learning should not be merely an abstracted generalization of the concrete cases of apprenticeship – or any other educational form. Further, coming to see that a theory of situated activity challenges the very meaning of abstraction and/or generalization has led us to reject conventional readings of the generalizability and/or abstraction of 'knowledge'. Arguing in favour of a shift away from a theory of situated activity in which learning is reified as one kind of activity, and toward a theory of social practice in which learning is viewed as an aspect of all activity, has led us to consider how we are to think about our own practice. And this has revealed a dilemma: How can we purport to be working out a *theoretical conception* of learning without, in fact, engaging in just the project of abstraction rejected above?

There are several classical dualist oppositions that in many contexts are treated as synonymous, or nearly so: abstract–concrete; general–particular; theory about the world, and the world so described. Theory is assumed to be general and abstract, the world, concrete and particular. But in the Marxist historical tradition that underpins social practice theory these terms take on different relations with each other and different meanings. They do so as part of a general method of social analysis. This method does not deny that there is a concrete world, which is ordinarily perceived as some collection of particularities, just as it is possible to invent simple, thin, abstract theoretical propositions about it. But these two possibilities are not considered as the two poles of interest. Instead, both of them offer points of departure for starting to explore and produce an understanding of multiply determined, diversely unified – that is, complexly concrete – historical processes, of which particularities (including initial theories) are the result (Marx 1857; Hall 1973; Ilyenkov 1977). The theorist is trying to recapture those relations in an analytic way that turns the apparently 'natural' categories and forms of social life into challenges to our understanding of how they are (historically and culturally) produced and reproduced. The goal, in Marx's memorable phrase, is to 'ascend (from both the particular and the abstract) to the concrete'.

It may now be clearer why it is not appropriate to treat legitimate peripheral participation as a mere distillation of apprenticeship, an abstracting process of generalizing from examples of apprenticeship. (Indeed, turned onto apprenticeship, the concept should provide the same analytical leverage as it would for any other educational form.) Our theorizing about legitimate peripheral participation thus is not intended as abstraction, but as an attempt to explore its concrete relations. To think about a concept like legitimate peripheral participation in this way is to argue that its theoretical significance derives from the richness of its interconnections: in historical terms, through time and across cultures. It may convey better what we mean by a historically, culturally concrete 'concept' to describe legitimate peripheral participation as an 'analytical perspective'. We use these two terms interchangeably hereafter.

With legitimate peripheral participation

We do not talk here about schools in any substantial way, nor explore what our work has to say about schooling. Steering clear of the problem of school learning for the present was a conscious decision, which was not always easy to adhere to as the issue kept creeping into our discussions. But, although we mention schooling at various points, we have refrained from any systematic treatment of the subject. It is worth outlining our reasons for this restraint, in part because this may help clarify further the theoretical status of the concept of legitimate peripheral participation.

First, as we began to focus on legitimate peripheral participation, we wanted above all to take a fresh look at learning. Issues of learning and schooling seemed to have become too deeply interrelated in our culture in general, both for purposes of our own exploration and the exposition of our ideas. More importantly, the organization of schooling as an educational form is predicated on claims that knowledge can be decontextualized, and yet schools themselves as social institutions and as places of learning constitute very specific contexts. Thus, analysis of school learning as situated requires a multilayered view of how knowing and learning are part of social practice – a major project in its own right. Last, but not least, pervasive claims concerning the sources of the effectiveness of schooling (in teaching, in the specialization of schooling in changing persons, in the special modes of inculcation for which schools are known) stand in contradiction with the situated perspective we have adopted. All this has meant that our discussions of schooling were often contrastive, even oppositional. But we did not want to define our thinking and build our theory primarily by contrast to the claims of any educational form, including schooling. We wanted to develop a view of learning that would stand on its own, reserving the analysis of schooling and other specific educational forms for the future.

We should emphasize, therefore, that legitimate peripheral participation is not itself an educational form, much less a pedagogical strategy or a teaching technique. It is an analytical viewpoint on learning, a way of understanding learning. We hope to make clear as we proceed that learning through legitimate peripheral participation takes place no matter which educational form provides a context for learning, or whether there is any intentional educational form at all. Indeed, this viewpoint makes a fundamental distinction between learning and intentional instruction. Such decoupling does not deny that learning can take place where there is teaching, but does not take intentional instruction to be in itself the source or cause of learning, and thus does not blunt the claim that what gets learned is problematic with respect to what is taught. Undoubtedly, the analytical perspective of legitimate peripheral participation could – we hope that it will – inform educational endeavours by shedding a new light on learning processes, and by drawing attention to key aspects of learning experience that may be overlooked. But this is very different from attributing a prescriptive value to the concept of legitimate peripheral participation and from proposing ways of 'implementing' or 'operationalizing' it for educational purposes.

Even though we decided to set aside issues of schooling in this initial stage of our work, we are persuaded that rethinking schooling from the perspective afforded by legitimate peripheral participation will turn out to be a fruitful exercise. Such an analysis would raise questions about the place of schooling in the community at large in terms of possibilities for developing identities of mastery. These include questions of the relation of school practices to those of the communities in which the knowledge that schools are meant to 'impart' is located, as well as issues concerning relations between the world of schooling and the world of adults more generally. Such a study would also raise questions about the social organization of schools themselves into communities of practice, both official and interstitial, with varied forms of membership. We would predict that such an investigation would afford a better context for determining what students learn and what they do not, and what it comes to mean for them, than would a study of the curriculum or of instructional practices.

Thinking about schooling in terms of legitimate peripheral participation is only one of several directions that seem promising for pursuing the analysis of contemporary and other historical forms of social practice in terms of legitimate peripheral participation in communities of practice. There are central issues that are only touched upon in this monograph and that need to be given more attention. The concept of 'community of practice' is left largely as an intuitive notion, which serves a purpose here but which requires a more rigorous treatment. In particular, unequal relations of power must be included more systematically in our analysis. Hegemony over resources for learning and alienation from full participation are inherent in the shaping of the legitimacy and peripherality of participation in its historical realizations. It would be useful to understand better how these relations generate characteristically interstitial communities of practice and truncate possibilities for identities of mastery.

* Chapter 3 first appeared in *Situated Learning: Legitimate Peripheral Participation*, 1991, published by Cambridge University Press.

References

Hall, S. (1973) A 'reading' of Marx's 1857 'Introduction to the Grundrisse'. General Series: Stencilled Occasional Paper No. 1. Birmingham: Centre for Contemporary Cultural Studies, University of Birmingham.

Ilyenkov, E.V. (1977) *Dialectical Logic: Essays on its History and Theory.* Moscow: Progress Publishers.

Lave, J. (in preparation) *Tailored Learning: Apprenticeship and Everyday Practice among Craftsmen in West Africa.*

Marx, K. (1857) Introduction to a critique of political economy. Version of the introduction to the *Grundrisse* published as supplementary text in C.J. Arthur (ed.) *The German Ideology*, 1988. New York: International Publishers.

Chapter 4

Looking beyond the interface

Activity theory and distributed learning

David R. Russell

Introduction

In this chapter, I first outline some basic principles of activity theory and then explore some ways it has proved valuable for analysing distributed learning, in both schooling and workplace training. Activity theory was developed out of the Russian developmental psychologist L.S. Vygotsky's (1994) cultural–historical approach to learning by one of his two main collaborators, A.N. Leont'ev (1981), beginning in the late 1930s. It has evolved into a major direction in psychology (called 'cultural psychology') and now has adherents worldwide.

Activity theory (AT) (see also Billett, Chapter 5) has for many years been used in studies of human–computer interaction, such as computer interface design and computer-supported cooperative work (Nardi 1996). In the past 5 years, it has begun to be used to understand distributed learning, as technological innovations in education have often 'seemed to be designed to exploit the capabilities of the technology rather than to meet an instructional need', to be technology-driven rather than theory-driven (Koschmann 1996: 83). As a result, instructional designers have often overlooked the cultural and historical aspects of education, focusing instead on individual learners encountering the machine interface (Kapetin and Cole 1997; Lewis 1997; Bakardjieva 1998; Guribye and Wasson 1999).

AT, like many of the other theories in this volume, attempts to go beyond the theories of learning that seem so obvious when teachers or instructional designers look at a person in front of a computer 'learning' the 'material' that appears on the screen. At first glance we imagine, perhaps, an individual responding to stimuli on the screen, internalising 'material' through repetition. In this view, the behaviourist stimulus–response learning theory seems a good enough explanation. Or we imagine, within the mind of the individual looking at the screen, inborn structures of thought being activated, in a communication of ideas between minds, as in idealist theories (like Plato's or Kant's) or structuralist theories (like Piaget's). Yet when we look further back over time, things often seem much less tidy. Some people do not learn at all but turn away from the screen, lacking motivation. Some interpret that 'material' in ways we may not expect (and may not like). People learn (and forget) to different degrees and in different ways, or put that learning to unexpected uses which thwart our object as teachers/designers. Faced with these problems, the old and still-dominant educational theories that focus on individuals are often inadequate to the daunting complexity of the task designers of distributed learning face. Distributed learning is often, in a word, messy – despite the seeming simplicity of person–screen–content.

AT understands this complexity as the effect of tool mediation. Human learning, unlike much animal learning, is mediated by cultural tools. Most human learning, from a very early age, is not the simple result of stimuli or inborn cognitive structures, but rather a complex result of our interactions with others mediated by tools in the culture, including language. Vygotsky expanded the behaviourist theory of learning by introducing the concept of tool mediation (see Figure 4.1). When people encounter some object in the environment, a stimulus, they interpret and act on it not directly, but through the mediation of tools used by others. For example, a child learns to use a ball as part of joint activity – by watching others use the ball in a game, by listening to their words (another kind of tool) and perhaps by becoming involved in the game, the joint activity.

Some instructional designers and educational researchers have found AT useful because it looks beyond the individual learner, the interface and the 'material' to understand the social and material relations that affect complex human learning, people's interactions with others as mediated by tools, including symbols.

AT understands learning not as the internalisation of discrete information or skills by individuals, but rather as expanding involvement over time – social as well as intellectual – with other people and the tools available in their culture. 'The question of individual learning now becomes the question of how that which is inside a person might change over time as a consequence of repeated social interactions with' other people and their tools, including the very powerful tools of words, images and gestures (Hutchins 1995: 290).

If learning with computers is – despite the surface appearance – profoundly social and cultural, then we who design distributed learning need to theorise how people use cultural tools to teach and learn, to change and be changed, through our interactions with others. In sum, AT can provide a richly descriptive answer to the question: Why and how do people learn (or fail to learn)

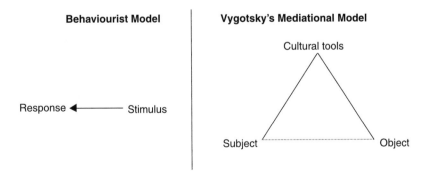

Figure 4.1 Two models of cognition and learning.

using computer networks? AT has been criticised as a 'loose' theory, more valuable for understanding what went wrong than doing predictive work (Nardi 1998; Roschelle 1998). Indeed, AT is less a tight theory than 'a philosophical framework for studying different forms of human praxis as developmental processes, both individual and social levels interlinked at the same time' (Kuuti 1994: 52). AT is a heuristic framework for asking important questions that other theories may not raise so clearly, and for seeing relationships among those questions that may guide design and evaluation.

When we see students encountering course materials via liquid crystal displays, it is easy to forget that there is much more going on. AT helps us remain aware of the intersections with the very dispersed activities and trajectories of the participants engaged in activity together – designers, teachers, students, technicians and others. AT prompts us to ask how we can 're-mediate' our interactions by changing our tools or the ways we share them with others. The questions AT invites us to ask grow out of some basic principles of behaviour, communication and learning. These principles push us to look beyond the interface to wider tool-mediated social interactions.

Basic principles

Although AT is a dynamic and evolving theory, several basic principles are shared by its adherents. Here I draw mainly on Cole's (1996) important book, *Cultural Psychology*.

- Human behaviour is social in origin, and human activity is collective (Cole and Engeström 1993). Human–computer interactions are also social in origin. Even when we are alone in front of a screen, we are in a profound sense engaging in collective activity, although that activity may be widely distributed in time and space, mediated by complex networks of tools.
- Human consciousness – 'mind' – grows out of people's joint activity with shared tools. Our minds are in a sense co-constructed and distributed among others. Our thoughts, our words and our deeds are always potentially engaged with the thoughts, words and deeds of others. Through involvement in collective activity, however widely distributed, learners are always in contact with the history, values and social relations of a community – or among communities – as embedded in the shared cultural tools used by that community or communities.
- AT emphasises tool-mediated action in context. Human beings not only act on their environment with tools, they also think and learn with tools. At a primary level these tools are material, 'external' – hammers, books, clothing, computers, telecommunications networks. But we also fashion and use tools at a secondary or 'internal' level – language, concepts, scripts, schemas. Both kinds of tools are used to act on the environment collectively (Wartofsky 1979). This suggests that distributed learning must take into account *all* the tools people use, not just the computer, as well as the relations among tools of various kinds as they mediate joint activity.
- AT is interested in development and change, which it understands broadly to include historical change, individual development and moment-to-

moment change. All three levels of analysis are necessary to understand people learning with computers.

- AT grounds analysis in everyday life events, the ways people interact with each other using tools over time. It looks beyond the student-with-computer to understand the (techno-) human lives we live and their broad potential for learning and growing together.
- AT assumes that 'individuals are active agents in their own development but do not act in settings entirely of their own choosing' (Cole 1996: 104). Individual learners learn, of course, but they do so in environments that involve others, environments of people-with-tools that both afford and constrain their actions. Telecommunications networks always do both.
- As Cole states, AT 'rejects cause and effect, stimulus response, explanatory science in favor of a science that emphasises the emergent nature of mind in activity and that acknowledges a central role for interpretation in its explanatory framework'. Accordingly, it 'draws upon methodologies from the humanities as well as from the social and biological sciences' (Cole 1996: 104). As we shall see, AT studies of distributed learning often combine traditional comparison-group studies with case studies, ethnographic observation, discourse analysis and rhetorical analysis to make sense of – rather than 'control for' – the complexity of human learning mediated by telecommunications networks.

An activity system: the basic unit of analysis

When we look at the myriad people, and the tools and relationships among them that affect distributed learning, it is difficult to know what to focus on, how far to go beyond the learner and the interface. What are we really looking at when we see students attempting to learn with electronic information technology? What, in other words, is the unit of analysis? According to AT, it is not a collection of individuals and stimuli. AT suggests we focus on a group of people who share a common object and motive over time, and the wide range of tools (including computers) they share to act on that object and realise that motive – what AT calls an 'activity system'. The activity system is a flexible unit of analysis (theoretical lens), which allows us to train our gaze in different directions and with different levels of 'magnification' to help us answer the questions that puzzle us. The world is not neatly divided into activity systems. It is up to the researcher or designer to define the activity system based on the purposes of the research study or the design task, to focus the theoretical lens AT provides.

For AT, the activity system – not the individual – is the basic unit of analysis for both cultures' and individuals' psychological and social processes, including learning. As Vygotsky's basic mediational triangle (Figure 4.1) suggests, any time a person or group (subject) interacts with tools over time on some object with some shared motive to achieve some outcome, one can analyse their interactions as an activity system. We might, for example, view as an activity system a hobby club, a religious organisation, an advocacy group, a political movement, a school, a discipline, a research laboratory, a profession, a government agency, a company – even a group of friends who gather regularly at a pub for conversation (Engeström 1987; Cole and Engeström 1993). But one can also focus the 'lens' more tightly: on activity systems that are part of a larger activity or institution, such as a course of study or a distributed learning design group.

In one sense, an activity system might be thought of as a context for behaviour and learning, but not in the sense of something that *surrounds* the individual's behaviour and learning. Rather, it is a functional system of social/cultural interactions that constitutes behaviour and produces that kind of change called learning. In this AT view, context is not a container for a learner, but rather a weaving together of the learner with other people and tools into a web or network of sociocultural interactions and meanings that are integral to the learning. (It is helpful to recall that the word 'text' is from the Greek word 'weaving' – as in 'textile'. In this sense, con-text is what is 'woven together'.) By viewing context as a functional system rather than a container, the designer of distributed learning can identify behaviours and try to explain their meanings in terms of the activity systems in which they are produced and understood. This is why learning is conceived of as expanding involvement with an activity system(s) (Cole 1996).

Engeström (1987) has developed Vygotsky's basic mediational triangle to represent more fully the essential social relations that teachers and designers need to account for to understand learning (Figure 4.2). This diagram suggests the various elements of an activity system (the nodes) and their connecting relations (the lines). By understanding joint activity that results in change (learning), we can perhaps ask more effective questions about how an activity functions (or fails to function) for an individual or group – the subject in the diagram.

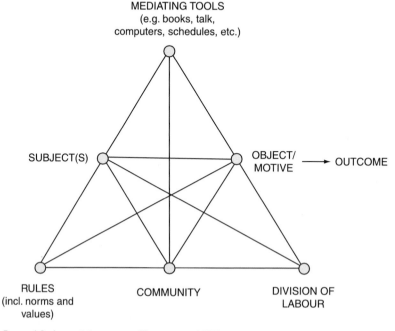

Figure 4.2 An activity system (Engeström 1987).

Let us look first at the elements of an activity system, using Engeström's version, and note the possible relations between them. To illustrate how AT may help us to understand distributed learning, I will refer to a course in media studies I have taught for 10 years and have recently put online. I will view the course as an activity system to help me answer the very broad question: How does distributed learning shape the teaching and learning? (AT analysis, like any other, begins with questions or problems.)

Activity systems have a *subject(s)* – an individual or sub-group engaged in an activity – in this case the students and the teacher. It is crucial to remember here that each of us participates in many activity systems (home, school, work, clubs, political parties, etc.) and each brings a different history of diverse involvements to a particular activity system. One must recognise 'where students are coming from' – their history of previous involvements – to understand their distributed learning. As the subjects (people) engage in some joint activity over time – an activity system – they change (and learn) as they negotiate new ways of acting together. Again, learning is viewed as expanding involvement – social as well as intellectual – with some activity system over time, rather than the internalisation of discrete information or skills. In terms of my course, the re-mediation of distributed learning made it more difficult, in one sense, for the subjects to get to know one another, because the tools for teaching and learning changed from primarily oral to entirely written; however, in another sense, students' postings about themselves on the first day provided a more permanent reference point than first-day introductions in a conventional course. And we often referred back to these. The tool–subject relationship allowed me to see many affordances and constraints, such as these, as the course moved online.

The *object* refers to the 'raw material' or 'problem space' on which the subject brings to bear various tools. This might be the 'object of study' of some discipline (e.g. cells in cytology, literary works in literary criticism) or the object of some production process (automobiles in an automobile company). In my course, it is the 'content': mass media studies. The object is more than raw stimuli; it is a culturally formed object with a history, however short or long. The object or focus of activity implies an overall direction of that activity, a (provisionally) shared purpose or *motive* (e.g. analysing cells or literary works, building and selling automobiles). In my case, the motive is officially learning about mass media studies. Of course, the direction or motive of an activity system and its object may be understood differently or even contested, as participants bring many motives to a collective interaction and as conditions change. Dissensus, resistance, conflicts and deep contradictions are constantly produced in activity systems, as we shall see. Students approach the course with different understandings of media studies and different motives for studying it, as I found out when they responded to my online questions with answers that often made me wonder if they were enrolled in the same course! I had to design interactions to make these differences evident and come to a generally shared understanding of the object – media studies – and the motives for studying it. Again, this was both afforded and constrained by the distributed electronic tools. Moreover, the object/motive of the course for the first 2 weeks unexpectedly became learning to use computers, not the 'content', as students and I

(I have to confess) primarily focused our attention on getting used to the interface. What was expected to be a mediational tool, the computer interface, became instead the object – although we were able to work that out in time and focus on the desired object/motive.

Finally, people who use tools act on the object to produce some *outcome*, which may be anticipated or surprising (e.g. research articles in cytology and literary criticism, automobiles made and sold in an automobile company, etc.).

Tools are understood as anything that mediates subjects' action upon objects. Like other species, humans act purposefully to meet biological needs; but unlike other species, human behaviour may differ radically among groups because we use tools, cultural artefacts. (Think of all the different ways of meeting the biological need for shelter in different cultures, in contrast to the bee's hive or the robin's nest.) There are many means (tools) that may be used by humans to achieve a similar outcome – for example, to send a message or teach arithmetic – and how these differ culturally and historically. The use of tools (including writing, speaking, gesture, architecture, clothing, as well as conventional tools) mediates humans' interactions, separating biological motives from the socially constructed – human – objects and motives of activity. And the tools that people in some activity system share and the ways they use them change over time, as they borrow new ways of working together from other activity systems or invent entirely new ways, potentially transforming the activity. Introducing computers, for example, has often changed the activity of teaching and learning, as was the case in my course. But there were many other tools in the course, both physical and conceptual – readings, images, video, theories, questions, and so on – which had to be re-thought in relation to the computer tools.

As Engeström has extended the analysis of activity systems (the bottom triangles in Figure 4.1), we can see the essential elements of the social relations necessary to activity. The subject is (or is part of a larger) *community*, which conditions all the other elements of the system. Although people engaged in the same activity may be separated by great distances, as in distributed learning, or by differences of many kinds – including deep conflicts – if they act together on a common object with a common motive over time, they form a community. In my course, the community was the students and myself. But in a wider sense, we were part of the community of scholars in media studies (in which the students were neophytes), and our reading and writing, collectively and individually, made us interact with that wider community, the discipline. We were linked, electronically through the World Wide Web and e-mail, as well as through print media, to others engaged in mass media studies, beyond the participants in the class. The mediation of the computer allowed us to be in wider and more sustained contact both with examples of mass media (on the web) – the object of study – and with the community of scholars who study it.

Moreover, we see that activity systems also have a *division of labour* that shapes the way the subject(s) acts on the object (and potentially all the other elements of the system). People take on different roles in the activity. In traditional schooling, for example, the labour is divided between a teacher (who teaches) and students (who learn). But new affordances and constraints, arising at any of the other nodes, may change the division of labour. For example, new tools, such as computerised communication, may drive changes that allow the division of labour to change and students to function more as teachers of other students, or even as teachers of the teacher. This happened in our course, often to my surprise. The new tool, the computer, mediated the division of labour in new ways. It allowed students to quickly bring new materials to the attention of the teacher and other students, through links to websites. And, as I mentioned before, it allowed students' comments to remain for inspection and further written discussion. The division of labour moved in such a way that I became (sometimes reluctantly) much more of a facilitator, coordinating the posting and written discussion of various mass media materials the students brought from the web. The re-mediation also made the division of labour more complex in that the software tools allowed groups of students to carry on sustained (and preserved) interactions during the course that would have been impractical without these new electronic tools.

Activity systems always have *rules*, broadly understood not only as formal and explicit but also as unwritten or tacit – what are often called norms, routines, habits and values. These rules shape the interactions of subject and tools with the object. Of course, these rules can also alter, tacitly or explicitly, with changes in other nodes in the system, but the rules allow the system to be 'stablised-for-now'. The re-mediation of the course through computer tools necessitated a host of new rules and norms. In one sense, it made the rules more explicit, firmer, because they could not be communicated tacitly or negotiated quickly in face-to-face interaction. The norms for 'discussion', largely assumed in the face-to-face classroom, had to be worked out explicitly with the new tool, requiring written procedures for carrying on asynchronous discussion to maintain the subjects' focus on the object and realise the motives of the course. But the re-mediation of the course also allowed certain rules (e.g. schedules and routines) to be built into the interface and become invisible (though less negotiable) for participants.

Contradictions: when people are at cross-purposes

As we have noticed, activity systems we human beings make are constantly subject to change. The version of AT I describe sees these changes as driven by *contradictions* within and among activity systems. An activity system 'is constantly working through contradictions within and between its elements' (Engeström 1987). In this sense, an activity system 'is a virtual disturbance- and innovation-producing machine' (Engeström 1990: 11). A change in any element of the activity system may conflict with another element, placing people at cross-purposes.

Contradictions can emerge between and among any of the elements of the activity system. Let me illustrate this with a different example. One may analyse as an activity system the teachers in my university English department who had over time used web-based teaching materials they created themselves. These tools were very loosely structured, with a range of links among them through which students could access the materials along different paths. Indeed, we valued this flexibility so highly that it became a norm (rule) for teaching. When my department wished to offer distributed learning courses, the university

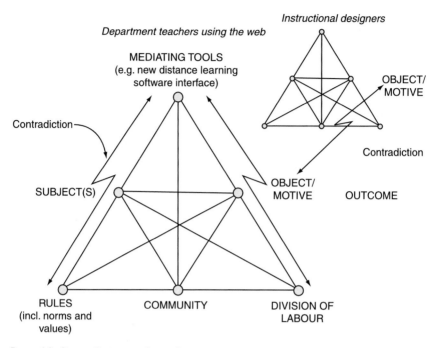

Figure 4.3 Contradictions within and among activity systems.

required my department to use a 'distance learning' software program supported by the university's instructional design unit. The program required us to organise teaching materials along a linear 'learning path' which students had to follow in order, lockstep. This produced a contradiction between the activity systems of instructional design and departmental teachers of mass media (see the broken arrow between the object/motive of the two activity systems in Figure 4.3).

Moreover, contradictions may arise between and among activity systems. Because the required distance learning web program was more complex and time-consuming to use, it required English teachers to turn to an instructional designer from another activity system, the instructional design unit, who was familiar with the software program – but not with our teaching content or methods (object/motive, rules). This new web tool required a new *division of labour* in our teaching, which produced conflict that had to be resolved over time (see the broken arrow between tools and division of labour in Figure 4.3).

Contradictions may also arise when participants from different activity systems have different objects and motives. For example, the instructional designer's object/motive was the software and its efficient functioning. The object/motive of the department's teachers was the students' learning about mass media. For teachers, the software was a tool, not an object/motive, and one that we wished to think about as little as possible. This produced a contradiction between the activity systems of instructional design and mass media teaching (see the broken arrow on the right in Figure 4.3). There was and is a great deal of conflict (pedagogical and political) that we are trying to understand and deal with as we 're-mediate' our teaching using the new software – and the new relationships with people who have a different object and motive.

Zones of proximal development: construction zones for learning

We have seen how AT answers the question: What are we looking at? I now turn to the question: What are we looking for – and hoping to design – in using AT for distributed learning? We are looking for (and designing) times and places where people's involvement in a shared activity with cultural tools can produce that kind of change called learning.

Because the activity systems that form (and are formed by) our lives are dynamic, they constantly present opportunities for learning. Vygotsky called these opportunities 'zones of proximal development' (ZPD), which he defined as the difference between what one could do alone and what one could do with assistance. That assistance might come from teachers, peers, co-workers or others. In these 'construction zones', learning takes place as people using tools mutually change themselves and their tools (Newman *et al.* 1989: 61). People change and learn as they expand their involvement with others in a community, and the tools that community uses in certain ways. In this view, learning is social. What appears first in the social or interpersonal plane is then (perhaps) internalised, appearing on the cognitive or intrapersonal plane. It may then be externalised in future social activity, leading to further change and perhaps learning. It is, in Engeström's (1987) phrase, 'learning by expanding'.

In Vygotsky's classic experiment, for example, an adult asks a young child to fetch a toy (object/motive) from a shelf that is too high for the child to reach without the aid of a stool and a stick placed in the room (cultural tools). When the child cannot immediately reach the toy, she may ask for aid from the adult, who then shows her how to use the tools to reach the toy. A zone of proximal development has formed between what the child could do without and what she could do through social interaction using certain cultural tools (tool, stick, words, gestures).

To extend this basic concept to distributed learning, we might imagine a course that consisted merely of readings posted on the web, compared to a course that provided opportunities for interactions with teachers, other students and perhaps outside experts. It is those human interactions, mediated by a range of tools, that allow zones of proximal development to emerge.

The significance of AT for distributed learning lies in its ability to analyse the dynamic human interactions mediated by computers at both the micro (psychological and interpersonal) and the macro (sociological or cultural) levels to understand – and construct – zones of proximal development. Computers are thus viewed as one tool among many others (architecture, clothing, speaking, writing, money, schedules, etc.) through which knowledge, identity, authority and power relations are continually (re)negotiated. Learning is therefore not a neat transfer of information but a complex and often messy network of tool-mediated human relationships that must be explored in terms of the social and cultural practices which people bring to their uses of the tools they share.

How AT has been used: three examples

I give below three examples of instructional designers using AT to understand and restructure (re-mediate) distributed learning. AT has mainly used qualitative and historical research methods, although all three projects I describe also used some quantitative methods. Space does not permit me to elaborate either. URLs in the references below provide details of each project.

AT in evaluating distributed learning: the Docta Project

A group of Norwegian researchers are using AT to study the design and use of collaborative telelearning scenarios, the Docta Project (2000). For them, AT offers an insight into 'the processes of collaboration, enabling us to identify collaboration patterns and further our understanding of how instructors, students and other learning facilitators organise their learning and work' (Wasson and Morch 1999). For example, Andreassen (2000) followed three graduate students taking teacher training courses at universities in different cities. The students collaboratively used a web-based shared workspace called TeamWave. They had two goals, the first of which was to learn Salomon's (1992) techniques for creating 'genuine interdependence' in work; that is, collaboration where the group can achieve more collectively than individually, as distinct from mere 'cooperation' where the result is merely the sum of individual efforts – 'ganging up on the task'. The second goal was to use 'genuine interdependence' to collaboratively create a web-based learning environment on endangered animal species for primary school science students.

Andreassen (2000) found that the students did not use the software tools to produce genuine interdependence, a 'partnership of collaborating peers', but rather 'ganged up on the task'. They merely 'cooperated' with each other, working individually 'to get the whole task over with as easily and fast as possible', and they did not recognise the potential of the software for creating genuinely interdependent collaboration.

At first glance, this seemed to be the fault of the software (perhaps it was too difficult to learn) or of the students (perhaps they found the task uninteresting, did not get on with each other, etc.). However, using AT, Andreassen traced the failure to *contradictions* within and among activity systems. He was able to discern a deeper set of relationships and a more useful analysis of the problem to guide future efforts.

In the first phase of the project – training on the software – the students did use genuine interdependence to create a zone of proximal development to learn to use the software for collaboration. Early on, the students co-constructed *rules* for interacting, first through e-mail (a tool with which they were familiar) and then through the synchronous 'chat' tool and the asynchronous 'brainstorming' communication tool in the TeamWave program. Using the synchronous chat tool, they scheduled 'chat' meetings, where they decided to create six rooms, each on a different ecosystem, reflecting the interests of the three members. Because the asynchronous brainstorming tool did not automatically indicate the author's name on each posting, they quickly developed a new unwritten rule when one of the students included her name after each sentence: add names to postings (later shortened to initials). In AT terms, they 're-mediated' their inter-actions using a different tool, and formulated different rules of interactions, which initially proved to be more productive of collaboration in the training phase. Clearly, the software tools were not at fault, since the group created a zone of proximal development for learning, and the students were able to use genuine interdependence to do so.

AT also helped Andreassen understand the change the group experienced as it moved from the first phase – training in the software and in Saloman's guide-lines for genuine interdependence – to the second phase – the design of the web learning environment on endangered species. Andreassen analysed these phases as two linked activity systems. The object of the first phase – the software – became a tool for the second phase – the web learning environment.

However, two contradictions appeared in the transition from the training phase to the design phase, which suggested that the cause of the failure lay beyond the software and the participants' willingness to collaborate. First, there was a contradiction between the motive of the activity system of their collabor-ation and the motives of the activity systems of the different courses in which they were individually enrolled. Although they found the task engaging and the other group members congenial, their collaboration was not part of the regular curriculum of the courses and was not evaluated by the instructors. Little was actually at stake for the students, so as time pressures from these courses and other activities in their everyday lives impinged on the collaboration, they did not maintain a shared *motive* sufficient to engage in 'genuine interdependence' in completing the teaching materials. They lacked 'a common motivational factor, which attainment requires sharing of information, pooling of roles, and joint thinking, might be regarded as important if one is to facilitate a genuine collaboration effort' (Andreassen 2000).

The second contradiction was between *division of labour* and *rules*. In the training phase, the students set up a division of labour based on genuinely interdependent collaboration and rules (scheduling, communication pro-cedures, etc.), where all three students worked on each of the rooms; but in the design phase, time constraints led them to a different division of labour. 'Labour was divided among the members for them to finish individually and the work turned asynchronous.'

> The need to share information was reduced or even diminished. Even though the students acknowledged the value of feedback and agreed to provide it throughout the design activity, this hardly ever happened . . . When the division of labour paved the way for individual rather than team work, the new meeting rules, set subsequent to the division of labour, were perceived as inflexible and cumbersome.
>
> (Andreassen 2000)

Although new rules were proposed for regular synchronous contact, these were never agreed or implemented.

> Although having the same overall object, that of designing the learning environment, one can argue that the students put the main focus on

achieving the goals of their individual actions. In other words, the preparation and commissioning of the separate rooms by the individual student took precedence over completing the learning environment as a joint team effort of information sharing, pooling of roles, and joint thinking.

(Andreassen 2000)

Andreassen concluded that the students did not use the software tools to create a zone of proximal development that took advantage of a 'partnership of collaborating peers' for creating the rooms. Neither did they realise the potential of the software for creating interdependent collaboration in qualitatively different zones of proximal development, although the problem was not 'in' the software. AT guided Andreassen to suggest that the outcome might have been more successful had the activity system of the collaboration been more firmly linked to the activity systems of the courses in their home universities (*motivation*), and had the three participants retained the more collaborative *division of labour* with which they began, using synchronous communication regularly throughout with the *rules* they originally agreed among themselves.

Activity theory in technical training: learning a geographic information system

Spinuzzi (1999) observed a group of 13 third-year university students in Community and Regional Planning, who were taking a course in geographic information systems (GIS). Late in the course, they were learning to use a government computer program that plots traffic accident locations and provides statistics on accidents (e.g. road conditions, injuries, vehicle damage), from data entered by police in their accident reports. The GIS program is called Accident Location and Analysis System (the apt acronym is ALAS). Although the students had become familiar with other GIS programs, they found it extremely difficult to use this program to find information on specific accidents, experiencing numerous 'breakdowns' (points at which they could not proceed without the help of the instructor).

At first glace, the students' difficulties appeared to be caused by the greater complexity of this program as compared to other GIS programs they had learned: more instruction and practice seemed to be the solution. However, using AT, Spinuzzi was able to trace these breakdowns to fundamental contradictions in the interface (tool), which in turn reflected historical contradictions in the whole activity system of accident location and analysis – now reflected in the GIS ALAS program. The cultural history of this activity system proved crucial to developing improvements in the GIS ALAS interface to help students and new employees to learn the program. To reduce breakdowns, Spinuzzi had to look beyond training 'in the software', to training in the ALAS activity system, its history and institutional uses.

One breakdown arose when students viewed accidents that appeared to have occurred in cornfields or in houses, not on roads. Experienced users knew that the records on which the GIS ALAS system was built were gathered before the invention of computerised maps. Accidents were plotted using less precise paper maps, divided into coordinates. Each accident was given a numerical coordinate, called a 'node', corresponding to the paper maps. In the late 1990s, the system was put on to a computerised GIS map. However, the history of the system had produced a *contradiction* between representations: the old node/ coordinates system of locating accidents and the geographic system of the new GIS ALAS program's electronic map. The nodes did not precisely correspond to the electronic map location because of the contradiction. The contradiction between tools for representing accidents, growing out of two historical periods of the activity system of ALAS, led students to mistake the geographic representation for the underlying node system and thus experience break-downs. The experts knew that one sometimes had to refer to the older, paper representation, or to one's knowledge of the area.

To redesign the software tool to reduce breakdowns for learners (whether students or new employees), Spinuzzi proposed that the interface should explain the contradiction and display it directly, by including both node/ coordinate and GIS representations. One could then teach students or new users to see the relation between the two. By acknowledging the contradiction rather than trying to bury it in the interface or work around it, the interface would then allow students to expand their involvement with the whole accident location and analysis activity system and negotiate it with fewer breakdowns. It would create new zones of proximal development.

Students also experienced breakdowns in accessing records from pull-down menus. They could not access all the information on a single accident without undertaking numerous steps. Again the cultural history of ALAS reveals why this was so. People from different activity systems use different types of infor-mation from the ALAS database: traffic sign designers (accident frequency by location and direction), insurance companies (severity of injury and property damage), road designers (road conditions at accident by location), police (fatal-ity, violation, time), and so on. The interface was designed to provide quick access for users from these different activity systems, each with a different object and motive in using the software tool; while students (or new employees) needed an overview of the shape of individual accident records to understand the structure of the records and the uses of the information. They needed to expand their conceptual understanding not only of the software tool and data-base, GIS ALAS, but also of the whole accident location and analysis activity system, in its interactions with other activity systems that used portions of the data. They needed the big picture. The AT analysis suggested that software designers should add a function for accessing complete records of individual accidents, as a learning tool, although it would serve little purpose beyond that.

AT's cultural historical analysis guided Spinuzzi in developing suggestions for redesigning not only the software tool – to 'fix' things that seemed to cause breakdowns – but also for redesigning the training process. Both the interface and the training had to take into account the historically evolved complexity of the activity system mediated by the software tool, and incorporate features into the system specifically to facilitate learning it – to construct zones of proximal development. Instructional designers must look 'beyond the interface to the activities in which information systems are used' (Spinuzzi 1999: 226).

Activity theory in children's learning: Fifth Dimension after-school program

The Fifth Dimension is an after-school program for disadvantaged children aged 6–14 years, with sites in 12 cities in four countries. Many of the children have great difficulty learning in formal schooling. At first glance, this seemed to be a problem with the children or their family and peer environments. Indeed, the ordinary response of many schools is to require students to spend more time doing school activities, either longer (after school) instruction or additional homework. But using AT, the Fifth Dimension program was able to see ways to 're-mediate' school activities as a mix of activities, some from schooling, some from computer games, some from web-mediated social interaction.

The goal of the Fifth Dimension program is to produce learning outcomes desirable in formal schooling within a very different activity system – to re-mediate learning using different tools, object/motive, rules, community and division of labour. From the point of view of the children participating in the program, the object/motive is to play the games together successfully – that is, to have fun. However, the designers of the program have re-mediated the activity of school learning by deliberately mixing activity choices (some school-like, some game-like, some creative play) to avoid contradictions in motives. The re-mediated system produced an outcome similar to – often better than – that produced in the activity system of formal schooling.

As Blanton *et al.* (1999) describe it:

> The heart of the Fifth Dimension is a three dimensional maze containing computer games and educational tasks. The maze is divided into twenty 'rooms', and each room provides access to either computer or non-electronic activities. In all, the maze contains over 120 educational and computer games. Children make progress through the maze by completing tasks set for them in each game or activity. Adventure Guides provide directions for how to play games and complete tasks. Children decide on goals, where they will begin their journey in the maze, how long they will stay in a 'room', where they will go next, and how they will complete the tasks in the maze.

A 'real make-believe' Fifth Dimension Wizard, an anonymous electronic entity that 'lives' in the Internet, writes and chats with the children via modem, performing the role of patron.

> The Wizard has a home page, and helps the children gain access to the World Wide Web, where they may display their own creative work. The wizard also affords a locus for conflict resolution, helping to mediate typical power relations between children and adults, and preserving the mobility of expert and novice roles.
>
> (Brown and Cole 1999)

The Fifth Dimension Wizard is in fact operated by the staff, consisting typically of a director and a group of prospective teachers, often second-year university students planning a career in teaching. The staff also give face-to-face guidance and support to children in their progress through the Fifth Dimension maze – and in their learning, of course.

Standard experimental–control group comparisons found that extended participation in the Fifth Dimension program had positive effects on children's learning of cognitive skills, transfer of learning to school settings, computer use and standardised school-administered tests of achievement (summarised in Brown and Cole 1999). Research also found strong evidence that prospective teachers 'transform their beliefs about education away from the belief of learning as a linear process towards a definition of learning as a social process involving active participation of children in socially constituted practices' (Blanton *et al.* 1999). This is remarkable, since previous research has shown that it is extremely difficult to change teacher education candidates' preconceptions of teaching, learning and pupils.

The many studies of the program are based on AT, which provides a useful framework for understanding *how* the changes in the students and their 'guides' occur. For example, in the study of prospective teachers, the researchers charted the communication flow among three activity systems in which the students were involved: university teacher education, the local school system and the Fifth Dimension program. Researchers constructed a pre- and post-test of attitudes and beliefs towards teaching, learning and pupils based on the different *rules* (norms) obtaining in the three activity systems. The researchers used qualitative methods to follow the prospective teachers as they moved among the three activity systems, noting zones of proximal development that grew out of the contradictions among them. For example, in interacting with children in the program, prospective teachers encountered moments where children who were further along in the Fifth Dimension maze than the teachers – and more familiar with the software tools. The students began to teach them how to perform the tasks. In these zones of proximal development for the prospective teachers, positive changes in attitudes about disadvantaged students' capabilities occurred. It is not surprising that students can teach teachers, but what AT contributes is an analysis of *how* that change in the division of labour occurred (how zones of proximal development were created) and how that change led to a change in attitudes towards disadvantaged students in the circulation of discourse among the three activity systems in which the prospective teachers participated.

The qualitative research on the Fifth Dimension program suggests that distributed learning is best accomplished when it accommodates a diversity of individual interests – in other words, when learners have choices. Moreover – and perhaps paradoxically – distributed learning appears to be most successful when people can better achieve their chosen goals by acting together than by acting alone. Yet creating activity systems where this mutual help in zones of proximal development is possible (or even essential for success) takes a great deal of time, especially in distributed systems where asynchronous or infrequent communication replaces face-to-face. Finally, collaboration does not mean there will be no conflict, only that there are means of resolving – or of constructively using – conflicts to further the learning. Indeed, distributed learning, like all learning, must take into account the fact that people have many different emotions which affect their interactions and their learning.

Conclusion: what AT can and cannot do

I began this chapter by saying that AT can have heuristic value for planning and 'trouble-shooting' redesigns of distributed learning, although it is a 'loose' theory that does not attempt firm predictions. I wish to conclude by posing some questions (following Lewis 1997) highlighted by various triads of nodes (a study that discusses each question is cited for each).

- *Subject–community–object/motive*. Motivation is particularly difficult to address in distributed learning environments, where participants may not have face-to-face support from teachers or peers. Do individual learners (or sub-groups) understand themselves as part of a disciplinary or learning community focused on a common object? Or do they feel disenfranchised, able only to learn discrete information for their own personal motives rather than being engaged in expanding involvement with a community and its activity (zones of proximal development) (Dirckinck-Holmfeld 1995)?
- *Subject–tools–object*. What tools do subjects bring to bear on the object of the learning, both those tools the course provides *and* those which subjects might bring from their previous involvements in other activity systems? This is a particular problem for distributed learning, as the computer is such a pervasive tool that it may crowd out others, or make them less visible (Fifth Dimension).
- *Subject–tools–community*. How do the computerised tools (such as groupware) afford – and constrain – students and teachers in forming a community where differences can be negotiated and mutual support (ZPDs) constructed? If some students use e-mail while others employ a different asynchronous tool, different communities may form among the students (Lewis and Collins 1995).
- *Subject–rules–community*. How do participants understand (and agree upon or dissent from) the interactional rules (norms) of the activity system, especially when (as in distributed electronic learning) there is no face-to-face communication to clarify and negotiate those rules? This is particularly difficult in distributed learning because participants may bring different assumptions – often unconsciously so – about ways of working (Andreassen 2000).
- *Subject–community–division of labour*. How will the teaching–learning labour in distributed electronic learning be divided (and renegotiated) in the community, when members of that community bring different histories and skills to the activity (Hoyles *et al.* 1994)? If the division of labour is exclusively teacher/individual students, then opportunities for creating community (and new zones of proximal development) are diminished.
- *One activity system interacting with others*. What other activity systems are participants engaged in which might create contradictions that afford or constrain their learning? How can teachers and others learn about these in the absence of face-to-face interaction (Spinuzzi 1999)?

These questions suggest only some of the many that AT analysis can high-light for designers of distributed learning environments. Because AT is a flexible framework (albeit complex), and compatible with many of the other theories in this volume, it is helpful in understanding what happens when students encounter course materials via liquid crystal displays. AT makes it hard to forget that there is much more going on – dispersed activities and trajectories of the participants engaged in activity together, whether designers, teachers, students, technicians or others. Where we are at cross-purposes, we must ask how we have come to be that way, and how we might use those contradictions to experience each other in more human and productive ways. By focusing on various relationships among participants and their tools, AT prompts us to ask better questions for designing distributed learning environments and understanding and evaluating where and why they work or break down. If something unexpected – or messy – happens when people use those environments, AT can provide analytical lenses to understand what has occurred, and perhaps use it productively for teaching and learning.

References

Andreassen, E.F. (2000) Evaluating how students organise their work in a collaborative telelearning scenario: an activity theoretical perspective. Masters dissertation, Department of Information Science, University of Bergen, Norway. Online at: http://www.ifi.uib.no/docta/dissertations/andreassen/.

Bakardjieva, M. (1998) Collaborative meaning-making in computer conferences: a sociocultural perspective, in M. Bakardjieva, T. Ottmann and I. Tomek (eds) *Proceedings of ED-MEDIA/ED-TELECOM 98*. Charlottesville, VA: Association for the Advancement of Computing in Education.

Blanton, W. E., Warner, M. and Simmons, E. (1999) The Fifth Dimension: application of cultural-historical activity theory, inquiry-based learning, computers, and tele-communications to change prospective teachers' preconceptions. Online at: http://129.171.53.1/blantonw/5dClhse/publications/tech/effects/ undergraduates.html.

Brown, K. and Cole, M. (1999) Socially shared cognition: system design and the organization of collaborative research. Online at: http://129.171.53.1/blantonw/5dClhse/publications/tech/cognition.html.

Cole, M. (1996) *Cultural Psychology*. Cambridge, MA: Harvard University Press.

Cole, M. and Engeström, Y. (1993) A cultural–historical approach to distributed cognition, in G. Salomon (ed.) *Distributed Cognitions: Psychological and Educational Considerations*. Cambridge: Cambridge University Press.

Dirckinck-Holmfeld, L. (1995) Project pedagogy as a foundation for computer-supported collaborative learning, in B. Collis and G. Davies (eds) *Innovative Adult Learning with Innovative Technologies*. IFIP Transactions A-61. Amsterdam: Elsevier.

Docta Project (2000) Design and use of collaborative telelearning artifacts. Department of Information Science, University of Bergen, Norway. Online at: http://www.ifi.uib.no/docta/index.html.

Engeström, Y. (1987) *Learning by Expanding: An Activity Theoretical Approach to Developmental Research*. Helsinki: Orienta-Konsultit Oy.

Engeström, Y. (1990) *Learning, Working, and Imagining: Twelve Studies in Activity Theory*. Helsinki: Orienta-Konsultit Oy.

Guribye, F. and Wasson, B. (1999) Evaluating collaborative telelearning scenarios: a sociocultural perspective, in B. Collins and R. Oliver (eds) *Proceedings of Educational Multimedia, Hypermedia & Telecommunications 1999 (EdMedia '99)*. Charlottesville, VA: Association for the Advancement of Computing in Education.

Hoyles, C., Healey, L. and Pozzi, S. (1994) Groupwork with computers: an overview of findings, *Journal of Computer Assisted Learning*, 10(4), 202–15.

Hutchins, E. (1995) *Cognition in the Wild*. Boston, MA: MIT Press.

Kapetin, V. and Cole, M. (1997) Individual and collective activities in educational computer game playing. Online at: http://129.171.53.1/blantonw/5dClhse/publications/tech/Kaptelinin-Cole.html.

Koschmann, T. (1996) Paradigm shifts and instructional technology, in T. Koschmann (ed.) *CSCL: Theory and Practice of an Emerging Paradigm*. Mahwah, NJ: Lawrence Erlbaum.

Kuuti, K. (1994) Activity theory as a potential framework for human–computer interaction research, in B. Nardi (ed.) *Context and Consciousness: Activity Theory and Human–Computer Interaction*. Cambridge, MA: MIT Press.

Leont'ev, A.N. (1981) *Problems of the Development of Mind*. Moscow: Progress Publishers.

Lewis, R. (1997) An activity theory framework to explore distributed communities, *Journal of Computer Assisted Learning*, 13(4): 210–18.

Lewis, R. and Collins, B. (1995) Virtual mobility and distributed laboratories: supporting collaborative research with knowledge technology, in B. Collis and G. Davies (eds) *Innovative Adult Learning with Innovative Technologies*. IFIP Transactions A-61. Amsterdam: Elsevier.

Nardi, B. (ed.) (1996) *Context and Consciousness: Activity Theory and Human–Computer Interaction*. Cambridge, MA: MIT Press.

Nardi, B. (1998) Activity theory and its use within human–computer interaction (response to Rochelle), *Journal of the Learning Science*, 7(2): 257–61.

Newman, D., Griffin, P. and Cole, M. (1989) *The Contraction Zone: Working for Cognitive Change in School*. Cambridge: Cambridge University Press.

Roschelle, J. (1998) Activity theory: a foundation for design (review of Nardi), *Journal of the Learning Science*, 7(2): 241–55.

Salomon, G. (1992) What does the design of effective CSCL require and how do we study its effects? *SIGCUE Outlook (Special Issue on CSCL)*, 21(3): 62–8.

Spinuzzi, C. (1999) Designing for lifeworlds: genre and activity in information systems design and evaluation. Ames, IA: Iowa State University. Online at: http://english.ttu.edu/spinuzzi/spinuzzi-dissertation.pdf.

Vygotsky, L.S. (1994) *The Vygotsky Reader* (edited by V. der Veer and J. Valsiner). Oxford: Blackwell.

Wartofsky, M. (1979) *Models: Representation and the Scientific Understanding*. Dordrecht: Reidel.

Wasson, B. and Mørch, A. (1999) DoCTA: design and use of collaborative telelearning artefacts. Online at: http://www.ifi.uib.no/staff/barbara/papers/edmedia99.html.

Chapter 5

Workplaces, communities and pedagogy

An activity theory view

Stephen Billett

Working and learning

New forms of work practice emerge as workplaces are transformed by changes in technology, global competition and employment practices. Consequently, learning for work becomes an ongoing project throughout individuals' working lives as they seek to maintain and develop further their work practice. In this chapter, I examine learning as participation in work from an activity theory (AT) perspective. I propose that work practice, the requirements for performance at work and the learning of those requirements, are both constituted in and distributed across the circumstances where the work is enacted – the workplace. Therefore, understanding how individuals learn at and through work necessitates accounting for how workplaces afford individuals opportunities to develop the capabilities to address these requirements. Moreover, as workplaces are contested rather than benign environments, these affordances are likely to be distributed asymmetrically across the workforce.

I begin by adopting the view that learning and participation in work are irreducible; that is, work requires engagement in activities and interactions whose outcomes are not restricted to task completion. Learning arises from these engagements. This is no more so than when individuals are actively and willingly engaged in demanding activities that extend what they already know. In contemporary psychological accounts, the view that thinking and acting – and therefore learning – are patterned and structured by and distributed across social practices, such as workplaces, has become increasingly accepted. Understanding learning at work therefore necessarily includes considering factors that shape participation in work activities and interactions. Although the contributions of everyday engagement and the use of intentional workplace learning strategies (e.g. coaching, modelling, questioning, etc.) provide potent bases for the development of working knowledge (Billett 1999), how these are afforded to and distributed among workers is determined by the norms, values and practices of the workplace. These include how work is undertaken, how the requirements for work activities are constituted situationally and whether individuals are able to participate in ways that will allow the development of the capacities required for effective performance. Perceiving the relations between social practice and individuals' thinking, acting and learning (cognition) within social practice sits within a larger project to understand relationships between human development and the social world. Accounting for these relations requires going beyond psychological concerns about the internal processes of the mind (Säljö and Wyndhamm 1993). Such an account needs to illuminate relations between the social sources of knowledge and the means by which humans construct (learn) that knowledge. In terms of individuals' learning for work, some key concerns are the extent to which thinking and acting (and learning) are shaped by the requirements and practices of particular workplaces, how these requirements are constituted and manifested in work practice, and how learning through work proceeds.

Drawing on cultural historical activity and cognitive theory, sociology and anthropology, I discuss the associations between participation at work and learning. I propose that, if the knowledge required for effective participation in work is also constituted there, even in part, it is necessary to understand individuals' participation in work and its consequences for learning and development. Here, communities of work practice and the activity systems that constitute these communities are used to focus the discussion. These concepts fit well within and assist in reconciling some of the emerging views about learning as participation. Rather than rehearse all these ideas at length, the overview that follows is intended as a short cut to position this chapter within current debates about the relationship between individuals' thinking, acting and learning, and social practice such as workplaces. Following this, 'co-participation at work' is advanced as a means to understand participation and learning at work. From a review of recent studies of work, categories of interdependencies within work practices are advanced to provide bases of how workplaces afford individuals' participation at work, and therefore learning. Relations between community of work practice and pedagogy are advanced as being central to understanding how knowledge is distributed across work practice and how access to this knowledge is mediated by both the workplace and individuals' agency. From these, a pedagogy of community is briefly proposed.

Work, community and activity

Recently, there has been some conciliation between those who emphasise the internal processes of the mind – the cognitive – and those who privilege the social and cultural contributions to thinking and acting – the sociogenetic (e.g. Rogoff 1990, 1995; Resnick et al. 1991, 1997; Valsiner 2000). This reconciliation was precipitated by and has energised the discussion about relations between the cognitive and social contributions of thinking and acting (e.g. Lave 1991; Anderson et al. 1996, 1997; Greeno 1997; Cobb 1998). For instance, developments in cognitive theory are seen to view situations as contexts in which thinking and acting occur in particular ways (e.g. Resnick et al. 1991, 1997), rather than situations in which individuals act, shaping and constituting learning. Conversely, the enthusiastic embrace of a wholly situational basis for cognition has been criticised (Salomon 1994; Cobb 1998; Valsiner 2000) for attempting to reduce the individual from being an active agent in cognition to just another element in a system that is distributed (Hutchins 1991; Pea 1993), or 'stretched' (Lave 1991) across the social practice in which individuals engage.

The situative perspective (Greeno 1997), at its strongest, proposes that all learning is located and embedded in the situations where it is encountered

(Hutchins 1991; Lave 1991). Other views propose that the knowledge to be learned arises historically from cultural practice (Scribner 1985; Cole 1998; Wertsch 1998; Valsiner 2000) and is constituted by situational factors. Consequently, a focus on locating the mind and behaviour in historical, cultural and situational contexts has developed, with the cognitive consequences of participation in particular social practices becoming the subject of fresh interest (e.g. Engeström and Middleton 1996; Billett 1997, 1998; Resnick *et al.* 1997). Within these deliberations, communities of practice (Lave and Wenger 1991) and activity systems (Leont'ev 1981; Engeström 1993) have become popular bases whereby social practices may be identified and their influence on thinking and acting analysed.

Concepts of particular social practice as 'communities of practice' originated in the work of Lave and Wenger (1991) and were extended by Wenger (1998). These communities are defined as 'a set of relations among persons, activity and world, over time and in relationship with other tangential and overlapping communities of practice' (Lave and Wenger 1991: 98). This concept, which emphasises relationships between persons and the social world, may be applied to workplaces, or even to different work areas within the same workplace. It suggests there are norms, values and procedures which are identifiable with particular work. These may be distinct from other workplaces or other areas in the same workplace. These practices determine how work progresses, the division of labour and how opportunities are distributed to participate in workplace activities that lead to new learning and the refinement of existing knowledge. In other words, the requirements for work, how activities are distributed, performance judged and opportunities to learn – those situational factors that constitute the community of practice, its boundaries and its relations – are evident in different forms within and across the workplace.

Whereas communities of practice may be seen as the manifestation of particular situational factors that constitute a social practice, AT (Leont'ev 1981) assists in identifying and understanding these factors. AT holds that human actions are the product of social practices that are historically and culturally constituted. Some AT perspectives focus on the historical and cultural contributions to human activity, including the sociogenesis of knowledge (e.g. Leont'ev 1981; Cole 1998), whereas others focus on how situational factors shape human actions (e.g. Engeström 1993). The latter, in particular, assists in delineating what comprises a social practice and identifying the factors that constitute that practice. More broadly, AT provides a basis to understand how the activities in which humans engage shape their thinking and acting. To understand learning from this perspective is to consider that the goal-directed activities in which individuals engage have cognitive consequences of reinforcing or refining what individuals already know, or of generating new knowledge if the activity is novel. Put succinctly, activities structure cognition (Rogoff and Lave 1984). Further, interactions between social sources (e.g. others, artefacts, symbols) are seen by Vygotsky (1978) and Meade (1934) as the source of cognition.

Unlike other approaches to mental functioning, activity theory views cognitive and motivational processes as embedded within larger activity structures whose goals they serve. Activity structures involve mediators – tools and symbol systems – that have deep implications for the way that intellectual tasks are accomplished.

(Martin and Scribner 1991: 583)

Paid work provides a useful illustration of the application of AT. Concepts of vocational practice are historically and culturally developed in responding to particular cultural needs (Scribner 1985), such as the products and services that are the focus of workplace activities. Nevertheless, the actual instance of vocational practice is constituted in particular ways by the circumstances of its enactment. Vocational practices such as nursing, medicine and hairdressing are not enacted uniformly. Instead, they are shaped by the circumstances in which these vocations are enacted and include factors that are external to the work-place (e.g. clients' needs) as well as those within it (e.g. rules, division of labour). These factors shape the kinds of procedures favoured in the work practice, the norms for task enactment as well as how actions are judged. Thus there are likely to be particular and possibly unique requirements for practice arising from each work situation. Consequently, what is required for performance in a particular community of work practice (i.e. what counts as expertise) is situationally constituted, and not a general attribute of the vocation (e.g. proficient nurse, doctor, hairdresser). Performance is judged on whether an individual is able to perform expertly in the particular nursing, medical or hairdressing context (Billett 2001).

Work practice as contested terrain

As noted above, diverse views exist about individuals in a social basis of cognition: sociogenesis; that is, human thinking and acting, particularly higher forms of cognitive activity, have social sources. They are not the product of human physiological development. Hutchins (1991) adopts a radical position in proposing that cognition is distributed across the social situation, including the individuals and artefacts that comprise the situation. In this view, the elements of the social system collectively contribute to knowing and learning, with the individual regarded as but one element in this system. These elements include goal-directed activities, interpersonal encounters and interactions with physical artefacts. More than being a mere context in which thinking and acting occur, situations shape activities, the goals for activity and the cognitive activities of individuals' thinking, acting and learning. However, other views propose greater agency for individuals (e.g. Engeström and Middleton 1996; Cobb 1998), with these perspectives examining how individuals engage in social practice. These views suggest that access to situationally constituted knowledge is held to be a reciprocal albeit complex and contested process. From this viewpoint, learning is not a unidirectional flow of knowledge from the source to the individual, nor does the individual engage with the social system comprehensively or uniformly. Instead, individuals are active and selective about what they appropriate from sources (i.e. event, activity or interaction). This active selective process might even result in outcomes (intra-psychological attributes) that are contrary to what was intended. This is likely to be so if there is a clash between what is being proposed and the individuals' values and beliefs (Hodges 1998); for instance, coal-miners rejected what was proposed in a safety course when they believed it was aimed to pass the responsibility of safe working practice solely to the miners.

Communities of practice are often proposed as being benign, with shared understanding, and supportive and benevolent interactions. However, this does not appear to reflect the relations that constitute most work practices. The recent literature on work and work practice identifies workplaces as contested terrain. Whether it is between 'newcomers' or 'old-timers' (Lave and Wenger 1991), full- or part-time workers (Bernhardt 1999), teams with different roles and standing in the workplace (Darrah 1996; Hull 1997), individuals' personal and vocational goals (Darrah 1996) or among institutionalised arrangements such as those representing workers, supervisors or management (Danford 1998), contestation is an enduring feature of work practice. Participation at work will be influenced by the individual's standing in the workplace and the extent to which their participation is afforded (i.e. either aided or inhibited) by the workplace. Opportunities to participate and access guidance are not distributed equally (see below). Consequently, it would be derelict to view learning as participation in work activities without trying to understand the bases for access to activities and their consequences. Access to guidance and support to learn (i.e. to reinforce, refine and construct new knowledge), especially the valued close guidance of more expert others (Vygotsky 1978; Werstch 1998), will be shaped by how individuals are invited to participate in the workplace. However, this very access to activities and guidance, the opportunities to become a full participant, are all grounds for contestation. As Lave has proposed:

> The heterogeneous, multifocal character of situated activity implies that conflict is a ubiquitous aspect of human existence. This follows if we assume that people in the same situation, people who are helping to constitute 'a situation' together, know different things and speak with different interests and experience from different social locations.
>
> (Lave 1993: 15)

Given the need to understand how individuals participate in and learn at work, the relations between and among individuals, teams and key interest groups become a central concern for understanding how learning at work proceeds. These relations pervade work, conceptions of performance, and influence how individuals act in, and learn the knowledge distributed across, the social system that comprises the workplace or practice. They are at the heart of the social division of labour (Scribner 1997). Importantly, such considerations are not peculiar to paid work. Social structures in domestic settings (homes) determine participation in another social practice: the family and the allocation of domestic tasks (Goodnow 1996). Regardless of whether a radical distributed view of cognition or one that accepts greater individual agency is adopted, participation at work is contested but remains imperative for learning. However, in considering relations between the individual and social practice such as work, it is necessary to account for the agency of individuals. A strongly socially distributed view may not adequately account for differences in individuals' engagement or how individuals make judgements about what the workplace affords.

Individuals as co-participants at work

Having considered how workplaces offer opportunities for participation, it is necessary to consider how individuals elect to participate in work activities. Individuals' engagement and what they learn from participation is unlikely to be uniform, given their existing knowledge, values, goals and preferred procedures for their work. These are products of their personal history or ontogeny (Billett 1997) constructed through unique combinations of their encounters with the social world throughout their ontogenies. Individuals' engagement may be determined by the perceived benefits of participation. For instance, some parents of schoolchildren may feel compelled to participate in organising the school fete or working the tuck shop roster, yet their engagement may be less intense than in activities which they prize more highly (e.g. work, social or sporting activities). For another, whose interests are linked to the community, such activities might be more central to their principal interests; thus participation might be more effortful and intentional.

Consequences for learning arise from how individuals elect to participate. First, Wertsch's (1998) concepts of 'mastery' and 'appropriation' describe different kinds of learning outcomes arising from participation in social practice. With the former, the learner remains unconvinced of and uncommitted to what they have learned, although they are able to perform the required task. The latter involves the learner making the socially generated knowledge they encounter in the social world 'their own'. Consider supermarket checkout operators who offer customers the standard greeting, 'How are you today?' These individuals have mastered the requirements to perform this salutation, but there is often little evidence of their appropriation of its intended value. The important point here is that individuals are active, discerning and that they construct their own meaning even when strongly enculturating circumstances prevail. The association between the inter-psychological (between the individual and a social source) and the intra-pyschological (attributes within the individual) processes, to use Vygotsky's terms, are not the passage of external sources internally. Rather, intra-psychological outcomes are mediated by social interactions with tools, signs and others' interpersonal interactions as proposed above and by individuals' existing knowledge, including their dispositions (e.g. attitudes, values). The social and cognitive psychological contributions are enmeshed in this process of knowledge construction.

Second, learning is an effortful activity. Individuals usually only engage in intentional effortful activities when there is strong motivation or interest to do so; their agency directs the expenditure of effort. Third, identity formation is a salient outcome of participation in work practice (Lave and Wenger 1991). However, participation may lead to dis-identification (Hodges 1998) when the norms of practice clash with individuals' values (e.g. Darrah 1996). Thus participation cannot be assumed to lead to the individual accepting and adopting the norms, values and beliefs of the social practice. Fourth, contestation between the individual and social sources arises through everyday thinking as individuals seek to understand what they encounter to overcome disequilibrium, such as that provided by the inevitable changes in work environments and tasks. Disequilibrium is probably premised on the degree and frequency of impasses that threaten individuals' knowing; however, the effort expended on addressing disequilibrium is directed by individuals' concern about that dissonance. Therefore, although knowledge may be distributed across the individuals and the artefacts that constitute a community of work practice, the agency of individuals shapes how they engage in and learn within that community.

Therefore, notwithstanding the affordance of the workplace, individuals' agency mediates workplace actions, thereby moderating the interdependence between the social and cognitive lines of psychological experience. Thus there is little to suggest that individuals unquestioningly engage in social practices, merely appropriating what is afforded of them. Instead the relationship between the social practices that individuals engage in and the individuals themselves is co-participative. In other words, social practices and individuals are interdependent; and this is manifest both in terms of how the social practices invite individuals to participate and how individuals decide to engage in the social practices. All this will be premised on how individuals conceptualise what is being afforded to them.

Bases of interdependency at work

To illuminate the bases for participation in workplaces and their consequences for learning, a scheme of interdependencies in workplaces has been generated from a review of recent studies of work in sociological, anthropological, economic, industrial relations and human resource development literatures (Billett 2000). Using an AT analysis of interactions between individuals and social sources, this review identified interdependencies in workplace settings that determine how participation and learning could proceed. The categories of interdependencies are now used to elaborate and illustrate how participation in work can be described. These categories are:

- *Working with others* – how work activity is premised on interactions with others.
- *Engagement* – bases of employment:
  - *status of employment* – the standing of the work, its perceived value, the support it attracts;
  - *access to participation* – attributes that influence participation;
  - *reciprocity of values* – prospects for shared values between individuals and the workplace.
- *Homogeneity* – the extent to which tasks in work practice are homogeneous. Similarities may contribute greater support (modelling, etc.) for the ability to perform at work.
- *Artefacts/external tools* – physical artefacts used in work practice and upon which performance is predicated (Billett 2000).

I now elaborate upon and illustrate these interdependencies.

Working with others

Inevitably, participation in work involves negotiating and interacting with others. These interactions are premised on 'formalised' structures associated with work (e.g. airline crews, dental teams), other forms of demarcation (e.g. trade or professional practice) or those negotiated collaboratively with peers, as in self-managed teams. In addition, there are affiliations associated with cliques, gender and interest groups that also shape participation. These structures influence access to activities and guidance; for instance, there are no pathways for dental assistants to become dentists or flight attendants to become pilots, yet there are opportunities for apprentices to become tradeworkers and flight engineers to become pilots. These sociohistorically derived structures establish the scope for participation in work activities. In other, less 'formalised' ways, rules about individuals and whether they should be permitted to participate determine the basis for participation and interaction. For instance, an aircrew member, police or military officer from a non-traditional background (e.g. female, aboriginal, migrant) may find their participation inhibited: a female police officer may have more difficulty being accepted under the values of male-dominated police services. Overlaps in participatory structures appear widespread. In one workplace, self-managed teams were established with leaders nominated on the basis of their expertise (Billett 1994). Yet in some work areas professionals intervened, thereby reducing workers' participatory discretion (e.g. range of tasks, possibilities) and causing dis-identification with their practice.

Working with others is premised on historically, culturally and situationally derived structures, and in ways that influence participation and learning. Given that learning higher orders of knowledge is a process shared with others, inclusion in or exclusion from participation premised on working with others may have consequences for this learning.

Engagement at work (employment basis, status of employment, access to participation)

Individuals' engagement at work has at least three dimensions. First, the bases of their employment will influence their participation. Whether they are full- or part-time employees or whether they are located at the centre or periphery of decision-making will influence the kinds of participation they may be able to secure. Second, workers' status and their standing will influence the support they receive and their access to opportunities for participation and support. Darrah (1996) describes how the production work in a computer manufacturing company was taken for granted, despite its complex demands, whereas work in the design area was the subject of attention, praise and support. Perhaps a legacy of Taylorism, expectations of and support for workers are premised on their work being categorised as professional or manual (Barley and Orr 1997). Workers' standing also influences the participatory discretion afforded them, including the kinds of activities in which they are able to engage. Third, access to participation will be shaped by workers' ability to engage fully. Those who work in isolation (e.g. home workers) or are separated from other workers by time (e.g. shift workers) and space (e.g. different offices) may have difficulty in participating fully. Part-time, home-based or isolated workers may find it difficult to engage in the workplace discourse and the currency of workplace goals required for full participation or advancement (Hull 1997). Certainly, part-time work has been shown to lower women's lifetime employment prospects (Tam 1997). In addition, part-time workers, as peripheral participants, are more likely to engage in routine tasks, thereby limiting their opportunities for development (Forrester *et al*. 1995). Participation by those with poor literacy skills is also likely to be restricted. In this way, language and writing skills become bases for social regulation and control (Whalley and Barley 1997), with those whose skills are perceived as deficient or who are unable to negotiate in mainstream discourses being potentially marginalised. Therefore, part-time, contingent or contracted workers or those whose language and literacy skills present barriers to participation may find their participation constrained compared with full-time workers, and those whose standing in the workplace is core.

In these ways, participation at work is influenced by individuals' employment, the status of their work and their standing in the workplace.

Reciprocity of values

The norms and values of workplaces will be more or less consonant with those who work within them; for instance, for professional reasons, many educators may feel unsympathetic towards changing policies and goals of educational systems. This influences how educators conduct their practice and how they interact with administrators and colleagues (e.g. Hodges 1998). Some commentators propose that, in an era of high competitiveness, employees and employers have never needed each other more (Rowden 1995). Therefore, reciprocity of values is important. Similarly, 'new workplaces' are characterised by worker involvement (Davis 1995) that aims to capture their enthusiasm, commitment and loyalty.

However, although some view the reciprocity of values between individuals and their workplace as being important, this is a remote prospect. Even if the whole historically grounded mess of differences in values between employees and employers, between supervisors and supervised, between 'old-timers' and newcomers, and between part-time and full-time workers were resolvable, other values need to be reconciled. For instance, part-time bank workers are quitting because limited prospects for promotion exist in restructured banking work (Hughes and Bernhardt 1999). Moreover, employees' cultural values may be antagonistic to the workplace's values. Vietnamese workers in a US manufacturing plant rejected teamwork because it valued their contribution only as team members not as individuals (Darrah 1996). These workers claimed to have escaped Vietnam only to find a system they believed to be analogous to communism had followed them to the USA. Cultural differences also made opportunities for Korean workers remote (Hull 1997), as their beliefs about self-sufficiency were not always consistent with workplace team values. Therefore, the degree of similarity between workplace practices and the values of the individuals who act in those practices may influence how workers engage in and commit energy to their work.

Homogeneity

The degree of similarity of workplace activities will also influence access to direct and indirect guidance. In Lave's (1990) study of tailoring apprenticeships in Angola, the apprentices learned through participation in workshops where tailors and other tailors' apprentices performed tailoring tasks, hence deriving both direct and indirect guidance. The apprentices also lived in the master tailors' houses which, with the workshops, occupied a district full of such houses and workshops. Consequently, the apprentices were immersed in tailoring practice, which provided a rich environment to participate in tailoring and learn the trade. Conversely, individuals might be the sole practitioner of their speciality in their workplace. For example, small regional vocational colleges may have only one teacher of a particular vocation (hairdressing, electrical work, metal fabrication). These teachers' access to guidance from others is more restricted compared with their counterparts in large metropolitan colleges. Therefore, the homogeneity of workplace activities will influence the range of participatory interaction and support available. Where access to expertise and observation of other workers is easy, since all are engaged in similar activities, guidance may be more accessible than where the learner is isolated from experts and other workers.

Artefacts/external tools

Opportunities to interact with technologies, equipment and tools in the work environment influence participation and access to the knowledge required for work. Artefacts and tools do more than extend human capacities: they are components of participation, performance and learning. It is not possible to practise a vocation without considering tools and artefacts, a relationship Wertsch (1998) describes as being irreducible. Performance is premised on the worker and artefact interacting. Moreover, technologies can shape both the practice and engagement in that practice, as they configure workplace tasks, the division of labour and shape workplace communications (Heath and Nicholls 1997). For instance, with the introduction of information technology, 'old-timers' might find their expertise superseded and displaced by new understandings and 'newcomers'. Electronics can open channels of visual, voice and text-based communication, providing instantaneous access that cannot be controlled by supervisors. Heath and Nicholls (1997) illustrate how real-time interactions mediated by technology (video shots of aircraft docking facilities) provide simultaneous visual access for workers whose performance needs to be coordinated. However, this technology renders decision-making public and interactive. In other ways, technology can also provide broader discretion and access to previously opaque knowledge. For instance, in hospitals, bedside computers focus patient care and provide access to records that enhance nurses' discretion (Cook-Gumperez and Hanna 1997). One worker, in a study of workplace learning (Billett 1994), used the two-way communication device to listen in and follow the problem-solving of the trades workers he wished to emulate. Conversely, technology can also separate workers from the means of production (Zuboff 1988; Martin and Scribner 1991). In these instances, opportunities to engage with artefacts and tools may either enhance or restrict participation and learning in the workplace.

These categories of *interdependence* describe and illustrate factors that determine individuals' participation in workplaces and the learning of knowledge distributed across the workplace. Together, these factors describe and illustrate how workplaces afford individuals' participation at work.

Co-participation as a pedagogy of community

As has been proposed above, workplaces are not only venues where individuals merely engage in tasks; they are also a constituted component of individuals' thinking, acting and learning. They furnish activities, interactions with others, physical tools and symbols that mediate learning, secured through the individuals' cognitive and social psychological experiences. As has been illustrated above, contributions to cognition are distributed across workplaces. Nevertheless, individuals are active in their engagement with work, albeit at different times and in different ways, depending on the relations and purposes of their engagement. These relations are not unidirectional – they are reciprocal or co-participative. Individuals are more than mere internalisers of knowledge sourced in the social systems that comprise workplaces – they are critical participants and appropriators. Therefore, co-participation is proposed as a basis for a pedagogy of community founded on engagement in activities and interactions that are constituted in communities such as workplaces. Instead of a pedagogy being premised on instructional techniques and the norms and practices of educational institutions, the pedagogy of community is premised on reciprocal bases for participation, access to activities and the particular requirements of the community. Participation in a community of work practice is a key premise to understanding learning at work, including learning values and appropriating a vocational identity.

However, the pedagogic principles that arise from discussions about learning in the workplace are similar to those about learning in educational institutions. Concerns about activities directed towards intended goals, access to support of more experienced others (e.g. teachers, co-workers) and how the setting promotes learning are common to both educational institutions and workplaces, as is the enduring concern about engaging individuals in its activities. Moreover, learning in both kinds of environment is structured by their activity systems (i.e. the activities to be engaged in and the guidance provided). This structuring renders redundant descriptions of workplace experiences and learning as being 'informal', 'unstructured' or *ad hoc*. Indeed, the above discussion might lead one to conclude that workplaces are too structured and formalised for learning to be distributed equally. The differences between workplaces and educational institutions may also be identified through an AT analysis; in particular, the objects and goals across the two environments may be seen as distinct (i.e. students versus products or services), as may the emphasis on intentional learning. Therefore, a pedagogy of community may be seen as constructed by and enacted in social practice such as work. Such a pedagogy is premised on activities and guidance, with access to these forming its basis. For the kind of learning required to participate and learn fully at work, individuals need to be richly engaged and shape the practice as well as being shaped themselves (Lave and Wenger 1991). Whereas the contributions of everyday activities and interventions such as guided learning in the workplace may develop a rich understanding and refined procedures (Billett 1999), it is the extent to which the workplace allows the individual to engage in activities and be guided that is important. Therefore, the concept of participation in the community is central to this pedagogy, and is proposed as a basis for interdependence between situations and learners. Together, these relations form a tentative basis to understand how the physical and social contexts, previously considered secondary or unimportant (Säljö and Wyndhamm 1993), contribute to individuals' development.

To conclude: I propose that understanding how learning occurs – initially to learn the skills required for work and then to develop further throughout one's working life – is salient. I propose that it is premised on participation in social practice, such as the workplace. The knowledge learned for vocational practice has sociohistorical geneses, yet will be constituted in particular ways in a particular workplace setting. Each workplace will have different requirements for performance and different bases for participation, which comprise the bases for the community of work practice. Proposing a pedagogy for the workplace necessitates going beyond the contributions of everyday activities in the workplace and of guided interventions to understand how the workplace invites workers to participate in its activities and guidance, and how individuals elect to engage with what is being afforded by the workplace.

References

Anderson, J.R., Reder, L.M. and Simon, H.A. (1996), Situated learning and education, *Educational Researchers*, 25(4): 5–11.

Anderson J.R., Reder, L.M. and Simon, H.A. (1997) Situative versus cognitive perspectives: form versus substance, *Educational Researcher*, 26(1): 18–21.

Barley, S.R. and Orr, J.E. (1997) Introduction: the neglected workforce, in S.R. Barley and J.E. Orr *Between Craft and Science: Technical Work in US Settings*. Ithaca NY: Cornell University Press.

Berhhardt, A. (1999) *The Future of Low-wage Jobs: Case Studies in the Retail Industry*. Institute on Education and the Economy Working Paper No. 10, March. New York: Columbia University.

Billett, S. (1994) Authenticity in workplace learning settings. In J.C. Stevenson (ed.) *Cognition at Work: The Development of Vocational Expertise*. Adelaide: National Centre for Vocational Education Research.

Billett, S. (1997) Dispositions, vocational knowledge and development: sources and consequences, *Australian and New Zealand Journal of Vocational Education Research*, 5(1): 1–26.

Billett, S. (1998) Situation, social systems and learning, *Journal of Education and Work*, 11(3): 255–74.

Billett, S. (1999) Guided learning in the workplace, in D. Boud and J. Garrick (eds) *Understanding Learning at Work*. London: Routledge

Billett, S. (2000) Coparticipation at work: knowing and work practice, in *Learning Together, Working Together*, Vol. 1. Proceedings of the 8th Annual International Conference on Postcompulsory Education and Training. Centre for Learning and Work Research, Griffith University, Brisbane, Australia.

Billett, S. (2001) Knowing in practice: re-conceptualising vocational expertise, *Learning and Instruction*, 11(6): 431–52.

Cobb, P. (1998) Learning from distributed theories of intelligence, *Mind, Culture and Activity*, 5(3): 187–204.

Cole, M. (1998) Can cultural psychology help us think about diversity, *Mind, Culture and Activity*, 5(4): 291–304.

Cook-Gumperez, J. and Hanna, K. (1997) Some recent issues of professional literacy and practice, in G. Hull (ed.) *Changing Work, Changing Workers: Critical Perspectives on Language, Literacy and Skills*. New York: SUNY Press.

Danford, A. (1998) Teamworking and labour regulation in the autocomponents industry. *Work, Employment and Society*, 12(3): 409–31.

Darrah, C.N. (1996) *Learning and Work: An Exploration in Industrial Ethnography*. New York: Garland.

Davis, D.D. (1995). Form, function and strategy in boundaryless organisations, in A. Howard (ed.) *The Changing Nature of Work*. San Francisco, CA: Jossey-Bass.

Engeström, Y. (1993) Development studies of work as a testbench of activity theory: the case of primary care medical practice, in S. Chaiklin and J. Lave (eds) *Understanding Practice: Perspectives on Activity and Context*. Cambridge: Cambridge University Press.

Engeström, Y. and Middleton, D. (1996) Introduction: studying work as mindful practice, in Y. Engeström and D. Middleton (eds) *Cognition and Communication at Work*. Cambridge: Cambridge University Press.

Forrester, K., Payne, J. and Ward, K. (1995) Lifelong education and the workplace: a critical analysis, *International Journal of Lifelong Education*, 14(4): 292–305.

Goodnow, J. (1996) Collaborative rules: how are people supposed to work with one another?, in P.B. Baltes and U.M. Staudinger (eds) *Interactive Minds: Life-span Perspectives on the Social Foundations of Cognition*. Cambridge: Cambridge University Press.

Greeno, J. (1997) On claims that answer the wrong questions, *Educational Researcher*, 26(1): 5–17.

Heath, C. and Nicholls, G. (1997) Animated texts: selective renditions of news stories, in L.B. Resnick, C. Pontecorvo, R. Säljo and B. Burge (eds) *Discourse, Tools and Reasoning: Essays on Situated Cognition*. Berlin: Springer-Verlag.

Hodges, D.C. (1998) Participation as dis-identification with/in a community of practice, *Mind, Culture and Activity*, 5(4): 272–90.

Hughes, K. and Bernhardt, A. (1999) *Market Segmentation and the Restructuring of Banking Jobs*, IEE Brief No. 24, February. New York: Institute on Education and the Economy.

Hull, G. (1997) Preface and introduction, in G. Hull (ed.) *Changing Work, Changing Workers: Critical Perspectives on Language, Literacy and Skills*. New York: SUNY Press.

Hutchins, E. (1991) The social organization of distributed cognition, in L.B. Resnick, J.M. Levine and S.D. Teasley (eds) *Perspectives on Socially Shared Cognition*. Washington, DC: American Psychological Association.

Lave, J. (1990) The culture of acquisition and the practice of understanding, in J.W. Stigler, R.A. Shweder and G. Herdt (eds) *Cultural Psychology*. Cambridge: Cambridge University Press.

Lave, J. (1991) Situated learning in communities of practice, in L.B. Resnick, J.M. Levine and S.D. Teasley (eds) *Perspectives on Socially Shared Cognition*. Washington, DC: Americal Psychological Association.

Lave, J. (1993) The practice of learning, in S. Chaiklin and J. Lave (eds) *Understanding Practice: Perspectives on Activity and Context*. Cambridge: Cambridge University Press.

Lave, J. and Wenger, E. (1991) *Situated Learning: Legitimate Peripheral Participation*. Cambridge: Cambridge University Press.

Leont'ev, A.N. (1981) *Problems of the Development of the Mind*. Moscow: Progress Publishers.

Martin, L.M.W. and Scribner, S. (1991) Laboratory for cognitive studies of work: a case study of the intellectual implications of a new technology. *Teachers College Record*, 92(4): 582–602.

Meade, G.H. (1934) *Mind, Self and Society from the Viewpoint of a Social Behaviouralist*. Chicago, IL: University of Chicago Press.

Pea, R.D. (1993) Practices of distributed intelligence and designs for education, in G. Salomon (ed.) *Distributed Cognitions*. New York: Cambridge University Press.

Resnick, L.D., Levine, J.M. and Teasley, S.D. (eds) (1991) *Perspectives on Socially Shared Cognition*. Washington, DC: American Psychological Association.

Resnick, L.B., Pontecorvo, C., Säljo, R. and Burge, B. (1997) Introduction, in L.B. Resnick, C. Pontecorvo and R. Säljo (eds) *Discourse, Tools and Reasoning: Essays on Situated Cognition*. Berlin: Springer-Verlag.

Rogoff, B. (1990) *Apprenticeship in Thinking: Cognitive Development in Social Context*. New York: Oxford University Press.

Rogoff, B. (1995) Observing sociocultural activities on three planes: participatory appropriation, guided appropriation and apprenticeship, in J.V. Wertsch, P. Del Rio and A. Alverez (eds) *Sociocultural Studies of the Mind*. Cambridge: Cambridge University Press.

Rogoff, B. and Lave, J. (eds) (1984) *Everyday Cognition: Its Development in Social Context*. Cambridge, MA: Harvard University Press.

Rowden, R. (1995) The role of human resources development in successful small to mid-sized manufacturing businesses: a comparative case study. *Human Resource Development Quarterly*, 6(4): 335–73.

Säljo, R. and Wyndhamm, J. (1993) Solving everyday problems in the formal setting: an empirical study of the school as context for thought, in S. Chaiklin and J. Lave (eds) *Understanding Practice: Perspectives on Activity and Context*. Cambridge: Cambridge University Press.

Salomon, G. (1994) Whole individuals in complex settings: educational research reexamined. Invited Address presented at the *Annual Meeting of the Australian Association for Research in Education*, Newcastle, NSW, November.

Scribner, S. (1985) Vygostky's use of history, in J.V. Wertsch (ed.) *Culture, Communication and Cognition: Vygotskian Perspectives*. Cambridge: Cambridge University Press.

Scribner, S. (1997) Mental and manual work: an activity theory orientation, in E. Tobah, R.J. Falmagne, M.B. Parlee, L.M. Martin and A.S. Kapelman (eds) *Mind and Social Practice: Selected Writings of Sylvia Scribner*. Cambridge: Cambridge University Press.

Tam, M. (1997) *Part-time Employment: A Bridge or a Trap?* Aldershot: Brookfield.

Valsiner, J. (1994) Bi-directional cultural transmission and constructive sociogenesis, in W. de Graaf and R. Maier (eds) *Sociogenesis Re-examined*. New York: Springer-Verlag.

Valsiner, J. (2000) *The Social Mind: Construction of an Idea*. Cambridge: Cambridge University Press.

Vygotsky, L.S. (1978) *Mind in Society: The Development of Higher Psychological Processes.* Cambridge, MA: Harvard University Press.

Wenger, E. (1998) *Communities of Practice: Learning, Meaning, and Identity.* Cambridge: Cambridge University Press.

Wertsch, J.W. (1998) *Mind as Action.* New York: Oxford University Press.

Whalley, P. and Barley, S.R. (1997) Technical work in the division of labor: stalking the wily anomaly, in S.R. Barley and J.E. Orr *Between Craft and Science: Technical Work in U.S. Settings.* Ithaca, NY: Cornell University Press.

Zuboff, S. (1988) *In the Age of the Smart Machine: The Future of Work and Power.* New York: Basic Books.

Chapter 6

Distribution and interconnectedness

The globalisation of education

Richard Edwards

Introduction

Educational organisations and practices are being transformed by the introduction and ever-increasing use of information and communications technologies. Whereas education was once associated with the bringing together of teachers and students into classrooms, what Lankshear *et al.* (1996) refer to as 'spaces of enclosure', increasingly there are now possibilities for people to be distributed across vast distances, yet be interconnected through the use of technologies. Although this is not an entirely new phenomenon – people have been able to have telephone tutorials for many decades – there is something new in the density of possible interconnections and the fact that they are not simply one-to-one. There is the possibility for collaborative forms of learning, despite the greater potential for learners to be vastly distant from each other. Rather than face-to-face tutorials as a means to, at least in part, overcome the isolation of learning in more conventional forms of distance education, distributed learning provides important virtual contexts for interaction.

It also provides opportunities for educational provision to emerge. Partnerships between educational institutions and private companies in the development of distributed learning are not uncommon, as we have seen with the emergence of corporate universities, such as McDonald's University in the USA. Information and communications technologies, and other media companies, rightly see a commercial opportunity in such developments (Cunningham *et al.* 1997). Learning is no longer perceived as having a monopoly of education institutions, and different forms of knowledge production based on bringing people together across distance are emerging (Gibbons *et al.* 1994). Here, distributed learning is making an important contribution to the wider policy-led goal of lifelong learning.

Moves in these directions raise many issues. Who has access to the technology and is able to participate in these forms of provision? What are the implications for curriculum in distributed learning? What are the implications for pedagogy and assessment of distributed approaches? How can we best explain and support learning in these settings? And what is the significance of distributed learning in relation to wider trends in the economy, politics and culture? It is the latter that provides the focus for this chapter. In particular, I want to explore how distributed learning may be positioned in relation to wider debates about globalising processes. In what ways does distributed learning contribute to globalisation? How might the debates about globalising processes help us to examine the implications of adopting distributed learning approaches?

Globalisation is often seen as resulting in a shrinking of the world through greater interconnectedness (Tomlinson 1999). This is often referred to as space–time compression, wherein distance and time are no longer significant barriers to bringing (certain groups of) people together as they might have been in the past. Things happen more quickly, they do not require as much time and thus distance becomes less of a problem. This bringing together can be seen as part of a homogenising of the world, where western forms of economics, politics and culture colonise ever more deeply the daily lives of people around the globe. Alternatively, the very act of bringing together may be seen as manifesting the difference and diversity of ways of life around the globe, making problematic these western perspectives. In what ways may distributed learning be examined as a colonising practice, or one that results in a richer more diverse curriculum and learning experience?

This chapter comprises two parts. First, I explore the attempts to interpret globalising processes, focusing in particular on arguments over the nature and extent of economic, political and cultural globalisation. This sets the context for the discussion in the second part. Here, I outline some of the implications of the analysis of globalisation for our understanding of the significance of developments in distributed learning. I am not concerned with how to improve the practices of distributed learning, but what those practices contribute to wider economic, political and cultural processes.

Globalising processes

As a child in the 1960s, I remember the awe I experienced sitting in front of the television watching the first moon landings and the strange sight of the globe hanging there in space. Reflecting back on this, the significance of those events strikes me even more, and how symptomatic they were for changes taking place in contemporary society and social theory. In conceptions of the nature and importance of space and in relation to the way our experience of space can alter sensibilities and identities, the moon landings were a significant occurrence.

The capacity to look at the earth from the moon helped to alter conceptions about space. Although notions of 'the earth' were encapsulated by the partial perspectives of earth-based humanity, space was a form of enclosure – the sky was literally the limit. By contrast, being able to see the earth as a minute part of a galaxy within a universe created an openness in the conception of space. Assumptions about the space 'we' occupy were thereby disrupted by the moon landings. In a sense, 'the globe' came on to the stage in this period in a way that had been only hinted at previously. Furthermore, considerations about the space of which 'we' are part also linked into considerations of time, for the space that the lunar walkers looked out upon – and which we see in looking at the night sky – is not the present. We look at the sky in the present but, because of the time it takes for light to travel across space, we are looking at what happened in the past – or more correctly pasts, as differences in distance result in differences in time. The need to consider space and time together as space–time rather than as separate categories came to the fore, a position many scientists will accept as mundane, but which has had profound effects in certain branches of the social sciences.

Until relatively recently, 'the world' was largely discussed either as an aspect of international relations or what is termed 'world systems theory'. The former focuses on the relations between nation states, the latter on capitalist economic relations. Each has been subject to the criticism that their particular foci marginalise and exclude large and important trends in the world, in particular the cultural dimensions and the impact of information and communication technologies. In response to these limitations, different conceptions of globalisation have emerged that have stimulated debate about its nature, extent and novelty as a phenomenon, particularly in relation to the economy (Hirst and Thompson 1996a, b), but also in relation to politics and culture (Waters 1995; Edwards and Usher 2000).

At its simplest, the notion of globalisation may be expressed as 'the compression of the world and the intensification of consciousness of the world as a whole' (Robertson 1992: 8) or, as Waters (1995: 3) suggests, 'a social process in which the constraints of geography on social and cultural arrangements recede and in which people become increasingly aware that they are receding'. It signifies the shrinking of the world where people, services and goods are connected to each other across the globe through a variety of means and in increasingly immediate ways. Airline tickets bought in England are processed in India. CNN and McDonald's are available on a global scale. People migrate for work, leisure and increasingly as refugees. The Internet, fax and telephone put people instantly in touch with each other, even though they may be in different hemispheres. Investment decisions taken in one country may well affect workers and investors in several other countries. What in the past would have taken months to move around the globe now takes days or even seconds. The economic, political and cultural dynamics of these processes are the focus of much debate and dispute.

Popular discussion of globalisation treats it as an entirely new phenomenon arising from the conditions of the immediate present. However, globalisation has a history and geography of its own. In this context, the contemporary interest in globalisation is the result of an intensification of certain processes and the awareness of the globe as a single environment. Robertson (1992), for example, provides one outline of the historical phases of the long, uneven and complicated process of globalisation. First, he identifies the Germinal Phase that lasted in Europe from the early fifteenth to the late eighteenth century. Although this is associated with the growth of national communities, it also embraces the spread of ideas about humanity and, perhaps more importantly, the Gregorian calendar, a step towards a global conception of time. The Incipient Phase lasted until the 1870s, once again mainly grounded in Europe, and saw the consolidation of the nation state and the development of international relations. The Take-Off Phase lasted until the mid-1920s, in which there were increasing global assumptions about what a nation state should be and how it should act. There was the implementation of 'world time', a sharp increase in the amount and speed of global communication, and a growth in global competitions, such as the Olympic Games. The mid-1920s to the late 1960s saw the Struggle for Hegemony Phase, particularly between the Second

World War and the cold war adversaries seeking to determine the direction of the globalising processes in line with their own ideologies. The Holocaust and atom bomb provided defining perspectives on the prospects for humanity within this period. The current phase since the late 1960s is what Robertson (1992) terms the Uncertainty Phase, in which global consciousness has become heightened, with international systems more fluid, the prospects for humanity more fraught in the light of environmental and other risks, and with the increase in global communications and the consolidation of the global media. Alongside and in response to trends towards global integration, white, 'western' male assumptions that underlie dominant conceptions of humanity and society have been called into question by considerations of gender, sexual, ethnic and racial differences, the increased multiculturalism of societies and notions of the hybridity of cultures.

Robertson claims these phases to be an outline in need of more rigorous analysis; this is certainly the case, for, in relation to commerce, Hirst and Thompson (1996a, b) argue that globalising processes were more intense 100 years ago than they are now. For many, it is the capitalist economy that is the driving force of globalising processes (Harvey 1989). For instance, Reich (1993) argues that much economic thinking is based on the 'vestigial thought' of national interest that no longer reflects the reality of contemporary economic life. He suggests that new ideas and fresh conceptualisations are necessary to help explain the current condition. Reich argues that economic interests nowadays are not about supporting particular 'national' companies, but in making geographical areas attractive for inward investment by transnational global capital. Ensuring a skilled labour force is one such way of attracting investment and thus the importance given to notions of lifelong learning, learning regions, learning cities, and so on – 'in a world in which inter-urban competitiveness operates on a global scale, cities are propelled into a race to attract increasingly mobile investors (multinational corporations), consumers (tourists), and spectacles (sports and media events)' (Robins 1993: 306).

However, evidence for Reich's thesis is lacking. For instance, Ashton and Green argue that:

> though trade has increased its importance in the post-war economic life of most countries, the largest economies are still served by national-based firms . . . the truly transnational corporation which has no national bases and no concern for national specificities remains in a small minority.
>
> (Ashton and Green 1996: 71)

Like Hirst and Thompson (1996a, b), they argue that this raises questions about the extent of globalising processes. However, they seem to see the latter as an undifferentiated process of integration of the world economy. Massey's view is more considered. She argues that while there is a national origin for most companies and with that a clear direction of flows in foreign investment, 'the geography of these flows has been changing and becoming more complex' (Massey 1994: 159). There is a greater degree of interconnectedness, and the alignment of certain corporate interests with those of specific nation states has indeed become questionable. The growth of trans-national corporations without commitment to any national economy may be more limited than Reich suggests, but the influence of more general globalising tendencies – for instance, in consumption – should not be underestimated. Thus, 'the increasing importance of targeting consumers on the basis of demography and habits rather than on the basis of geographical proximity' (Morley and Robins 1995: 110).

Economic globalisation is usually held to be central to globalising processes. This raises questions not only about the competence of the nation state to govern, but also about what and who constitutes civil society. We thus enter debates about political globalisation. Although economic globalisation provides the basis for an increase in the power of the market, in the face of which national governments sometimes appear relatively powerless, different possibilities for globalised forms of oppositional politics also emerge. This is termed 'globalisation from below' (Falk 1993; Korsgaard 1997). Here the link between nation state and citizenship may be loosened, with people playing an active role in more global networks to address issues of shared concern, such as global warming. National governments become only a partial focus for certain forms of popular intervention, as demonstrated by Greenpeace and certain humanitarian groups. Globalisation therefore provides political possibilities as well as threats in the spread of capitalist relations. On the one hand, for instance, there is the feminisation of labour, where:

> global assembly lines are 'manned' by women workers in free trade zones; subcontracted industrial homeworking is performed at kitchen tables by women who 'have time on their hands'; home-based teleworking is carried out by women who can't afford day-care costs and are grateful to have paid work.
>
> (Manicom and Walters 1997: 72)

However, practices also develop to bring together groups affected by economic restructuring in new ways, such as trade unions funding labour and community projects outside their own national base (Marshall 1997). Similarly, communications technologies may be utilised by differing groupings:

> Affinity groups of 'senior' or retired citizens, feminist scholars, individuals who share knowledge on health afflictions, hobbyists, professionals, political organisations and many others are . . . using the Internet to educate, prosyletise and organise, cutting across national boundaries with apparent ease.
>
> (Goodenow 1996: 200)

People may be geographically distributed, but politically interconnected and active.

There is thus a reconfiguration of governance and the political in the intensifying processes of globalisation. Waters (1995) suggests that there is evidence for the aggregation and decentralisation of state powers and the growth of international organisations, although the latter are relatively powerless at present. Scott, however, argues that it is deregulation which undermines the ability of nation states to protect themselves and the community they represent from the social destructiveness of markets, but it is also the nation state that is the key actor in bringing deregulation about both internally (e.g. through privatisation and lowering social costs within its borders) and externally (e.g. by participating in and agreeing to proposals emerging from international fora – GATT negotiations etc.).

(Scott 1997: 10)

In other words, if political globalisation does undermine the capacity of the nation state to intervene in the economy, it is in part an outcome of the policies adopted by nation states themselves. Cunningham and Jacka (1996: 14) argue that globalisation has 'gradually led to the erosion of the appearance of congruity between economy, polity and culture within the nation-state'. However, a continued role for the nation state is taken by some (Hirst and Thomspon 1996a; Green 1997) to be evidence against globalising processes.

In his detailed argument for the role of the nation state in supporting different forms of nationalism – civic, ethnic and economic – through education, Green (1997) is cautious in his assessment of globalisation. However, this is in part because he views the argument to be whether there is an increased or decreased role for the nation state and nationalism. However, it is also possible to explore the changing role of the state as part of globalisation. It is part of the paradoxes of globalisation rather than a refutation of it that the role of the nation state and specific nation states might be enhanced in certain ways. Here it is a question of whether one sees attempts to protect national interest against international trends as a rejection of globalisation or part of globalising processes.

Globalisation is often taken to have a single trajectory or logic that results in increased uniformity across the globe. However, despite the powerful effects of transnational capital and international media conglomerates, this is not sustainable. To assume that globalisation results in homogenisation is to simplify the processes at work and, in a sense, to distance oneself from the complex effects of interconnectedness that globalising processes highlight. As Giddens (1990) among others suggests, while globalisation has resulted in the spread of 'western' institutions across the globe, that very trend produces a pressure for local autonomy and identity which may be asserted in a range of ways – economic, political, cultural. In other words, globalisation is about examining places as simultaneously traversed by the global and local in ways that have been intensified by the contemporary compression of space and time. Thus, alongside the global availability of satellite television, McDonald's and Arnold Schwarznegger films, there is the affirmation of, for instance, local, regional and ethnic identities. Indeed, some transnational companies have explicitly adopted strategies of 'glocalisation', extending their influence around the globe while situating themselves and their products and services within the local contexts (Robertson 1992). 'Time–space distanciation, disembedding, and reflexivity mean that complex relationships develop between local activities and interaction across distances' (Waters 1995: 50). The integration of the globe therefore reconfigures rather than supplants diversity. Globalisation 'does not necessarily imply homogenisation or integration. Globalisation merely implies greater connectedness and de-territorialisation' (Waters 1995: 136).

The assertion of heterogeneity by the locale or region may take many forms; for instance, it may involve the protection/assertion of a specific identity as a reaction against the perceived homogeneity introduced by the global (Castells 1997). As Turner (1994: 78) argues in relation to contemporary religious fundamentalism, it 'is a two-pronged movement to secure control within the global system and also to maintain regulation of the lifeworld'. Fundamentalism attempts to contain the assertion of difference and secular consumerism through the deployment of notions of religious community bounded together by spiritual belief and sentiment. This is a cultural response to globalising processes. Paradoxically, however, such religions also take their own world views to be universal and, through the use of new technologies, seek to promote themselves more effectively as global religions. 'Islam is now able to self-thematise Islamic religion as a self-reflective global system of cultural identity over and against the diversity and pluralism involved in the new consumer culture' (Turner 1994: 90). Here fundamentalism is as much part of globalisation as a response to it.

Although clear differences about the nature and significance of globalisation do exist, there is a shared sense of the centrality of the contribution of media, communication and transport to these processes. In many ways, it is the development of these technologies that has underpinned globalising processes. Perhaps most importantly it has enabled financial flows around the globe to be speeded up on an almost continuous basis. However, the globe also enters our homes through the media with which we engage and the products and pollutants we consume. Most arguments regarding globalisation therefore focus on the significance of the development of technology and particularly the speeding up of communication and transportation made possible by this development. Here 'globalisation has reordered both time and space and "shrunk the globe"' (Held 1993: 5). Globalising processes have brought different cultures into contact and collision with each other through information technology, travel, migration and the media. Aeroplanes, satellites and computer networks have assisted in this shrinking process, bringing about what Rowan et al. (1997) term a greater range of '(en)counters'. This has occurred to such an extent that Castells (1996), in his monumental analysis of contemporary trends, suggests that we increasingly live in a 'network society', one in which information is a key resource, and within which there are increasing disparities between those included and excluded from the powerful networks.

Depending upon which part of the globe one inhabits and one's position therein, lifestyles, life courses and decision-making are increasingly mediated and reinscribed through globally integrated and integrating processes. However, care should be taken in the framing of the centrality of information and communications technologies to contemporary globalisation, since the result is often a crude form of technological determinism. Technological development may be necessary to these processes but it is not sufficient, and their development and deployment is subject to a range of factors and possibilities.

As suggested above, central to globalising processes is the re-ordering of space and time and in particular the compression of space–time. Soja (1989) suggests that the restructuring of space–time in contemporary capitalism does not simply displace previous conditions but rather overlays them. This undermines established patterns of uneven development and produces new centres of urbanisation, but does not completely replace what existed previously. Notions of a post-industrial world are therefore partial and misplaced. What has become generally accepted is the experience engendered by space–time compression. Basically, the world feels smaller and in a sense *is* smaller, since more people, goods and services are now able to travel around it and communicate across great distances more quickly and easily than ever before.

Space–time compression and responses to it are neither uniform nor homogenising. They present several contradictory positions, in which the importance of distance and place appear to be reduced, even as their importance is reasserted as a reaction to the perceived unifying effects of global integration. Thus, 'the globalisation of social relations is yet another source of (the reproduction of) geographical uneven development, and thus of the uniqueness of place' (Massey 1991: 29). The strength of these processes is dependent upon the intensity of the space–time compression and one's place in the global–local nexus: 'different social groups, and different individuals, are placed in very distinct ways in relation to these flows and interconnections' (Massey 1994: 149). However, as Lemert (1997: 20) argues, 'it is not just that technology allows people closer communication with each other . . . but that globalising processes are of such a nature as to have fundamentally changed the way the world is experienced'. This is the cultural dimension of globalisation (Tomlinson 1999).

Thus, Waters (1995) argues that claims for globalisation rest on a relationship between social organisation and territoriality, and that this link is established through the forms of exchange that predominate in any one period. Central to contemporary globalisation is the dominance of symbolic exchange over material and political exchange and the extent to which the latter two themselves become subject to culturalisation. For Waters, a globalised culture

> is chaotic rather than orderly – it is integrated and connected so that the meanings of its components are 'relativised' to one another but it is not unified or centralised . . . [it] admits a flow of ideas, information, commitment, values and taste mediated through mobile individuals, symbolic tokens and electronic simulations.
>
> (Waters 1995: 125–6)

While suggestive, a certain caution is also necessary, for, as Cunningham *et al.* (1997: 12) suggest, there is a 'need to desegregate the different elements of what is referred to as global media into: global media events; service delivery platforms; media corporations; and distribution of content'. However, Waters finds the evidence for cultural globalisation well advanced and Massey argues that

> each geographical 'place' in the world is being realigned in relation to the new global realities, their roles within the wider whole are being reassigned,

their boundaries dissolve as they are increasingly crossed by everything from investment flows, to cultural influences, to satellite TV networks.

(Massey 1994: 161)

The economic and political are therefore increasingly understood as mediated by the symbolic and cultural. Here, the cultural interconnectedness of globalising processes becomes more significant than the economic and political practices.

There is a complex interplay of the economic, political and cultural in the debates about the nature, extent and significance of globalising processes. In what ways do they help us to assess the significance of distributed learning? What issues do they highlight that we may need to address in adopting such approaches?

Distribution and interconnectedness

The forms of interconnectedness possible through the extension of networking undermine the need for people to attend specific places for learning, even while it brings to the fore their own place as a learning setting. Distributed learning brings people together, yet provides the possibility for their ever wider dispersal. Learners and tutors no longer need to be in the same place, or even the same nation state, but may communicate on a global scale through the mediations of technology. As with the wider debates about globalising processes, this can have paradoxical effects, as it enables people to be kept 'in their place', while at the same time enabling them to be brought together across great physical distances. It also provides the potential for them to be on the move as they learn; the mobile subject in the many senses of that notion.

Place therefore has a continuing significance even if at one level the provision of learning opportunities makes it less important in principle. The very distance covered by distributed learning brings places together and compresses space. It can therefore shrink the globe in many and varied ways. Of course, this is dependent on the media through which the learning is made available. Thus, sending printed material by post brings about a specific form of interconnectedness, one that is transformed through, for instance, the use of computer conferencing. The mail and the computer conference may link the same two places, but the time it takes for this to happen and the nature of the interconnection is radically different.

The precise form distributed learning takes is part of the hidden curriculum. In relation to distance education, Evans (1989: 181) has suggested that this 'is partly about "choreographing" a myriad of personal and collective movements in time–space'. This applies equally to distributed learning, where the notion of choreographing reflects the looser organisation of space–time within forms of distributed learning than where more conventional forms of education are governed by the timetable. Thus, while there is still the possibility for the dance to be timetabled with synchronous online activities, there is also the possibility for less control over where and when the person undertakes their learning with asynchronous communication access to the Internet wherever possible. Thus, airports and cafés become sites for distributed learning: one engages with virtual rather than physical dance partners.

In creating extended networks of interconnectedness, distributed learning is theoretically able to bring together people from diverse educational and cultural backgrounds. Whether it does so at present is another matter, but the potential for more diverse groups raises questions about the assumptions made about learners and learning among those who design these types of learning opportunities. Does distributed learning contribute to homogenising or heterogeneity in learning? This bringing together can serve to raise awareness of diversity and differences – for example, in religion, language, ethnicity and culture. It may not be surprising, therefore, that the opportunities for greater interconnectedness across distance provide a context for the more extensive use of sociocultural theories of learning to find purchase, which are sensitive to place and context. However, the very bringing together can also result in a disembedding of learners from their context as they (en)counter each other in mediated forms across space and place.

Having mentioned the hidden curricula, it is also important to consider the formal curricula, since distributed learning opportunities are developed in certain spaces and places and for certain purposes. At present, it is evolving from a phenomenon within the business community and the global business elite to become a mainstream part of tertiary education – as the UK's e-university initiative suggests. In part, then, distributed learning might be said to be part of economic globalisation, enabling elites to conduct their business and learning wherever they may be. Indeed, distributed learning is itself becoming an important global business, not only within the commercial sector but also in the support national governments are giving to educational institutions to increase their export income. It is therefore possible to view distributed learning as part of the massive growth in the distributive services industries – for example, leisure, hospitality, tourism – in recent years. Here, the extensive and intensive use of information and communications technologies, modularisation and the plethora of innovations to increase 'openness' may be construed as developments to satisfy the demands of consumers for educational and training products.

The learning opportunities also largely emanate from the capitalist centres of power. To what extent does distributed learning result in the universalising and homogenising of the curricula, a further extension of economic and cultural colonisation? To sit in south-east Asia studying materials produced in the UK is certainly a feat of access and enterprise, but what is excluded from the curricula through such acts of distribution and interconnections? This issue may vary from subject area to subject area, but even in the field of management, whose reach does seem to be truly global, there is the question over what and whose view of management is being conveyed.

The argument that the current phase of space–time compression is integral to capitalism's shift towards a more globally integrated set of market relations is compelling, and raises the question about the political implications of the adoption and expansion of distributed learning. This is not simply the question of the support for geographical dispersal and labour market control that distributed forms of learning enable in the support of more flexible labour markets (Harvey 1989). It is also about how this dispersal might be seen to undermine senses of solidarity and opposition to exploitation and oppression. Thus, as Harvey observes, the non-financial zones of inner cities, which have quite rightly been the focus of so much attention in the past, have increasingly become, therefore, centres of unemployment and oppression . . . rather than creatures of labour exploitation and working class political organizations of the classic sort.

(Harvey 1993: 89)

Although this is not the direct result of distributed learning, it is engendered by the reconfiguration of space–time of which it is a part and to which it contributes. Distributed learning may therefore be considered as one of those actions at a distance, the ' "indirect" mechanisms of aligning economic, social and personal conduct with socio-political objectives' (Miller and Rose 1993: 76) that make the governing of modern social formations by consent possible. Here, governments

rely upon a complex network of technologies – in management, in market-ing, in advertising, in instructional talks on the mass media and communi-cation – for educating citizens in techniques to govern themselves. Modern political power does not take the form of the domination of subjectivity . . . Rather, political power has come to depend upon a web of technologies for fabricating and maintaining self-government.

(Miller and Rose 1993: 102)

Implicitly or explicitly, distributed learning may play a role in such processes, although, given the discussion of globalisation from below, there is also the possibility for oppositional spaces to be created, wherein the curricula may be deconstructed and reconstructed.

Conclusion

This discussion has indicated the range of issues and some of the competing interpretations of them. Innovations in distributed learning cannot be taken as a given; they need to be examined for their significance in relation to wider trends. In relation to the economy, politics and culture, globalising processes are having profound impacts. It appears there is nowhere to hide from capitalist economic relations. The interdependence of states is manifesting itself in a growing number of regional groupings and a general consensus around policy across political divides. The spreading influence of the media and of western forms of culture is having a profound impact on people's values and lifestyles. We have the growth of hugely wealthy transnational companies and the devel-opment of globalisation through the activities of activist groups such as anti-globalisation demonstrators at world summits. While huge inequalities remain in relation to wealth, health and housing and the Internet continues to be primarily a vehicle for the well-off and well educated in certain geographical locations, there is no denying the intensifying forms of interconnectedness around the globe. It is not surprising that these trends have also prevailed in the provision of learning opportunities. Precisely because of the compression of space–time in the practices of distributed learning, it can be located as part of the more general trends in globalisation identified above. Many of the issues and paradoxes raised by wider globalising trends may therefore be seen in relation to distributed learning. Castells (1998: 378) characterises the thrust of current trends as producing 'informed bewilderment'. Many important issues and questions have been raised in the process, and require far more extensive debate than has taken place to date. Distributed learning may provide opportunities for access and collaboration for people geographically dispersed, but for what, to whom, why and with what effects remain important questions that need to be addressed.

References

Ashton, D. and Green, F. (1996) *Education, Training and the Global Economy*. Cheltenham: Edward Elgar.

Castells, M. (1996) *The Information Age: Economy, Society and Culture. Vol. I: The Rise of the Network Society*. Oxford: Blackwell.

Castells, M. (1997) *The Information Age: Economy, Society and Culture. Vol. II: The Power of Identity*. Oxford: Blackwell.

Castells, M. (1998) *The Information Age: Economy, Society and Culture. Vol. III: End of Millennium*. Oxford: Blackwell.

Cunningham, S. and Jacka, E. (1996) *Australian Television and International Mediascapes*. Cambridge: Cambridge University Press.

Cunningham, S., Tapsall, S., Ryan, Y., Stedman, L., Bagdon, K. and Flew, T. (1997) *New Media and Borderless Education: A Review of the Convergence Between Global Media Networks and Higher Education Provision*. Canberra: DEETYA.

Edwards, R. and Usher, R. (2000) *Globalisation and Education: Space, Place and Identity*. London: Routledge.

Evans, T. (1989) Taking place: the social construction of place, time and space in the remaking of distances in distance education, *Distance Education*, 10(2): 170–83.

Falk, R. (1993) The making of global citizenship, in J. Brecher, J. Brown Childs and J. Cutler (eds) *Global Visions: Beyond the New World Order*. Montreal: Black Rose Books.

Gibbon, M., Limoges, C., Nowotny, H., Schwartzman, S., Scott, P. and Trow, M. (1994) *The New Production of Knowledge: The Dynamics of Science and Research in Contemporary Societies*. London: Sage.

Giddens, A. (1990) *The Consequences of Modernity*. Cambridge: Polity Press.

Goodenow, R. (1996) The cyberspace challenge: modernity, postmodernity and reflections on international networking policy, *Comparative Education*, 32(2): 197–216.

Green, A. (1997) *Education, Globalisation and the Nation State*. London: Macmillan.

Harvey, D. (1989) *The Condition of Modernity: An Enquiry into the Origins of Cultural Change*. Oxford: Blackwell.

Harvey, D. (1993) Class relations, social justice and the politics of difference, in J. Squires (ed.) *Principled Positions: Postmodernism and the Rediscovery of Value*. London: Lawrence & Wishart.

Held, D. (1993) *Democracy and the New International Order*. London: IPPR.

Hirst, P. and Thompson, G. (1996a) *Globalisation in Question*. Cambridge: Polity Press.

Hirst, P. and Thompson, G. (1996b) Globalisation: ten frequently asked questions and some surprising answers, *Soundings*, 4: 47–66.

Korsgaard, O. (1997) The impact of globalisation on adult education, in S. Walters (ed.) *Globalisation, Adult Education and Training: Impacts and Issues*. London: Zed Books.

Lankshear, C., Peters, M. and Knobel, M. (1996) Critical pedagogy and cyberspace', in H. Giroux, C. Lankshear, P. McLaren and M. Peters (eds) *Counternarratives*. London: Routledge.

Lemert, C. (1997) *Postmodernism is Not What You Think*. Oxford: Blackwell.

Manicom, L. and Walters, S. (1997) Feminist popular education in the light of globalisation, in S. Walters (ed.) *Globalisation, Adult Education and Training: Impacts and Issues*. London: Zed Books.

Marshall, J. (1997) Globalisation from below: trade unions connections, in S. Walters (ed.) *Globalisation, Adult Education and Training: Impacts and Issues*. London: Zed Books.

Massey, D. (1991) A global sense of place, *Marxism Today*, June, pp. 24–9.

Massey, D. (1994) *Space, Place and Gender*. Cambridge: Polity Press.

Miller, P. and Rose, N. (1993) Governing economic life, in M. Gane and T. Johnson (eds) *Foucault's New Domains*. London: Routledge.

Morley, D. and Robins, K. (1995) *Spaces of Identity: Global Media, Electronic Landscapes and Cultural Boundaries*. London: Routledge.

Reich, R. (1993) *The Work of Nations: A Blueprint for the Future*. London: Simon & Schuster.

Robertson, R. (1992) *Globalization: Social Theory and Global Culture*. London: Sage.

Robins, K. (1993) Prisoners of the city: whatever could a postmodern city be?, in E. Carter, J. Donald and J. Squires (eds) *Space and Place: Theories of Identity and Location*. London: Lawrence and Wishart.

Rowan, L., Evans, T. and Bartlett, L. (eds) (1997) *Shifting Borders: Globalisation, Localisation and Open and Distance Learning*. Geelong: Deakin University Press.

Scott, A. (1997) Introduction – globalisation: social process or political rhetoric?, in A. Scott (ed.) *The Limits of Globalisation: Cases and Arguments*. London: Routledge.

Soja, E. (1989) *Postmodern Geographies: The Reassertion of Space in Critical Social Theory*. London: Verso.

Tomlinson, J. (1999) *Globalisation and Culture*. Cambridge: Polity Press.

Turner, B. (1994) *Orientalism, Postmodernism and Globalism*. London: Routledge.

Waters, M. (1995) *Globalisation*. London: Routledge.

Chapter 7

The English language and 'global' teaching

Barbara Mayor and Joan Swann

Introduction

In this chapter, we discuss some linguistic and cultural issues in the teaching and assessment of students who are distributed globally across place and time and who are thereby located in diverse local contexts; who are likely to bring different expectations and understandings to their learning; and who are, to a large extent, unknown, and perhaps unknowable, to course designers. Drawing mainly on our experiences as designers and producers of supported open learning materials at the Open University (UK), as well as related research on language and global communication, we focus on the problems and possibilities of using English, a 'global' language, as a medium for the design of teaching and assessment materials. For the purposes of this chapter, we are less concerned with issues related to local tuition and assessment, although we do make some reference to this. Although our teaching situation is the particular one of an English-medium institution delivering its courses to locations across the globe, we hope our experiences will have broader relevance for anyone working with linguistically or culturally diverse groups and/or in the context of distributed learning. The examples we refer to are generally from traditional print-based courses, but the points we raise will apply to courses using different modes of teaching/course delivery, including new information technologies.

Language and communication in a global context

The choice of language for course delivery is an important issue for anyone designing courses for distributed learning and, in particular, for global presentation. This inevitably raises issues to do with the relationship between languages and cultures, in particular the extent to which the choice of language affects the ways teachers and learners represent the world and the ways they relate to each other.

In this chapter, we adopt a socially oriented model of language. We focus on the different cultural meanings attributed to language varieties and, more critically, differences in their status and their social and economic power. A further concern is with the communicative practices engaged in by speakers and writers from different cultural contexts in communication with one another. We draw particularly on insights from sociolinguistics (broadly, the study of the relationship between language and society), applied linguistics (the application of linguistics, and sociolinguistics, to practical and policy issues such as language teaching) and inter-cultural communication (the study of communication between members of different cultural groups).[1] These will inform our discussion in this section of the role of English as a global language of education, and teaching and learning practices across different cultural contexts.

English as a global language of education

English   A Germanic language which has come to be spoken world-wide by a large and ever-increasing number of people – 800,000,000 by a conservative estimate, 1,500,000,000 by a liberal estimate. Some 350,000,000 use the language as a mother tongue, chiefly in the USA (c. 220 million), the UK (c. 55 million), Canada (c. 17 million), Australia (c. 15 million), New Zealand (c. 3 million), Ireland (c. 3.5 million), and South Africa (c. 2 million). A further 400 million use it as a second language, in such countries as Ghana, Nigeria, Tanzania, Pakistan, and the Philippines. It has official status in over 60 countries. Estimates also suggest that at least 150 million people use English fluently as a foreign language, and three or four times this number with some degree of competence. In China, India, and most of the countries of western Europe, the presence of English is noticeable or rapidly growing. English is also the language of international air traffic control, and the chief language of world publishing, science and technology, conferencing, and computer storage.

(Crystal 1992: 121)

[The] widespread use [of English] threatens other languages; [it] has become the language of power and prestige in many countries, thus acting as a crucial gatekeeper to social and economic progress; its use in particular domains, especially professional, may exacerbate different power relationships and may render these domains more inaccessible to many people; its position in the world gives it a role also as an international gatekeeper, regulating the international flow of people; it is closely linked to national and increasingly non-national forms of culture and knowledge that are dominant in the world; and it is also bound up with aspects of global relations, such as the spread of capitalism, development aid and the dominance particularly of North American media.

(Pennycook 1994: 13)

English is probably used by many more people, and in a wider range of contexts, than when David Crystal wrote his dictionary entry. It is particularly widely used as a language of higher education and of academia more generally – so that a vast range of academic books, journals and other resources is available in English. Given the prevalence of English, the likely competence in the language of a large number of students and the availability of resources, English seems the obvious choice of teaching medium for institutions operating in a global context. As a UK institution, the Open University has traditionally taught through the medium of English.[2] This fortuitous occurrence seems to have made it well placed to expand its teaching overseas. Such an expansion, however, is not without problems. We discuss below the extent to which the global spread of English (in which education through English necessarily plays a part) may be considered an 'imperialist' project, promoting the English language itself as well as 'western'[3] educational values and practices.

Pennycook (1994) comments that the development of English as a global language has conventionally been regarded as a 'natural', 'neutral' and 'beneficial' activity. It is 'natural' in that, while the colonial imposition of English is clearly recognised, its more recent spread is seen as the product of 'inevitable global forces' (primarily economic). The spread of English is 'neutral' because, as an international language, English has become detached from its earlier cultural contexts – its associations with nations such as the UK and the USA have loosened and it has become a lingua franca for communication across diverse groups for whom it is not a first language. English is 'beneficial' because it facilitates international communication across several important domains, such as commerce, science and technology. There are, however, several problems with this position. Both Pennycook (1994) and Phillipson (1992) argue that the spread of English did not simply 'happen'. They provide close documentation of the active promotion of English from colonial times to the present – for example, through institutions such as the British Council and as an aspect of development aid. Promotional activities were explicitly intended to further the cultural, political and economic interests of countries such as the UK and the USA. And the spread of English has had a detrimental effect on other languages and many of their speakers; for instance, in contexts where English dominates in domains such as science or technology, local languages may not expand to occupy those domains; as English spreads further, the viability of local languages may become threatened (a process known as 'language shift'; see e.g. Fishman 1964; see also discussion in Mesthrie *et al.* 2000). In relation to individual speakers, English offers many people an opportunity for social and economic advancement, but it also necessarily acts as a gatekeeper.

Phillipson sees the global dominance of English as an example of 'linguistic imperialism', by which he means that: 'the dominance of English is asserted and maintained by the establishment and continuous reconstruction of structural and cultural inequalities between English and other languages' (Phillipson 1992: 47). The term 'structural' here refers to 'material properties' such as institutions and financial allocations; 'cultural' refers to 'immaterial or ideological properties' such as attitudes and values. Phillipson's claim is that English linguistic imperialism is associated with other forms of imperialism (e.g. cultural, economic) that systematically assert the dominance of western 'Europeanised' countries and their cultures.

Phillipson and Pennycook are particularly concerned with the role played by English language teaching (ELT) in the global domination of English. They argue that alongside the spread of English as a language, the ELT industry exports 'western' pedagogical practices that may not be suitable in other teaching contexts. Difficulties may be caused, for instance, by inappropriate levels of informality in the classroom, the adoption of inappropriate communicative norms and the lack of recognition of multilingualism as a resource. Pennycook (1994: 152) comments: 'Teaching practices need to be seen as cultural practices, and thus the promotion of particular teaching approaches is closely linked to the promotion of English and to the promotion of particular forms of culture and knowledge.'

These arguments also have some relevance for institutions offering education through the medium of English. On the one hand, institutions such as the Open University are reflecting the current state of affairs – the global dominance of English; they are satisfying a 'market demand' for courses and qualifications in English; and they would no doubt argue that they are producing materials of a high quality. But they are thereby necessarily contributing to the dominance of English, and their teaching practices are also likely to be associated with 'western' educational and cultural values and principles. We return to this issue below.

Phrases such as 'linguistic imperialism' may suggest a monolithic process in which the spread of English has an inevitable and undifferentiated effect on communities and speakers of other languages who are the 'victims' of this spread. In practice, however, there is considerable diversity in the cultural meanings attached to English, how the language is responded to by speakers of other languages, and how it is used in different contexts. The spread of English has also given rise to several new English varieties – to the extent that the term 'Englishes' is often used to indicate the level of global diversity. Alongside traditionally monolingual varieties such as Australian English and New Zealand English, there are many 'second language' varieties, such as Indian English and Singaporean English. Not all of these are codified (i.e. described in dictionaries and grammars), but they do have systematically distinctive pronunciations, grammar and vocabulary that are passed on to new speakers. We have discussed elsewhere the establishment and characteristics of different varieties of English (see the examples in Graddol *et al.* 1996).

Across these different linguistic contexts, English may be experienced primarily as a language of education, or higher education; it may also be used in 'official' contexts; it may have made inroads into popular culture; it may be used among close friends. Speakers may use different varieties of English for these various communicative purposes – a local vernacular variety to talk to friends, a more standardised variety in the office. In terms of their responses to English, speakers may see English (or a particular variety of English) as a 'suit of clothes' that they put on to go to work and take off when they return home; they may actively resist what they see as the imposition of English or they may see this as a necessary evil; they may regard English as a language of social and economic advancement, as a means of asserting post-colonial defiance or simply as 'cool'; or their perceptions of English may be far more ambivalent and shifting than any of these statements would suggest. Speakers' experiences of, and feelings about, English will depend partly on where they live: Pennycook (1994) contrasts the relatively 'mainstream' position of English in Singapore with its more 'marginal' position in Malaysia. However, there will be different perceptions even within the same country: Kanyoro (1991) discusses ambivalent attitudes towards English in Kenya; in India, antipathy towards the language in many quarters is matched by support for it as an alternative to Hindi, and there are also conflicts over the validity of 'Indian English' as a distinct variety (see Verma 1982; Kachru 1986, 1992; Tripathi 1992). The 'global' nature of English therefore includes the fact that it is used, to very different effect, in countless local contexts.

For educators, the choice of English (or any language variety) as a medium for teaching and learning is significant, not just because of students' level of competence in that variety but also because of students' prior experiences of, and feelings about, language – the fact that they will bring to their study certain experiences, perceptions and expectations of the teaching/learning medium. But, in a global context, it is impossible to predict in advance what these will be.

Pennycook (1994) argues that teachers (he is focusing here on English language teachers) need to adopt a critical pedagogy. He emphasises that this means not promoting one's own political ideas and ideals, but listening to students, being sensitive to the context in which they live, and recognising what possibilities are offered to them by English. Teachers, he argues, need to enable students to appropriate English on their own terms: to develop their own forms of language, culture and knowledge that may be in opposition to dominant norms and values. The same degree of sensitivity, and critical awareness, might be called for in teaching any subject to a diverse student body through the medium of English. The difficulties of achieving this, however, will be exacerbated in a global context where the 'same' course is made available to a highly and unpredictably diverse student body that is, initially at least, unknown to the producers of course materials.

Language and culture in teaching and learning

The relationships between languages and cultures

Human languages are viewed by sociolinguists as symbolic practices that derive their meanings from layers of collective experience within a culture. Recent developments in the computer-based analysis of large bodies of text – an approach known as corpus linguistics – have demonstrated that even apparently straightforward words rarely have a simple denotative (or 'dictionary') meaning; rather, they acquire meanings in context, with all the attendant connotations (sometimes referred to as 'encyclopaedic' meaning). It follows that, for different speakers in different global contexts, the same word may be *differently* meaningful. Corpus analysis (for an overview, see Stubbs 1996) has revealed that this applies as much to apparently common points of reference such as 'hours' and 'days' as to more obviously culturally loaded terms such as 'freedom' and 'democracy'. In addition, many English words are metaphoric, deriving their meaning from some real-life comparison or analogy (e.g. the brow of a hill, mouth of a river, head of a pin, eye of a needle). Over time, the original metaphor may become de-activated (leading to examples such as *high brow, loud mouth, school head, private eye*) and ultimately the source may become obscure or inaccessible even to monolingual native speakers (e.g. *red herring, red letter day, in the red*). Different metaphors develop in different contexts, giving rise to local forms that have not yet achieved international currency (e.g. the Singaporean *void deck*, US *panhandling*, Australian *ratbag*). All this cultural baggage is lost on students for whom English is a relatively new language. Farmer (1997) describes how Open University Management students from Russia assumed '*offshore*

banks . . . were on stilts like oil rigs'. It would of course be impossible to eradi-
cate cultural reference altogether, since it is the essence of any living language,
but informal and literary language are more infused with connotation than are
formal and scientific language. Distance teaching materials are arguably in a
special position: because they stand in place of an oral relationship between
teacher and student, their interactional style tends to be relatively informal and
to draw pedagogically on shared points of reference (whether real or assumed).
The density of cultural reference in these materials is therefore likely to be high,
an issue to which we return below.

Ambiguity is intrinsic to all communication, but in real-life contexts we
filter out the less likely interpretations. In cross-cultural communication,
however, it becomes less easy to predict what inferences will be drawn by the
communicating partner:

> Where two people have very similar histories, backgrounds and experi-
> ences, their communication works fairly easily because the inferences each
> makes about what the other means will be based on common experience
> and knowledge. Two people from the same village and the same family are
> likely to make fewer mistakes in drawing inferences about what the other
> means than two people from different cities on different sides of the globe.
>
> (Scollon and Scollon 2001: 21)

Because English has come to function as a global family of languages, it is
probably more prone to misunderstanding than any other contemporary
language.

The relationships between cultures and learning styles

Early research on inter-cultural communication tended to conflate cultures
with *nationalities*. However, individuals vary greatly in the extent to which
they identify with national cultures: their primary allegiance may be to an
ethnic, linguistic or religious minority within a nation, their position as
women may marginalise them from the dominant culture, and so on. Hence
cultures are now more commonly defined in terms of communities of *discourse*, based on allegiance to more narrowly focused groups defined by ethnicity, occupation, and so on. Scollon and Scollon (2001: xii) have described
discourse in this sense as 'an envelope of language which gives us an identity
and makes it easier to communicate with those who are like us'. With regard
to cultural preference in learning style, the evidence is inconclusive. Sanchez
and Gunawardena (1998) argue that this is largely an *individual* trait. However,
such individual preferences are also overlaid by social experiences: some
national or religious educational systems may emphasise and reward collaboration over competition; many students have been brought up to believe that
learning equates with memorising 'the facts'; those from backgrounds with a
reverence for traditional wisdom, consensual attitudes or respect for authority may have difficulty coming to terms with learning as a developmental and
negotiated process (see Ndoloi 1994; Pardoe 1994; Cortazzi and Jin 1997). For
example:

constructivist learning meant nothing for many Portuguese because the transmission mode of learning was still in practice and actively encouraged in many institutions ... This may be a cultural factor, not so much an individual characteristic of the learner, because some cultures value reproduction of knowledge (as opposed to shared construction of it) as a sign of respect for the authority and knowledge of the teacher.
(Student on Open University MA in Open and Distance Learning, quoted by A. Kukulska-Hulme, personal communication)

Such models of teaching and learning originate in face-to-face situations, but, in a context of distributed learning, similar attitudes extend towards written texts: where the teacher is regarded as the authority, the text is also usually regarded as monolithic and beyond challenge (for a useful summary, see Kingsley 1997).

Interpersonal relationship in English language texts

Language is not simply used to express our thoughts and perceptions of the world: it also necessarily implies a relationship between reader and writer or speaker and listener. The linguist Halliday (1994; see also Bloor and Bloor 1995) uses the terms 'ideational' and 'interpersonal' to refer to these linguistic functions. The interpersonal function is manifested in texts through the use of interpersonal pronouns and expressions of affect, judgement, engagement or force, all of which attempt to co-opt the reader into a world view or call upon them to respond in some way. Both the interpersonal and the textual functions are seen in phrases such as 'As we have seen above' and 'We must therefore conclude', which imply that writer and reader are engaged on a common journey and have drawn similar conclusions from the evidence.

According to Scollon and Scollon (2001), relationship is also encoded in the topic structure of the discourse. They argue that English language texts – especially the model academic essay – are characterised by a 'deductive' style of argument, which presents its main thesis before arguing its case. This approach, they argue, assumes a relationship of 'symmetrical solidarity' between reader and writer in the common pursuit of truth. Although both writers and readers are expected to bring their individual engagement to the exercise, it is ironically the rationality and objectivity of the argument itself that is held up as the supreme authority. 'The authority of the person or of personal relationship is played down and is replaced by the authority of the text itself. One believes what is said not because of who is saying or writing it but because of how the text is written' (Scollon and Scollon 2001: 121). Many students from non-English-speaking backgrounds, however, are familiar with a rhetorical strategy that presents its rationale before advancing its thesis, an approach which Scollon and Scollon term 'inductive'. This kind of essay, they argue, assumes a hierarchical relationship between writer and reader: the person in the lower position in the social hierarchy (in this case, the student writer) has no right to introduce his or her own topic without first convincing the person in the higher position (in this case, the teacher reader) of the reasons for doing so. These ways, it is argued, the written relationship between teachers and learners is constrained by the specific linguistic resources and traditions of the language used. A field of research known as 'contrastive rhetoric' is exploring the ways in which such resources and traditions may vary across languages and cultures (for an overview, see Connor 1996).

Issues in teaching and assessment

So far, we have focused on some problematical cultural and linguistic issues associated with global communication through English, which may have implications for the global presentation of English language teaching materials. In the remainder of this chapter, we turn to more specific issues and examples that derive from our own teaching and research at the Open University (UK). These relate to the representation of academic knowledge; establishing and maintaining a relationship with students; and assessment policies and practices. We are particularly concerned with how producers of supported open learning materials may take account of, and respond to, culturally and linguistically diverse student groups, and with some continuing dilemmas that face global course providers.

Academic voices

Open University (henceforth OU) teaching materials may be viewed as polyphonic, or multi-voiced. Although printed texts (for example) usually have named authors, such texts will actually bear the imprint of numerous other voices.[4] Teaching texts necessarily draw on multiple sources, both explicitly (reference to or quotation from other texts) and implicitly (in the reproduction of academic ideas that are never the simple product of individual activity).[5] In the case of OU teaching, however, several people have a more direct hand in the construction of texts. Teaching materials go through several draft stages, and are subject to comments and suggestions from members of the course team responsible for the course, and from external readers and assessors. They include contributions from consultants as well as the main OU course team. All texts go through an editing and design process, which may affect both the wording and appearance of the finished materials, and courses are mediated by tutors, namely members of OU academic staff normally employed part-time to teach groups of students. Open University course production and presentation processes, then, open up potential spaces for the inclusion of alternative voices and perspectives in what may ostensibly be a British-based course team. At issue here, however, is on whose terms such voices and perspectives may be admitted.

Alternative voices

Teachers who work in certain areas (for example, in the social sciences and the humanities, with which we are most familiar) often face the problem that research fields are biased towards 'western' contexts and 'western' concerns. In our own teaching, we have found it necessary to acknowledge this bias – and we have tried to counterbalance it by including research from a broader range of contexts. This may involve the use of languages other than English, although in this case we would need to include a translation or subtitling. We have also tried to locate research studies, so that the sources of evidence and arguments are made explicit:

> . . . to quote the Canadian linguist and educationist Merril Swain, . . .

> Li Wei . . . has made extensive recordings amongst the Chinese community in Newcastle upon Tyne, England

> Gupta argues that, in Singapore at least . . .

Other voices may be brought more formally into the writing process by drawing on consultant authors, critical readers and advisers from different parts of the world. Given the dominance of 'western' traditions within published academic materials, however, it is still not easy to identify contributions from different cultural backgrounds which may offer alternative perspectives on academic knowledge. Perhaps even more significant for us has been the problematical nature of academic mediation. For instance, to what extent should all contributors to a course be encouraged to write 'in their own voice'? When editing material to make it more 'accessible' to students, or to make it conform to a 'house style', is there a danger of imposing a cultural blandness that stifles diversity?

The selection of examples and case studies

Our own conception of good teaching practice includes the use of case studies and examples that illustrate academic (frequently theoretical) discussion, make this discussion more accessible to students, and perhaps help students to relate rather abstract ideas to their own experiences. Particularly in a global teaching context, this would involve using examples that reflect cultural diversity. Given students' differing experiences, however, it is not always obvious how such examples will be received and acted upon. To give an illustration: in our teaching about language diversity, we have drawn on an audio recording of bilingual 'codeswitching' (when speakers alternate between two or more languages in the course of a conversation).[6] This was intended to illustrate the practice of codeswitching itself and also the social and cultural meanings different languages have for their speakers. We hoped the band would be of interest to all students, but felt it would be particularly relevant to the language experiences of bilingual students. Although subsequent research on our teaching showed this to be overwhelmingly the case,[7] some monolingual students also related directly to the bilingual example and were able to make connections that extended their awareness of their own language use:

> I found codeswitching interesting. I codeswitch dialects when with long-standing friends and relatives from the north. This is instinctive, and I only realised I do it, through studying section 8.

> This was fascinating . . . I have noticed how people's accents revert back to their roots when speaking to their families.
> (Both UK-based, monolingual English speakers)

More unexpectedly, one or two bilingual speakers did not find the band relevant to their needs. A student from Singapore, for instance, who would almost certainly use bilingual codeswitching in daily conversation, nevertheless felt that he could not identify with the particular example of codeswitching we had chosen:

> I found the block particularly interesting as the examples given to elaborate the concepts were very authentic, especially those pertaining to the local, Singaporean context.

> I did not quite find this band [on codeswitching] too useful perhaps because the experiences related are unique to a certain culture which I'm unable to identify with.
>
> (Singapore-based bilingual speaker, Hindi/Malay/English)

Another example where student response ran counter to expectation comes from the presentation of OU management courses to students in Russia. A member of a management course team commented:

> [Some of the Russian students] use our materials as a blue print for the new life, not as a way to develop their own management capacities in their existing lives (for example, they do not want boring Russian case studies to replace the lively tales of Western life appearing in our materials).
>
> (Thorne 1997)

Clearly, students, as active participants in the construction of their own academic knowledge, will bring differing expectations to teaching materials – and these will not necessarily conform to the expectations of course producers. While it seems useful, as a response to global diversity, to include a wide range of case studies and examples, one cannot always be certain how these will be taken up by students or how meaningful they will be. No less important is how these examples are represented in teaching, to which we turn below.

Relationships between teachers and students

The representation of examples

The writing of any pedagogic text is premised on the construction of an idealised reader. As Hill and Parry (1994) put it, we '[ascribe] an identity to these readers by virtue of the discourse [we] construct: the choice of particular vocabulary and syntactic patterns, the amount of background knowledge assumed and so on'. In working on draft course materials, we have found that examples from contexts such as the USA or the UK may be represented as part of common experience, whereas examples from other countries are represented as 'other', perhaps even exotic. Linguistically, this may be realised by a form of *deixis* – a means of indicating the spatial or temporal proximity of something referred to, relative to the speaker or writer. Deictic expressions include such terms as *here* and *there*, *now* and *then*, *this* and *that*. A teaching text may refer to the situation *here* (either explicitly or by implication in the UK) or *there* (in another part of the world). In addition to locating people, events and practices in relation to the teacher/writer, such devices may be used to position the reader. The reader may be included in the writer's here and now, contributing to a sense of commonality of experience between writer and reader.

The use of the first person pronoun *we* is a particularly powerful means of establishing commonality between writer and reader: 'we now have a national health service . . .'; 'in any high street we can see [street signs, shop displays – common in the UK]'; 'we are surrounded by such images . . .'; 'our news media frequently report . . .'; 'the kinds of facilities we have in Britain today'. A sense of common experience may also be constructed without recourse to specific deictic expressions – as when certain practices are represented as 'normal' or readily understandable, whereas others are carefully explained; or when an assumption is made that readers will share the writer's perspective (of an event in an Asian country): 'This is not such an unusual example as it may appear'.[8]

Such writing practices partly derive from a perceived need, particularly when teaching at a distance, to form a relationship with students through the teaching text. One way to achieve this is to emphasise commonality of experience and understanding. There is a danger, however, of appearing to co-opt students into experiences that are not, in fact, held in common; and perhaps of alienating certain students. OU 'global' course teams with which we have been involved have tried to adopt a more culturally located teaching voice; for example, using the first person singular *I* to refer to the writer's cultural context and experiences, with which readers may be able to compare or contrast their own. We have tried to describe other practices and events (including UK practices and events) from the outside: 'In Singaporean English, terms of address may include . . .'; or 'In British English, terms of address may include . . .'. Sometimes, however, this requires a considerable conceptual shift, and it may be experienced as disruptive to the writing process. One OU course author describes how he found himself temporarily unable 'to "map" between [the students'] everyday organisational discourse and the course's language of management – something I take for granted elsewhere as an important part of making connections and grounding ideas' (Paton 1997).

Attitudes towards the validity of evidence

The very grammar of English encodes subtle attitudinal markers towards the truth value of what is written. Academic discourse often requires a sophisticated distinction between the writer's evaluations of facts and those of researchers being discussed. One way in which this can be managed in English is through the use of a reporting verb, as in 'Chomsky *claimed* that humans produce an infinite variety of sentences'. Even though the subject of the verb *claim* is Chomsky, the selection of reporting verb is that of the writer. One key distinction with regard to reporting verbs is between those which are 'factive' (implying the truth of the statement following) and those which are 'nonfactive' (suggesting that the truth of the statement following could be or is in question). A factive version of the above sentence might be 'Chomsky *discovered* that humans produce an infinite variety of sentences'. Modality (the relative certainty or tentativeness of a claim) may also be signalled through the use of some other phrase which modifies the verb, as in 'Chomsky *supposedly* discovered . . .' or '*According to some commentators*, Chomsky discovered . . .'. In ways such as this, the reader is subtly called upon to enter into the world view of the writer.

However, there are important cross-cultural differences with regard to these features, even within English medium texts. According to a study one of us conducted into course materials and student work from various open learning institutions (Graddol and Mayor 1996), Open University (UK) texts – by the use of non-factive verbs such as *appears* and *suggests* – tend to present know-ledge not as something fixed and absolute, but as something produced and evaluated through institutionalised processes of research. On the other hand, the preference in texts from Indira Gandhi National Open University (IGNOU) in India is for factive verbs such as *found* and *revealed*. The predominance of past tense verbs also reinforces the impression of facticity. Not surprisingly, students from the two institutions are socialised into the use of such attitudinal markers and their underlying value systems, with the result that something of this difference is reflected in their assessed work.

Directness and indirectness

We have suggested that it is impossible to write in English without subtly pla-cing oneself in a position of equality or hierarchy relative to the reader. How-ever, the intended force of a delicately 'hedged' statement or directive can sometimes be lost on a student whose variety of English (even if it is their first language) is not sensitive to the same interpersonal signals as those of the writer. There was a lively e-mail discussion among tutors on an OU English Language course about how cultural and linguistic background – among monolingual as well as bilingual students – can influence students' interpretation of both teach-ing texts and tutors' written comments. Expressions such as 'You might like to think about X' or 'Have you read Y?', which are intended to carry the force of a polite directive, may be received literally, sometimes giving the student a wrong impression of what is required, and perhaps forcing the tutor into a far more direct version ('You really must do Z') which feels unnatural and rude. One tutor, in an archetypally indirect way, suggested that:

> Perhaps we need to be thinking of ways round this, perhaps by saying things like 'evidence of . . . is needed here' which is declarative so functions as a strong recommendation but is also passive making it less direct/harsh; if you were Spanish you would say something to your students like 'Con-vence me!' ('Convince me!'), a lot more direct.
>
> (M. Normand, unpublished)

This poses a continuing dilemma for native English-speaking tutors or course authors in whose varieties of English indirect forms are the norm and indeed are an intrinsic part of their strategies of politeness towards their adult students and of their educational philosophy. In the interests of (possibly short-term) com-municative effectiveness, how far should they accommodate the non-native speaker variety, thus producing a kind of 'interlanguage'? The risk of their not doing so is not only that the interpersonal meaning of the interaction may be lost on some students, but that the teaching materials themselves may be misinterpreted.

Assessment of learning outcomes

The setting of assignments

In a global context, course designers need to ensure that the assessment tasks they set are not only meaningful but also 'do-able' in the whole range of circumstances in which students may find themselves. This may mean setting alternative versions of assignments reflecting, for example, different teaching contexts. In ways such as this, course designers may seek to be culture-fair by being culturally *differentiated*. An alternative and equally valid strategy may be to strive for a level of generality that ensures maximum relevance in a wide range of contexts; in other words, an attempt at cultural *neutrality*.

There is, however, continuing debate within the OU about how best to ensure that what is required in assessment tasks is unambiguous and clear to students (see e.g. Stierer 1997). Terms such as 'describe', 'criticise' and 'analyse' have traditionally been used in a rather loose way within the UK education system and are increasingly open to misunderstanding by students educated in, for example, a North American or Australasian tradition, where the terms have acquired distinct and mutually exclusive meanings. OU course teams may believe that they have circumvented potential misunderstanding by drafting accompanying assignment guidelines, but experience shows that these may not be sufficient to allay concerns, and may even add to the confusion.

Explicitness in itself does not guarantee mutual understanding. As described above, out of respect for the autonomy of adult learners, the wording may be overly 'hedged' rather than directive, and consequently fail to communicate to some students exactly what is required. Moreover, some aspects of OU assessment policy may be in conflict with students' prior educational experience. For example, Hedge (1994) includes the following guidelines on what is meant by 'active learning' in the context of British management education:

Active learners . . .

Set out to understand what is to be learned by:
* *relating* what is being learned to what is already known, and by
* *relating* what is being learned to the workplace . . .

Set out to take control of learning by:
* *questioning* everything
* *personalising* everything . . .

You need to become self evaluators – to become aware of mistakes you might make and to learn how to mark your own work . . .

Tutors and examiners are not really interested in elegant prose. They need to see that you have understood course ideas and can apply them.

(Hedge 1994: 147–70)

Although the educational philosophy underpinning this advice may be second nature to a student raised within a culture where the teacher has primarily played the role of mentor or colleague, it represents a major challenge to those brought up to revere the teacher as authority and the text as sacred, who will have been socialised into, and rewarded for, a very different set of practices that did not entail the same amount of selection and/or application of knowledge. Thorne (1997) neatly sums up this mismatch of expectation when she writes, with reference to the OU's model of supported open learning:

> First, the materials are presented so that they can form a dialogue with the independently learning student; they are quite unsuitable for learning by heart. Second, the tutor plays a key supportive role in facilitating the student's learning; the tutor, however, does not tell the student what he/she must learn.
>
> (Thorne 1997)

This can be a difficult cultural shift to accomplish. As Mordaunt (1997) remarks with reference to a group of OU management students from Zambia: 'They were accustomed to a highly didactic approach to teaching in which they were passive recipients of knowledge imparted from the tutor. The notion that they could learn from each other was a novel one.'

Some pedagogical principles are sacrosanct within the OU's (and to some extent the UK's) educational philosophy, and are probably non-negotiable – principles such as racial or gender equality, for example, or the clear articulation of learning objectives. It has been a point of principle in the design of the English language/linguistics courses with which we have been involved that there should be maximum transparency both in assignment guidelines and marking criteria. This means that the same criteria are available both to the students who complete the assignments and to the teachers who grade them. This policy has not been without controversy, particularly in parts of the world where the authority of the teacher is highly guarded, but we have so far defended it. However, as the OU continues to expand the range of global contexts in which it works, course teams become increasingly aware of the need to make explicit underlying assumptions that they may previously have taken for granted, and to question them where necessary.

The grading of students' work

A further set of issues arises in relation to the grading of students' written work. This issue has been extensively debated elsewhere (see e.g. Leki 1995; Lukmani 1996; Cortazzi and Jin 1997) so we only touch on it here. A perennial dilemma for OU tutors is whether or how much to correct for surface errors in students' writing. Not only can it be time-consuming for a tutor and off-putting for a student to see their work covered with ink or electronic 'interruptions' (although this may be circumvented by the use of appended notes), there is also the risk that this practice will focus disproportionately on surface features rather than on the underlying structure of the discourse. In our view, the best practice would always be to negotiate the most helpful level of surface correction between the two parties. None the less, a dilemma remains for many tutors, as well as for those students who approach OU study with an expectation that it will 'improve their English' (Regan 1998); namely, what level and nature of writing ability is, or should be, indicated by an HE qualification from an English-medium, UK-based institution? And how should tutors (most of whom will not be language specialists) respond to non-standard or non-UK varieties of English with their different syntax and semantics? The guidelines developed in English language/linguistics courses over the years tend to downplay surface or presentational features, focusing instead on the effective communication of ideas. However, this is by no means standard practice across the OU – Arts courses, for example, set more store by elegance of style – and it is not known how far marking guidelines map on to the grading practices of individual tutors. It would be naive to assume that tutors remain uninfluenced by mismatches in communicative style and the consequent additional effort required on their part to interpret the student's meaning.

Critical engagement

In terms of course *content*, some OU courses have fine-tuned their guidelines on the use of personal experience and critical engagement with the course texts. For example:

> You are not expected to agree with everything that is said in course [materials]. Indeed [we] hope that you will engage in a critical dialogue . . . However, any criticism should be based on a sound knowledge and under-standing . . . [and] . . . should be supported by relevant argument and information . . .
>
> [E]nsure that any examples you include may be related to the question; try to use them to illustrate or address points from the course.
> (U(ZS)210 *The English Language: Past, Present and Future*, Assignment Booklet, 2000)

However, those students who do attempt to engage critically with course texts may not find this an easy (or ultimately rewarding) process. Mary Lea (1998) has commented that students on one OU course who adopted a 'challenging' approach to their study (i.e. drawing on their personal perspectives and inter-pretations to challenge academic conventions) often failed to meet their tutor's expectations, whereas those who simply reformulated course materials did rather better. One of us has discussed elsewhere (MacKinney and Swann 2001) the case of an OU student who tried to take issue with an assumption under-pinning a sociolinguistics text: that different varieties of language are, linguistic-ally at least, equal (for example, it is not possible on linguistic grounds to say that one variety is more 'correct' or 'logical' than another). The student found it difficult to muster sufficient resources to argue against this position in her essay, and commented finally:

It seems to me it's a good idea to take on and support the argument of the authors of a Block. They clearly state their opinions and substantiate them. Arguing against them does not appear to be penalised, still not everyone can present their argument in a favourable light. This is what might have happened in my case.

(UK-based bilingual speaker, Russian/English)

Although the course explicitly encouraged a critical response from students, it was difficult to provide adequate resources to support the critique of a 'core' sociolinguistic principle, precisely because the materials themselves were written within a sociolinguistic framework. It was thus inevitable that there were going to be weaknesses – from the point of view of linguists at least – in a 'critical' student's argument. This raises issues for how tutors respond to a student whose essay shows certain weaknesses, perhaps because the student has taken the risk of adopting a critical stance.

Attitudes towards plagiarism

An area where there is increasing pressure to develop an institution-wide policy within the OU, particularly in view of the increasing access to electronic sources, is the definition of, and response to, plagiarism. Pennycook (1996) argues that notions of plagiarism are related to contemporary 'western' concepts of creativity and originality in writing – which, ironically, are belied by the routine borrowing of ideas, words and phrases practised by all writers. There is a particular problem for student writers who, while they are constantly being told they must put things 'in their own words', are also 'required to acquire a fixed canon of knowledge and a fixed canon of terminology to go with it' (Pennycook 1996: 213). This may be more problematical for students whose own prior learning experiences have emphasised the accurate reproduction of ideas. Pennycook argues that teachers need to take account of different types of textual borrowing, different cultural meanings ascribed to the appropriation of words and ideas from authoritative texts, and students' own varied understandings of why they are incorporating others' words into their writing.

A set of draft guidelines for inclusion in the OU *Student Handbook* provoked a rich debate among tutors of the English Language course, partly because the guidelines needed to tread a careful path between admonishing the 'cheat' (who is assumed to have plagiarised deliberately and out of laziness) and counselling the student who is insecure in either subject knowledge or use of English (who may have plagiarised inadvertently by quoting verbatim from source material without observing bibliographic conventions). Although it was widely acknowledged that imitation can be a valuable learning strategy, especially when studying in a second or third language, it was recognised that OU assessment questions are rarely phrased in such a way that they can be answered by directly copying from or paraphrasing source materials, and that such practices are unlikely to lead to a fluent and logical answer (for a fuller discussion, see Goodman, forthcoming).

In discussions of assessment, it is important to remember that 'any communicative change is a change in identity' (Scollon and Scollon 2001: 284), so learning to write in new academic ways may represent as much a threat as an opportunity for the learner. As one student (in a face-to-face context) said:

> I have had to accept many things I do not approve of and it is such a shock to me because of my own customs. It is as though everything I have been taught at home and all my values do not count for anything here and I must become a different person.
>
> (Anonymous 1985, quoted in Harris 1997: 39)

Inter-cultural competence is more than just a linguistic matter: as Byram (1997) has argued, it involves a range of sociocultural competencies (ways of understanding, being, doing, learning). It may be timely to reconsider the kinds of cultural change that are an appropriate goal of education in an increasingly multicultural and global context.

Conclusion

In preparing material for presentation to global audiences, course designers and writers are clearly aware that they need to avoid parochial references and concerns (in the case of the OU, uniquely UK concerns). We have tried to demonstrate that the issues involved in global course design are rather more subtle. We have focused in particular on the use of English as a medium of teaching and learning, and on linguistic and cultural factors that affect communication between teachers and learners. We have suggested that, while English language qualifications bring many benefits to students in different parts of the world, the practice of teaching through English is also problematical: the use of English as a language of education necessarily contributes to the global dominance of English; English itself encodes certain values that may be unfamiliar or even unacceptable to students from certain linguistic and cultural contexts; and teaching through English, at least from our own (UK) starting point, is associated with a set of communicative and pedagogical practices that may not be universally shared in a distributed learning community.

There are no easy answers to the issues we have raised. We suggest, however, that those who teach globally through the medium of English need at least to be aware of their own cultural and pedagogical assumptions, and the fact that these will not be shared in all teaching contexts. This suggests, in part, a need for greater clarity – assumptions may be made more explicit so that students are more aware of what they are 'buying into'. Course providers should also, however, consider how far teaching and learning outcomes may be locally negotiated: to what extent may students be supported to negotiate their own pathway through course materials, to bring to bear their own experiences and understandings on their study, and perhaps to 'read against' the teaching text? What does it mean to offer the 'same' course in different parts of the globe? More crucially, perhaps, what does it mean to award the 'same' qualification?

Notes

1 On sociolinguistics as an academic area (including applied sociolinguistics), see Holmes (2001) and Mesthrie *et al.* (2000); on inter-cultural communication, see Scollon and Scollon 2001.
2 There are some exceptions to the OU's use of English as a teaching medium: on some courses, for instance, Welsh students have submitted assignments in Welsh; certain courses are also available in translation (e.g. business courses in parts of eastern Europe).
3 There are problems with the use of the term 'western'. This is unsatisfactory, first because it is inaccurate: 'western' countries include countries in several parts of the world (including North America, Europe, Australasia). The term also masks cultural and economic differences between and within countries, and, when used in a relationship of opposition to 'non-western' countries, it identifies such countries in terms of what they are not. Alternative formulations, however, do not seem to be much better. Because of its common currency, we have used 'western' on those occasions when we need to make (necessarily simplified) global generalisations.
4 Given the explictly collaborative nature of the production of OU texts, some OU course teams do not acknowledge individual authorship.
5 Contemporary sociolinguistic theory would say the same of any text. Any piece of speech or writing is heteroglossic, in the sense that it reproduces material (words and expressions, with their associated values) from other texts and other contexts (such ideas are attributed, most notably, to the Russian theorist Bakhtin; see Bakhtin 1981).
6 The codeswitching example comes from course U(ZS)210 *The English Language: Past, Present and Future*: Audio cassette 2, Band 8, 'Codeswitching between Hindi, Kannada and English'. Producers: Anne Diack and Paul Manners. Main contributor: G.D. Jayalaskshmi.
7 The research forms part of a project on academic literacy. The project as a whole is discussed in Goodman *et al.* (2000).
8 These are the kinds of examples we have seen in initial drafts of teaching materials, but they are not literal quotations. As sociolinguists we would normally set great store by 'authentic examples'. In this case, however, it did not seem reasonable to reproduce, word for word, extracts from the writing of other colleagues that were not in the public domain and that will, in most cases, have been redrafted to make the text more open to diverse audiences.

References

Bakhtin, M.M. (1981) *The Dialogic Imagination*. Austin, TX: State University of Texas Press.
Bloor, T. and Bloor, M. (1995) *The Functional Analysis of English: A Hallidayan Approach*. London: Arnold.
Byram, M. (1997) *Teaching and Assessing Intercultural Communicative Competence*. Clevedon: Multilingual Matters.
Connor, U. (1996) *Contrastive Rhetoric: Cross-cultural Aspects of Second-language Writing*. Cambridge: Cambridge University Press.
Cortazzi, M. and Jin, L. (1997) Communication for learning across cultures, in D. McNamara and R. Harris (eds) *Overseas Students in Higher Education: Issues in Teaching and Learning*. London: Routledge.
Crystal, D. (1992) *An Encyclopedic Dictionary of Language and Languages*. Oxford: Blackwell.
Farmer, E. (1997) The assessment process with partners, paper delivered to conference on *Cultural Adaptation of Distance Learning*, Milton Keynes, October.

Fishman, J. (1964) Language maintenance and language shift as a field of enquiry: a definition of the field and suggestions for its further development, *Linguistics*, 9: 32–70.

Goodman, S. (forthcoming) Plagiarism or writing problem? The views of teachers on a distance-taught English course, *CLAC Occasional Papers* No. 70. Milton Keynes: Centre for Language and Communications, the Open University.

Goodman, S., Lea, M.R. and Swann, J. (2000) *Academic Literacies in a Distance-taught English Language Course: Project Report*. Milton Keynes: Centre for Language and Communications, the Open University.

Graddol, D. and Mayor, B.M. (1996) Knowledge and modality in academic discourse, paper presented to inaugural meeting of the *English Language Teaching and Learning Research Group*. Milton Keynes, 10 June.

Graddol, D., Leith, D. and Swann, J. (eds) (1996) *English: History, Development and Change*. London: Routledge in association with the Open University.

Halliday, M.A.K. (1994) *An Introduction to Functional Grammar*, 2nd edn. London: Arnold.

Harris, R. (1997) Overseas students in the United Kingdom university system: a perspective from social work, in D. McNamara and R. Harris (eds) *Overseas Students in Higher Education: Issues in Teaching and Learning*. London: Routledge.

Hedge, N. (1994) Studying with English as a foreign language, in K. Giles and N. Hedge *The Manager's Good Study Guide*. Milton Keynes: The Open University.

Hill, C. and Parry, K. (1994) *From Testing to Assessment: English as an International Language*. London: Longman.

Holmes, J. (2001) *An Introduction to Sociolinguistics*, 2nd edn. London: Longman.

Kachru, B.B. (1986) *The Alchemy of English: The Spread, Functions and Models of Non-native Englishes*. Oxford: Pergamon Press.

Kachru, B.B. (ed.) (1992) *The Other Tongue: English Across Cultures*, 2nd edn. Chicago, IL: University of Illinois Press.

Kanyoro, M.R.A. (1991) The politics of the English language in Kenya and Tanzania, in J. Cheshire (ed.) *English Around the World*. Cambridge: Cambridge University Press.

Kingsley, J. (1997) Trials and tribulations of an ESL learner, paper delivered to conference on *Cultural Adaptation of Distance Learning*, Milton Keynes, October.

Lea, M.R. (1998) Academic literacies and learning in higher education: constructing knowledge through texts and experience, *Studies in the Education of Adults*, 30(2): 156–71.

Leki, I. (1995) Good writing: I know it when I see it, in D. Belcher and G. Braine (eds) *Academic Writing in a Second Language: Essays on Research and Pedagogy*. Norwood, NJ: Ablex.

Lukmani, Y. (1996) Linguistic accuracy versus coherence in assessing examination answers in content subjects, in M. Milanovic and N. Saville (eds) *Studies in Language Testing 3: Performance Testing, Cognition and Assessment*. Cambridge: Cambridge University Press.

MacKinney, C. and Swann, J. (2001) Developing a sociolinguistic voice?, *CLAC Occasional Papers* No. 69. Milton Keynes: Centre for Language and Communications, The Open University.

Mesthrie, R., Swann, J., Deumert, A. and Leap, W.L. (2000) *Introducing Sociolinguistics*. Edinburgh: Edinburgh University Press.

Mordaunt, J. (1997) Supporting the new learner: a case of chairing from the rear?, paper delivered to conference on *Cultural Adaptation of Distance Learning*, Milton Keynes, October.

Ndoloi, D.B. (1994) Writing one's way into university culture: the case of Dar es Salaam freshers, *Centre for Language in Social Life Working Paper* No. 59. Lancaster: Centre for Language in Social Life, University of Lancaster.

Pardoe, S. (1994) Learning to write in a new educational setting: a focus on the writer's purpose, *Centre for Language in Social Life Working Paper* No. 58. Lancaster: Centre for Language in Social Life, University of Lancaster.

Paton, R. (1997) Out of Africa, paper delivered to conference on *Cultural Adaptation of Distance Learning*, Milton Keynes, October.

Pennycook, A. (1994) *The Cultural Politics of English as an International Language*. London: Longman.

Pennycook, A. (1996) Borrowing others' words: text, ownership, memory and plagiarism, *TESOL Quarterly*, 30: 201–30.

Phillipson, R. (1992) *Linguistic Imperialism*. Oxford: Oxford University Press.

Regan, P. (1998) *A New Academic Community: Open University Students in Continental Western Europe: A Survey*. Newcastle upon Tyne: Open University in the North.

Sanchez, I. and Gunawardena, C.N. (1998) Understanding and supporting the culturally diverse distance learner, in C.C. Gibson (ed.) *Distance Learners in Higher Education*. Madison, WI: Atwood Publishing.

Scollon, R. and Scollon, S.W. (2001) *Intercultural Communication: A Discourse Approach*, 2nd edn. Oxford: Blackwell.

Stierer, B. M. (1997) Mastering education: a preliminary analysis of academic literacy practices within masters-level courses in Education, *CLAC Occasional Papers* No. 59. Milton Keynes: Centre for Language and Communications, the Open University.

Stubbs, M. (1996) *Text and Corpus Analysis: Computer-assisted Studies of Language and Culture*. Oxford: Blackwell.

Thorne, E. (1997) Crossing cultures: supporting the learner in Russia, paper delivered to conference on *Cultural Adaptation of Distance Learning*, Milton Keynes, October.

Tripathi, P.D. (1992) English: 'The chosen tongue', *English Today 32*, 8(4): 3–11.

Verma, S.K. (1982) Swadeshi English: form and function', in J.B. Pride (ed.) *New Englishes*. Rowley, MA: Newbury House.

Chapter 8

From independent learning to collaborative learning

New communities of practice in open, distance and distributed learning

Mary Thorpe

Introduction

The purpose of this chapter is to explore the effects of changes in practice that have been fuelled by the application of information and communication technology (ICT) both to campus and distance forms of higher education. These practices and their accompanying ideologies are presented from a practitioner perspective, in some cases drawing on educational research and theory to support particular views. The focus is on the contrast between the practices of distance education in the 1970s and 1980s and the current computer-mediated communication and web-based teaching designed to foster collaborative learning. The emphasis on collaborative learning is a key difference between how we attempt to enable learning at a distance now compared with practices of 20 years ago.

However, the question I want to address is about the extent of these differences. In so doing, I use Lave and Wenger's concept of a 'community of practice' to ask whether there are now new communities of practice, involved in different activities and with different concerns. This requires looking back to how learning and teaching were discussed and theorised over 20 years ago, in order to draw contrasts and comparisons with today. Campus-based practitioners without a background in open or distance learning may not be familiar with a literature that has addressed similar concerns, if in different material conditions, to those currently faced by educators. However, by reflecting on our immediate history, we are better able to identify both continuities and differences in current approaches.

Communities of practice

I begin by considering how Lave and Wenger's concept of a community of practice may be applied (Lave and Wenger 1991). The concept has been developed to describe groups that interact to achieve a shared purpose or enterprise. It is not used to define groups that physically share the same space but are not otherwise involved in achieving a shared purpose or outcome; for example, mere residence in the same locality does not qualify a neighbourhood as a 'community of practice'. However, workplaces and long-standing social activities, such as community playgroups, clubs, sports organisations, and so on, would all constitute communities of practice. Companies, universities, colleges and schools similarly qualify. The groups must exist for a period sufficient to generate patterns of interaction and significant learning among participants. As Wenger asserts:

> The development of practice takes time, but what defines a community of practice in its temporal dimension is not just a matter of a specific minimum of time ... [but] ... sustaining enough mutual engagement in pursuing an enterprise together to share some significant learning ... communities of practice can be thought of as shared histories of learning.
>
> (Wenger 1998: 86)

Wenger also defines communities of practice as having three major defining components or elements:

- *Mutual engagement*: participation in a shared task.
- *Joint enterprise*: negotiated interaction, with accountability.
- *Shared repertoire*: routines, tools, words, processes, concepts, genres, gestures, etc., through which practices are carried out.

Communities of practice – at two levels

Applying this concept to practitioners of on-campus or off-campus learning suggests that there are two overlapping communities of practice. The first is the relatively small group of practitioners and their students or learners who study and work together to achieve the goals of their particular course or programme. They share the task of ensuring that learning is effective and that the learning outcomes of the course are achieved. Their interactions affect each other and they are held accountable for what they do. They spend a considerable propor-tion of their time sharing the language of their discipline or learning goal, and working together to achieve the outcomes that have been set.

Such communities may exist within a wider organisation of which they are a part, and overlap with a second community of organisations and practitioners who have similar goals in terms of teaching and learning. University and college staff, for example, may feel they are part of 'the academy', and, since they write about our practice for journals or for our peers working elsewhere in different organisations, we engage in a kind of extended practice in the sense of partici-pating in a community seeking to achieve a shared literature about and under-standing of that practice. Certainly, the shared repertoire of flexible/open/distance/distributed learning is enhanced and extended through engagement with a network of practitioners that may include national and global connec-tions. This community of practice is more attenuated than that of the immedi-ate work team of tutors and their students, or trainers and trainees. Scholarship and writing about practice is usually engaged in only periodically, in the 'spaces' we create within our practice for reflecting on and recording its effects, but bulletin boards, computer-mediated communication and e-mail have put more social interaction into this discursive activity over the past 10 years, and its operation as a community has been strengthened as a result.

In what follows, I retain both contexts of use for 'community of practice'. I review several texts as examples of the shared repertoire that practitioners of the time were seeking to build among their wider network of peers in the academic and practitioner community. I discuss these accounts of practice to explore what they tell us about communities of practice in both senses outlined above: first, in the sense of how tutors or teachers interact with the learners for whom they have responsibilities and the kinds of learning environments they seek to establish; second, in terms of the research and theory drawn on in practitioner accounts at different periods, and in terms of the priority concerns and issues they identify.

Whose history?

Some contributors to the literature on distributed and flexible learning may experience little connection with open and distance forms of learning (ODL). However, in designing online learning to ensure that the learning goals of their course are achieved, they will face issues that have also been confronted within ODL, and (albeit under different conditions) often decades before the current widespread use of telecommunications and the web. Topics such as course design and technology selection, learner support, accessibility of materials and access to other learners are high priority issues for designers of virtual learning environments (Milligan 2000). These topics also have a history in open and distance learning, where many practitioners have analysed their implications for practice, compared it with others, provided rationales for what they do and sometimes evaluated the outcomes.

Although we could turn to the nineteenth century to review the origins of all these developments at the beginning of correspondence education, I propose a less ambitious review, concentrating on the last 30 years of the twentieth century. With the early success of the Open University in the 1970s, many other countries set up organisations to provide post-compulsory opportunities through mediated teaching. A growing range of technology and media has been used by many different organisations, with and without local support, to meet the varying needs of different audiences in the countries concerned (Tait 1994). It is this burgeoning of provision for the part-time adult learner, using varying combinations of media and technology, that provides the immediately relevant experience for all those now applying ICT to their practice, whether campus-based or otherwise. Self-evidently, relevance does not imply that we must copy the past unthinkingly, but we might sharpen what is distinct about our current thinking and practice if we identify both its similarities and its differences with what has been said and done before.

Independence and the independent learner

Innovative developments in the UK during the 1970s and 1980s began to take for granted the notion that independent learning was both a requirement for effective study at a distance and a good in its own right. There was often an unflattering comparison with conventional provision, which was assumed to rely upon an inappropriate degree of dependency by the learner on the tutor/lecturer, and upon other elements of institutionalised provision. However, one of the earliest accounts did not take such a simplistic stance, addressing head-on the relative merits of interaction and independence, and the extent to which both are necessary, to varying degrees according to the needs of system and learner. Daniel and Marquis (1979) took a systems approach to the design of distance provision, arguing that all such provision must balance interaction and independence as complementary modes of learning essential to the educational outcomes of any system. They defined interaction as the archetypal form of learning, drawing on Pask's conversational definition of learning (Pask et al. 1973) to argue that two-way interaction between people is essential, and can be mediated in various ways in open systems through pre-course counselling, tuition, tutorials, residential meetings, and so on. They accept that conversations are often internalised, as in the case of a text that stimulates the learner to think and to question. However, they used a working definition of interaction as person-to-person exchange (whether at a distance or face to face) to maintain a sharp distinction from independence in learning. Independence is defined as all those activities which do not involve interpersonal interaction of this kind.

Through a comparison between the practice of Canada's TeleUniversité and other distance institutions – the Open University in particular – Daniel and Marquis (1979) identified four key issues that frame decision-making around the balance to be struck between interaction and independence:

1   Choice of content: authority *vs* autonomy.
2   Economies of scale.
3   Does the activity suit the student? (access and flexibility issues).
4   To pace or not to pace?

I will discuss each of these issues in turn.

Content and control

Content is seen primarily as an issue of independence of mind. Without interaction, predetermined content risks authoritarianism and the imposition of frameworks that are not integrated into local and individual cultures. The authors assume here that learning requires the student to articulate the relationship between predetermined course content and his or her own understandings and needs. Local support via tutors or animateurs (the term they prefer over facilitator) is perceived to be the route through which to stimulate and support this personal grasp of knowledge by the learner. Thus interaction is seen as essential to ensure that an active response by the learner is encouraged and independence of mind is achieved.

Cost structures

Economies of scale are involved because of the cost differential between interactive options that require interpersonal exchange and independent study modes. Interpersonal learning relationships bring staff costs into the equation and therefore increase overall costs. Since many distance and open systems were introduced as a way of increasing access without increasing costs pro rata, there has been a trade-off in most cases between providing interaction and designing a cost-effective system around essentially independent modes of study. Crudely put, since interpersonal interaction can only add costs, making positive choices to increase interaction must always pose difficult decisions to increase costs – assuming the technological choices of earlier decades.

Pacing and workload

Pacing is also an issue with a difficult trade-off to accommodate. This time the trade-off is between 'respect for the freedom and autonomy of the individual student' (Daniel and Marquis 1979: 34) and providing the kind of structured environment within which pressured adult learners may be helped to complete the required amount of study to acceptable standards. Thus both independent and interactive components can be, and frequently are, used to pace the workload required: independent activities in the form of assignments, scheduled broadcasts and other deadlines; interactive components in the form of meetings, residential schools, conference calls, tutorials and so on, since all depend on synchronised activity.

Access and flexibility

Does the activity suit the student? is posed as a question to locate the crucial impact of learner availability, whether in terms of time or place. At the post-compulsory stage, most forms of learning compete with alternative roles and activities that put a premium on the use of students' time and limit their freedom to travel. Issues of flexibility and attendance are relevant here. Residential schools presented a barrier to approximately one-third of OU entry level students, who had good reasons for avoiding attendance if possible. By contrast, the supreme flexibility of text was even more apparent then than now in offering maximum value for hours spent and maximum flexibility in mode of access. The proverbial commuter making good use of every minute of their daily journey is but one example of the famed availability of print for most learners. Independent study in these contexts therefore gave learners maximum control and provided the means by which learning was made possible.

Daniel and Marquis (1979) locate their arguments primarily at the level of practical systems design, but also cover many of the tensions that are inherent in the relationship between interaction and independence. They offer an example of one TeleUniversité course where a good mix of independent and interactive strategies was used to pace learners through a French language and culture study option. Their view recognises both that independent study is a sine qua non for open and distance education and that it presents difficult challenges for systems that need to be accountable to their funders and to society, for reasonable rates of retention and success. Using the practical experience of distance providers, they argue that wholly independent forms of study (i.e. those lacking social interaction) are neither feasible nor desirable in terms of the quality of learning they support.

The conflicting meanings of 'independence'

The growth of open learning provision during the 1980s was accompanied by an increase in semi-promotional practitioner accounts which adopted a rather black and white approach to these innovations. Some practitioners asserted that open systems were a total break with the past in terms of substituting the acclaimed independence of their particular version of open learning in place of the dependence (on scheduled lectures/classes, etc.) of traditional education and training. In some cases, it has been difficult to view this apparent independence as anything other than a 'sink or swim' form of self-study, and prompted Morgan (1985) to assert that 'independent learning is not so much a technical term as a slogan. People use it differently with differing meanings and connotations.' He went on to argue that it was inappropriate to assume that such a term could be used as a proxy for learning that is automatically better than so-called 'dependent' learning. He draw up a list of good and bad associations with both terms (see Table 8.1) as a reminder of the need to question meanings and make assumptions explicit, rather than to use key terms as blanket forms of either approval or disapproval without justification.

By 1985, it was clear that 'independence' might mean many things to many people, but that there were two widely held views that could lead to very different forms of practice. First, independent learning was viewed effectively as self-study – learning on one's own, without help or indeed interaction of any kind with others. Such a view was associated with the promotion of open systems as a way of reducing costs through cutting out the local support and physical infrastructure typical of conventional provision. In constrast, 'independence' was seen by others as independence of mind – the ability to make one's own choices about what and how one studies, and to absorb influences without being dominated by them. At this stage, such approaches were still characterised as individually driven – *independent* rather than *inter*dependent, with the role of the tutor being to support students studying essentially on their own. As Morgan noted, much of the course design and regional practice of the OU at

Table 8.1 Associations for 'independent' and 'dependent' learning

	Independent	Dependent
'Good' associations	'gets on on his/her own' 'stands on his/her own feet' 'self-starting' 'resourceful' 'autonomous'	'willing to listen' 'responsive' 'able to take in "feedback"' 'flexible' 'manageable'
'Bad' associations	'won't listen to advice' 'opinionated' 'unable to take in opposing points of view to his/her own' 'pig-headed' 'won't take direction or guidance'	'passive' 'no ideas of his/her own' 'over-conscientious' 'conformist' 'needs to be told everything'

Reproduced with permission from Morgan, The Open University (1985: 39).

that time had built up a range of both stimulating and supporting activities and roles, through which the independence of the individual learner could be fostered and developed. It was embedded in the thinking of staff at all levels in the institution that the underconfident beginning student must not be allowed either to sink or to succeed by means of a low-level regurgitation of what was in the course units. The goal was certainly to pass the course, but to pass by demonstrating understanding and independence of thought.

Control and support

Morgan works through both of these competing notions of independence by raising what he feels to be more fundamental questions about any system of provision. In so doing he returns to the same issues raised by Daniel and Marquis (1979) earlier: Where is the control in what is being learned and in how that learning proceeds? What forms of academic support are available to learners, including both course and interpersonal support systems? However, whereas Daniel and Marquis focus on what it takes to create an effective system in terms of both quality of learning and economic viability, Morgan focuses solely on the quality of learning within an open higher education system.

Projects

Morgan focuses on projects as a mode of teaching and learning that offers real opportunities for self-direction and risk-taking by learners. He also tackles issues central to the curriculum, in terms of the constraints on learner freedom that arise from expectations around standards and the requirements of learning outcomes at different levels. These tensions are not avoided and, while questions are raised rather than solutions offered, projects are used to demonstrate how structure may be used to provide more support to the less experienced learner, and smaller projects incorporated into foundation courses to provide 'safe' opportunities to develop the kind of independence of mind that is the hallmark of high-quality learning.

Theories used in support of the independent learner model

During the 1970s and 1980s, practitioners were largely drawing on cognitive approaches to learning, such as the work of Ausubel et al. (1978), in which the importance of the learner's existing conceptions and knowledge is recognised. Ausubel's famous dictum – that the single most important factor influencing new learning was what the learner had already learned – was often used to justify practice that fosters an active approach by the learner. A narrow behaviourist approach, as exemplified by programmed learning, was rejected in favour of more holistic approaches to course design and the parallel use of multiple media to stimulate understanding and the personal construction of meaning.

The emphasis was placed on growth and development in the individual learner, and Perry (1970) demonstrated for many practitioners evidence of the kind of intellectual development ODL should aim for within the context of further and higher education. Perry's research – admittedly among the elitist populations of ivy league universities in the USA – demonstrated that students moved through a range of orientations to knowledge as they progressed from their freshman year to graduation. Their initial attitudes included the notion that their lecturers knew the truth, and their role was to ensure that their students learned it. By graduation, however, many had moved from this dependent approach to a more sophisticated grasp of the uncertainties surrounding what counts as knowledge, and awareness of the cultural influences on what counts as 'truth' or otherwise. Practitioners in ODL, such as those quoted in the previous section, were keen to demonstrate that ODL systems were capable of providing education challenging enough to ensure that its graduates had achieved the later stages of Perry's scheme in terms of their understanding and personal cognitive development.

Morgan (1985) drew not only on Perry's work but on that of Marton and Saljo (1976a, b), who had also researched the thinking and practice of university students. Their interviews of students who had completed a conventional study task in their discipline showed that individuals differed markedly from each other in terms of their orientation to the task and to university study more generally. Some were studying to understand and to experience personal sense of commitment to what they were learning. Others were more dominated by fear of failure and concentrated on the surface details of texts, attempting to memorise their reading and lecture notes. The schema developed by Marton and Saljo identified these contrasting approaches to learning as 'deep' and 'surface', respectively. They also identified a third approach, 'strategic', which they felt categorised those learners who were motivated by achievement and highly organised in terms of meeting the requirements for assessment and succeeding within the terms set by their university.

The identification of these phenomena in student learning led to the approach being labelled 'phenomenological', and the three orientations to study have been widely used by higher education practitioners both in campus and open systems. Entwistle (1994) has summarised the distinctions in the form of a framework (see Table 8.2). Gibbs et al. (1984) applied the approach to studies of OU students during the 1980s and verified its main findings in this context. They drew parallels between the growth of independence of mind and the process through which novice students become more experienced within a particular discipline or field of study. In seeking to understand material for themselves, not simply to remember and reproduce it, students are not only taking a 'deep approach' to study, but they are becoming independent learners in the best sense. The research at the OU also reflected the differences between the predominantly older (over-thirties) part-time student returning to higher education and the young adult of 18 to mid-twenties, typical of the US and Swedish research. OU students identified 'changing as a person' as one of the meanings of learning for them, and this again emphasised a broad conception of independence, rather than a mere accumulation of skills and knowledge.

Morgan (1985) also made connections with the idea of academic socialisation, which adds value to the whole cultural and social context of a discipline or a particular course within a discipline. It is the richness of these contexts, and

Table 8.2 Categorisation of approaches to learning

Approach to learning	Function
Deep approach	Transforming
Intention: to understand material for oneself	
Showing an active interest in course content	
Relating ideas to previous knowledge and experience	
Looking for patterns and underlying principles	
Adopting a cautious, critical stance	
Checking evidence and relating to conclusions	
Surface approach	Reproducing
Intention: to cope with content and tasks set	
Studying without reflecting on purpose or strategy	
Seeing the course as unrelated bits of knowledge	
Difficulty in making sense of ideas presented	
Memorising facts and procedures routinely	
Feeling undue pressure and worry about work	
Strategic approach	Organising
Intention: to excel on assessed work	
Alertness to assessment requirements and criteria	
Gearing work to perceived preferences of lecturers	
Putting consistent effort into studying	
Ensuring right conditions and materials for studying	
Managing time and effort to maximise grades	

Reproduced with permission from Entwistle, The Open University (1994).

the interactions they make possible, that offers learners multiple pathways and experiences through which they develop their own identity as learners within the culture of a particular academic discipline. Distance learning, therefore, has to communicate not just 'content' but the experiences and interactions of an academic community, in and through which the student can come to understand both what it means to learn and what there is to learn.

Theories that take us from independent to collaborative learning

As we have seen, the role of interaction in supporting the growth of independence in learning had been recognised, at least by some practitioners, in the 1970s. Daniel and Marquis (1979) referred in passing to Pask's conversation theory as evidence to support their positive valuation of interaction. However, Pask's work and the idea of a conversational theory of learning did not achieve any currency among practitioners until the publication of Laurillard's *Rethinking University Teaching*, where the core ideas were elaborated and explained in a model (Laurillard 1993: 103) that has been widely referenced within practitioner literature in higher education (Conole and Oliver 1998; Fowler and Mayes 2000). Pask's work was ahead of practice at the time and fits more as a bridge between independence and collaboration as the different goals of practice during these two periods.

Laurillard's conversational theory of learning shows the interaction between learner and teacher operating at two levels – through dialogues where learners' conceptualisations may be corrected and refined by a tutor, and through practical tasks set by the teacher, where learners' actions prompt intrinsic feedback on their understandings. The learners engage in internalised conversations as they work through activities framed by their explicit dialogue at the level of tutor–learner interaction. In other words, independence grows through both successful interaction and independent activity.

However, other theoretical influences have taken a more radical approach and broadened our appreciation of what learning is and how it happens. Pask's focus was on cognitive development and how it can be promoted successfully. Researchers in the late 1980s, however, were now publishing their studies of learning in work and community settings. Bereiter and Scardamalia (1989), for example, contrasted the approach to learning of adults and children. Adults were found to be oriented by their purpose and to take a problem-solving approach. Bereiter and Scardamalia identified a disjunction between institutionalised learning and 'real' learning:

> The work that characterises classroom life may have originally been conceived with learning goals in mind, and it may even achieve some learning objectives, but from the standpoint of the students, doing schoolwork is what school is about. It is their job, not attaining learning goals.
>
> (Bereiter and Scardamalia 1989: 377)

Resnick also identified a basic disjunction between what goes on in school and the requirements of intentional learning:

> Evidence is beginning to accumulate that traditional schooling's focus on individual, isolated activity, on symbols correctly manipulated but divorced from experience, and on decontextualised skills may be partly responsible for our schools' difficulty in teaching processes of thinking and knowledge construction.
>
> (Resnick 1989: 13)

In a paper on situated cognition, Brown *et al.* (1989) summarised the radical challenge of such work that had become one of the most referenced works in support of collaborative approaches to learning by the late 1990s. They began their 1989 paper with an attack on one of the core assumptions of most forms of schooling, namely that knowledge may be codified and abstracted from the contexts in which it occurs, and learned through a process that focuses on what may be abstracted and generalised from practice. They argue thus:

> Recent investigations of learning, however, challenge this separation of what is learned from how it is learned and used. The activity in which knowledge is developed and deployed, it is now argued, is not separable from nor ancillary to learning and cognition. Nor is it neutral. Rather, it is

an integral part of what is learned. Situations might be said to co-produce knowledge through activity. Learning and cognition . . . are fundamentally situated.

(Brown *et al.* 1989: 32)

The claim that 'all learning is situated', and the implications of that claim for how formal educational settings should rethink their practice, has roots in Vygotsky's cultural-historical approach to learning. This approach highlighted the role of the teacher as scaffolding the learning process so that learners can operate, in the area beyond their immediate capability, in a context of guided practice. Having achieved mastery, they become able to operate independently and can take the next step forward, again into territory just beyond their immediate independent capability. This idea of teachers and learners working together in a 'zone of proximal development' gave new emphasis to the role of others in the achievement of learning. Such an approach derived from educational research into learning in and out of school began to have a strong impact once the web became a real possibility for educational provision from the mid-1990s onwards.

In charting the development of practitioner thinking from a focus on individual independence to a focus on collaboration, it is interesting to question whether theory led practice or vice versa. My own interpretation is that many theoretical insights recognised collaboration as an immensely powerful context and stimulus for learning, but that they were not sufficiently identified in the practice of teaching and learning in the 1980s and early 1990s. However, by the turn of the century, collaborative learning had become a topic of great importance in practitioner accounts, reflecting the enormous impact of computer-mediated communication and the web, more than the power of particular theoretical perspectives. Nevertheless, such perspectives have been used to legitimise particular innovations: both practitioner accounts and theoretical perspectives have worked together in their effects. Practitioners have become more familiar with the ideas of social constructivism and situated cognition alongside using new technology more extensively in their teaching.

Collaboration and collaborative learning

Open and distance learning

Although the title of this chapter suggests a neat polarisation between independence and collaboration, the history of ODL demonstrates that this is not so. As we have seen, some of the most influential contributors argued for the necessary role of interaction (as distinct from collaboration) in achieving independence of mind, and did not promote a purely individualistic philosophy as either appropriate or possible for distance and open education. None the less, the constraints on interpersonal interaction, and the limited technologies available, narrowed practical options and emphasised the individual learner and what might support individual development as the primary goal of good instructional design.

However, the overlap of this dominant practice by the new possibilities for interaction occurred with the introduction of computer-mediated communication (CMC). In the distance education context, the availability of and the changes promised by CMC were seen as heralding a new generation of practice. Nipper's (1989) account of three distinct periods in ODL practice is one of the most referenced of such approaches. He distinguished between three generations of provision, each sparked off by some new potential offered by a combination of technology and media becoming widely available. The first generation was based on correspondence and textual communication alone, made popular and widespread by the expansion of print, rail and postal services in the late nineteenth century. This was followed by second-generation ODL, where broadcasting and two-way communication using the telephone to augment text and other media came into widespread use from the 1970s onwards. Third-generation ODL marks a radical break in bringing interactive communication and integrated multimedia within reach of systems delivering into homes as well as campuses and workplaces.

Nipper (1989) situates his analysis in the context of adult education in Denmark, where there is a strong tradition of face-to-face adult learning, emphasising oral communication and social action and interaction. This tradition includes nineteenth-century farmers' liberation groups that promoted 'the living word' as an expression of their opposition to the written language of the authorities. Such traditions are a common element in the ideology of adult learning across Scandinavia, and are at odds with the communication limitations of much first- and second-generation ODL. The introduction in 1983 of computer conferencing for updating Danish teachers therefore reflected a view of learning that had always been strongly social: 'Learning – although a very *personal* matter – must never be an *individual* matter – one learns best by and with others' (Nipper 1989: 66). In another reminder of the long history of recurring themes within education and pedagogy in particular, Nipper identifies CMC as a technology catching up with the insights and ideologies of Danish social movements of the preceding century: 'the social and educational requirements which were first formulated in the rural summer schools of the early nineteenth century are being fulfilled by a technology from the last part of the twentieth century' (Nipper 1989: 66).

A little behind the pioneering Danes, the OU launched its use of the CoSy conferencing system on course DT200, *Information Technology and Society*, in 1988, at a time when efforts to achieve independent learning were still being emphasised (Gaskell and Mills 1989). This course reached over a thousand students every year, and put firmly on the agenda the feasibility of new forms of connectedness between individuals, overcoming the constraints of synchronous events and physical meetings. Although many of the now commonplace themes and issues were explored in the book documenting this and related experiences (Mason and Kaye 1989), these researchers and practitioners were, at the time, well ahead of their field. They marked the beginning of what is now a tidal wave of web-based and online teaching and learning, in which dialogue and collaboration with others are routinely promised – much less routinely delivered.

Campus-based flexible and distributed provision

It is now axiomatic that the integration of telecommunications with computing is enabling methods of teaching and learning that are revolutionising campus-based learning as well as ODL. In campus-based provision, developments have progressed rather differently. From the late 1980s, universities and colleges have come under pressure to increase their student population without commensurate increases in the staff and accommodation required for conventional provision. Such expansion has been led by the state, in response to the growing realisation that a 'knowledge economy' requires a highly educated workforce and continual updating and retraining to match the demands of rising productivity. Gibbs and Jenkins (1992) demonstrated that, by the beginning of the 1990s, this expansion had directly affected the conditions within which teaching and learning are carried out.

Within this context, the UK Higher Education Funding Council also earmarked funding tranches for projects implementing new technologies in teaching, in three phases from 1992 to 2001, entitled the Teaching and Learning Technologies Programme. Over £33 million was allocated, and most projects in the first two phases were for discipline-based resources and software. The 1999 round of proposals was focused on embedding innovation within institutions. Experience in the two prior funding rounds demonstrated that creation of software products and course materials suffered from the effects of not being embedded within mainstream teaching, and often required heroic and, in the long term, unrealistic efforts on the part of a few enthusiastic individuals and teams.

One of the outcomes of this experience has been to encourage collaboration across institutions, to share costs but also to ensure that good ideas and good software 'travel' across the sector and thus bring change on a wider scale. A similar story could be told of many developed countries, where the state has tried to influence universities and the private sector to make as much use as possible of ICT (Perraton, 2000). Initially, the idea of saving costs was part of the motivation. Experience has led to the realisation that, in the immediate future, cost savings are unlikely. However, other motives have come into play, as governments see the need to educate the workforce to use ICT as part of an engagement with the knowledge-based economy and as a means of personal updating and lifelong learning.

Although computer-based software has not become widespread outside disciplines such as medicine, veterinary science and biochemistry, the web and e-mail are growing in use in most campuses (Haywood et al. 2000). Thus the practitioner literature of the late 1990s reveals a high preponderance of accounts of the use of CDROM and web-based resources, intranets and conferencing systems that specifically emphasise the values of collaboration and resource-based learning (Jones et al. 2000).

Many such accounts may be found in the *Association for Learning Technology Journal*. Kitts and Hancock (1999), for example, describe the use of Hypermedia Learning Tutorials (HLTs) at universities based in Bristol, UK. Students in final-year language degrees have 24-hour access to HLTs developed for Spanish studies. The HLTs include a range of texts from Spanish-speaking contexts, with associated 'tutorials', activities and self-assessment exercises. They may be accessed using either a guided linear approach or a more open and exploratory approach. Students have the freedom to use them according to preference, and non-assessed oral presentations and workshops have been linked to the issues they raise. However, they are also integrated with assessment, through independent and collaborative projects based on topics in the resources. Students are also encouraged to write their own materials for inclusion in the resources, and some project work is planned for inclusion in HLTs in the future.

The authors of the case study argued that the HLT may be seen as an application of Grabinger and Dunlap's (1995) idea of a Rich Environment for Active Learning (REAL). REALs are designed to encompass whole systems of teaching and learning, not just computer-based learning or microworlds, although Kitts and Hancock (1999) argue that the way in which the HLT is integrated with existing learning activities on campus ensures that it meets the requirements of a REAL. A constructivist approach is the starting point, with an emphasis on relevance and building correspondence between the learning context of the REAL and the context of use of the knowledge. REALs should:

- promote study and investigation within authentic contexts;
- encourage the growth of student responsibility, initiative, decision-making and intentional learning;
- cultivate collaboration among students and teachers;
- utilise dynamic, interdisciplinary, generative learning activities that promote higher-order thinking processes to help students develop rich and complex knowledge structures;
- assess student progress in content and learning to learn within authentic contexts using realistic tasks and performances (Kitts and Hancock 1999: 10).

HLTs, for example, include materials from sources in Spain and Latin America on topics relevant to current society. Assessment helps students make use of the resources, but there is also 'space' for students to use them in a manner that suits their preferences and modes of study. Clearly, the positive feedback reported from students is encouraging, but it would be premature to make large claims for this example.

What is important in this and other examples are the aspirations of the practitioners concerned, and their appeal to the literature on constructivist (Jonassen et al. 1995) and situated learning. Many efforts are being made, for example, to build virtual learning environments in which students will not only have flexible options for independent study, but be able to collaborate and communicate with others and manage their affairs as a learner. Such efforts attempt to go well beyond the mere add-on of an interactive facility, by harnessing the best features of web-based technology with communications and administrative functions integrated into a single platform, creating all the elements that could be predictably required in a learning and teaching system:

- access to resources, on- and off-line;
- user management capability;

- assessment;
- personal workspaces for users – learners, teachers, administrators;
- e-mail;
- discussion/conference spaces.

Fowler and Mayes (1999) provide an example of this approach. They describe a framework for the design of a Generic Learning Platform (GLP), intended to be available at all levels of education and across the private sector. The assertion is that learning is universal and that 'building sector specific solutions made little educational or commercial sense'. One of the authors (Fowler) represents British Telecom research at Adastral Park and their development of the GLP, a computer-based learning environment designed for lifelong learning needs wherever these occur. One of the key aspects about the GLP is the emphasis on the design of connections and collaborative links between learners, 'moving the emphasis of learning away from "what" we learn to the "who" we learn from' (Fowler and Mayes 1999: 14). This orientation also fits well with their aim to provide a learning environment that meets both organisational and educational learning contexts.

The developed and trialled platform included many familiar functions, such as modular coursework, e-mail and discussion groups, and public and private work spaces for learners and tutors. Trials were conducted to meet a variety of different learning contexts: an assessed English as a Foreign Language course at Hull University for 40 students worldwide; NVQ students working with Northern Colleges Network to assemble evidence for Level II in Information Technology; and Wickham Market Primary School where homes and school were provided with PCs to use the environment for improving home–school contact and activity.

The important point about this example is not primarily about whether the claims of its designers have been achieved, but what they were attempting to do, namely to enable the technology to support not only collaboration across learners, but also to support assessment of work-based learning and to enhance communication and collaboration between communities, such as schools and the home environment of pupils.

The evolution of new communities of practice

Practitioners and their learners

In this final section, I return to concerns about how these developments are affecting communities of practice in our field. Taking first the context of distance learning, if we consider the local community of practice constituted by a tutor and his or her group of learners, there are some noticeable differences in what that community can do now and how participants can interact within it. The ease with which people communicate not only enables more frequent contact with a tutor but also with other learners. Asynchronous communication makes it possible to build group work into the design of courses and to foster group support for the kind of encouragement and general support previously only available in a limited way from a tutor. Synchronous meeting environments are still not widely used, but offer some of the motivational effects of face-to-face meetings in 'second-generation' ODL and are set to increase.

In many ways, therefore, use of the web and CMC provides the conditions for tutors/facilitators and groups working at a distance from each other to become communities of practice for the purposes of achieving their learning goals. The idea of learners working together on a regular basis, negotiating meanings and building their practice of learning, is now becoming a possibility. In this sense, use of the new technologies enables us to try to support such communities in the first place, through the way we design and set up the interactive process in our courses. Collaboration has an even greater emphasis for distance than campus-based educators, if only because in the past such collaboration was effectively impossible on a regular basis.

In the context of campus-based study, collaboration may not be new, but asynchronous communication offers new possibilities. These possibilities may prove frustratingly difficult to achieve, where learners can subvert the aims or simply ignore the opportunities offered (Jones 1999; Jones et al. 2000). However, the benefits to be realised relate to valuable learning outcomes, and the search for good designs to support collaboration is likely to continue (McAteer et al. 1997). Student groups, for example, can create texts together or work on a shared task without the limitations of time and location (Thorpe 1998). This greater flexibility is particularly important because so many students are now studying part-time, or trying to work and study in parallel. There are also new opportunities for contact with those beyond the walls of the educational community, and the boundaries between institutions and communities and workplaces are being lowered by the use of the Internet.

Thus, in both distance and other contexts, new technologies are being used by practitioners to achieve new as well as established goals. Teamwork and collaboration are being valued in their own right, and assessment of students' abilities in these areas has become an important goal in higher education and one of the reasons for using the technologies in the first place. Furthermore, the kind of activity students engage in when they study is changing. As students have more access to extensive resources and databases on the Internet, the goals we set them are changing from sole emphasis on mastery of content towards developing skills in knowing how to use that content, and to find resources which meet specific needs. Lankshear et al. explore these aspects in Chapter 1.

Practitioner networks

Turning now to those extended networks between practitioners, in what sense may we claim that here also we see the evolution of the community? We might begin to answer this question by reflecting on the fact that so much more of the space within which learning occurs can be directly created by the designers of teaching and learning systems. This is surely a radical difference between what is now possible and the technologies of the 1970s and 1980s.

This factor is also bringing new participants into practitioner communities, with the growth of learning support staff in libraries, computer services, and learning and teaching units. Such staff play a major role in the mediation of teaching and in supporting learners in their use of software and computer-based resources. Teaching is increasingly about the existence of effective learning environments, and such staff play a major role in their design, delivery and support. Our practitioner networks have expanded to include these new staff roles, which are distinctive and increasingly important in making the best use of content experts.

A further outcome of the design of effective learning environments is that the clear boundaries which existed in 1979 between interaction and independence – the trade-offs between the two and the complex balancing act required between learner needs, costs and performance – are now less marked. A form of interaction is now possible simply by moving to a different area of the software interface to conference or e-mail, with an equally easy shift back into independent study mode by accessing online resources. However slow our computer, this is usually easier than telephoning or travelling to a study centre, both of which used to be our only mode of interaction in distance forms of study, and even campus-based interaction can have barriers of place and time.

Furthermore, the boundaries we saw between the institution and the learner's local community and identity are now also blurred and softened in efforts to enable virtual learning environments to support existing social activities and ways of working. Since the web is now also a powerful mode of access for large sectors of the population to goods and services of all kinds, there is a gradual process of familiarisation which reduces the barriers to using learning technology. As we have seen, private developers of learning environments are demanding a lifelong learning approach on commercial as well as educational grounds and seeking to support many different kinds of learning, not just learning appropriate to the different stages of schooling or to higher education

There are marked differences, therefore, between 1979 and 1999 in who counts as a practitioner, in what practitioners are doing and between the theoretical approaches from which they draw to both justify and help develop further their designs of environments to support learning. Such differences are, of course, more marked in some areas of practice than others, and there has been no sudden, radical departure in theoretical terms. We are able to trace a line of thinking from Pask's conversational model, through Morgan's emphasis on the role of dialogue in academic socialisation within higher education, through constructivism and into situated learning and the 'community of practice' approach to learning and teaching.

Practitioners now have an enlarged range of tools at their disposal, which they are using to create different kinds of learning experience from those available 30 years ago. Their repertoire is enlarged, and the collaborative learning components are currently more highly valued than others. They are setting themselves new goals and drawing on different theoretical approaches to elaborate and justify those goals. Their learners are able to demonstrate skills online and to create individual and group products as evidence of their learning. New literacies in on-screen reading, image and text creation are being developed. The attraction of constructivist approaches to learning is driving concentration on collaborative strategies that build in regular expectations of dialogue within groups and group task completion. The current emphasis is often on how independent study may be used to support and sustain group interaction, where in 1979–89 the roles were reversed; interaction was used to support and foster independence.

The analytical tools developed alongside this practice are also distinctive. At the micro level, issues of interface design and architecture are crucial for enabling learners to make the best use of the tools available. At the macro level, culture in the sense of institutional customs, the expectations of users of learning systems and communication norms across different communities all play a part in the actual performance of a learning environment (Musselbrook et al. 2000).

Conclusion

The communities of practice in our field for the twenty-first century are different in several important ways from those of the preceding three decades, itself a period of enormous change in scale and modes of provision of post-compulsory education and training. However, in outlining those differences, it has also been possible to recognise some continuing shared challenges in terms of the constraints of time and accessibility for learners. In revisiting the boundaries and distinctions characteristic of those earlier practices, we remind ourselves of the challenges still to be overcome in the design of learning, whatever the promise of our more powerful ICT tools and media. Although the creation of virtual learning environments promises to reduce the negative impact of location and time barriers, it has had only partial success as yet. It may also have diverted attention from the time barriers that still remain.

Distance educators have also found that students still value the control that working independently of others gives them, and that there are real limits to the extent to which collaborative work may be expected (Mason 1994). While to the designer of the system asynchronicity promises freedom from time constraints, in reality, the time constraints of learners do shape their behaviour and thus intrude very directly on the virtual learning environment. It may be a paradox, but only by factoring in the real-time availability of learners can educational designers move closer to achieving the time freedoms that online systems promise but find difficult to deliver.

In yet other ways, there are also similarities between the practice contexts of today and those of 30 years ago. Pacing is no less important, for example, simply because current systems offer the enhanced flexibility of electronic submission of assignments, e-mail and desktop access with multiple routes through diverse and rich resources. To leave the task of managing and prioritising learning activities wholly to the learner is to add more to the time constraints that then threaten the achievement of learning outcomes.

However, such reminders of the continuity of concerns should not be the last word. This would risk obscuring the major changes that have occurred in the communities of practice of teaching and learning practitioners themselves. One of the outcomes of these changes is the tendency towards convergence of teaching practitioners around the key shared concern of how best to apply ICT to teaching and learning. This convergence has operated across the diverse territories and modes of provision of post-compulsory education and training.

Where there were undoubtedly two distinct practitioner communities in 1979, based on the campus versus distance divide, this boundary is now much reduced. We use similar, sometimes the same, technology applications, and draw on the same research and theoretical literature for a sense of the broad direction in which teaching and learning should go, albeit with rather different groups of learners and learning goals.

As Brown and Duguid (1996) have argued, shared direction is being formulated in a new way, as providing access not only to accredited learning but also to the professional and academic communities in which learning and expertise develop. Their analysis provides reasons why we ought to reject both the old emphasis on delivery that has characterised much distance provision and the barriers of the traditional campus offering only privileged access for the few. They argue that the goal for any form of provision fit for the learning purposes of the twenty-first century should be to create 'essential access to authentic communities' (Brown and Duguid 1996: 8). Interactivity is the means to an end which is not now formulated in terms of independence in learning, but of participation in communities that generate knowledge and provide access to the learning process. In an evocative phrase that sums up the move away from a conceptualisation of independence in learning as the goal, they set down the challenge for campus and distance alike: 'Learning involves inhabiting the streets of a community's culture. The community may include astrophysicists, architects, or acupuncturists, but learning involves experiencing its cultural peculiarities' (Brown and Duguid 1996: 5).

If this does indeed sum up what is distinctive about our new communities of practice, we ought nevertheless to reflect critically on the path along which we have travelled to this conclusion and on the extent to which we can now achieve the challenging goal it sets. In generating our own community of practice, critical reflection upon our own claims and our own 'cultural peculiarities' should be at the core of what we do.

References

Ausubel, D.P., Novak, J.D. and Hanesian, H. (1978) *Educational Psychology: A Cognitive View*. New York: Holt, Rinehart & Winston.

Bereiter, C. and Scardamalia, M. (1989) Intentional learning as a goal of instruction, in L.B. Resnick (ed.) *Knowing, Learning and Instruction: Essays in Honor of Robert Glaser*. Hillsdale, NJ: Lawrence Erlbaum.

Brown, J.S. and Duguid, P. (1996) Universities in the digital age, *Change*, 28(4): 11–20.

Brown, J.S., Collins, A. and Duguid, P. (1989) Situated cognition and the culture of learning, *Educational Researcher*, 18(1):32–42.

Conole, G. and Oliver, M. (1998) A pedagogical framework for embedding C&IT into the curriculum, *Association for Learning Technology Journal*, 6(2): 4–16.

Daniel, J.S. and Marquis, C. (1979) Interaction and independence: getting the mixture right, *Teaching at a Distance*, 14: 29–44.

Entwistle, N. (1994) *Teaching and the Quality of Learning*. London: CVSP/SRHE.

Fowler, C.J.H. and Mayes, J.T. (1999) Learning relationships from theory to design, *Association for Learning Technology Journal*, 7(3): 6–16.

Fowler, C.J.H. and Mayes, J.T. (2000) Learning relationships from theory to design, in

D. Squires, G. Conole and G. Jacobs (eds) *The Changing Face of Learning Technology*. Cardiff: University of Wales Press with Association for Learning Technology.

Gaskell, A. and Mills, R. (1989) Interaction and independence in distance education: what's been said and what's being done?, *Open Learning*, 4(2): 51–2.

Gibbs, G. and Jenkins, A. (eds) (1992) *Teaching Large Classes in Higher Education: How to Maintain Quality with Reduced Resources*. London: Kogan Page.

Gibbs, G., Morgan, A. and Taylor, E. (1984) The world of the learner, in F. Marton, D. Hounsell and N.J. Entwistle (eds) *The Experience of Learning*. Edinburgh: Scottish Academic Press.

Grabinger, R.S. and Dunlap, J.C. (1995) Rich environments for active learning: a definition, *Association for Learning Technology Journal*, 3(2): 5–34.

Haywood, J., Anderson, C., Coyle, H., Day, K., Haywood, D. and Macleod, H. (2000) Learning technology in Scottish higher education – a survey of the views of senior managers, academic staff and 'experts', *Association for Learning Technology Journal*, 8(2): 5–17.

Jonassen, D., Davidson, M., Collins, M., Campbell, J. and Bannan Haag, B. (1995) Constructivism and computer mediated communication in distance education, *American Journal of Distance Education*, 9(2): 7–26.

Jones, C. (1999) From the sage on the stage to what exactly? Description of the place of the moderator in cooperative and collaborative learning, *Association for Learning Technology Journal*, 7(2): 27–36.

Jones, C., Asensio, M. and Goodyear, P. (2000) Networked learning in higher education: practitioners' perspectives, *Association for Learning Technology Journal*, 8(2): 18–28.

Kitts, S.A. and Hancock, J.T. (1999) Putting theory into practice: the creation of REALs in the context of today's universities, *Association for Learning Technology Journal*, 7(2): 4–14.

Laurillard, D. (1993) *Rethinking University Teaching: A Framework for the Effective Use of Educational Technology*. London: Routledge.

Lave, J. and Wenger, E. (1991) *Situated Learning: Legitimate Peripheral Participation*. Cambridge: Cambridge University Press.

McAteer, E., Tolmie. A., Duffy, C. and Corbett, J. (1997) Computer-mediated communication as a learning resource, *Journal of Computer Assisted Learning*, 13(4): 219–27.

Marton, F. and Saljo, R. (1976a) On qualitative differences in learning I: outcome and process, *British Journal of Educational Psychology*, 46(4): 4–11.

Marton, F. and Saljo, R. (1976b) On qualitative differences in learning, II: outcome as a function of the learner's conception of the task, *British Journal of Educational Psychology*, 46: 115–27.

Mason, R. (1994) *Using Communications Media in Open and Flexible Learning*. London: Kogan Page in association with the Institute of Educational Technology, The Open University.

Mason, R. and Kaye, A. (1989) *Mindweave: Communication, Computers and Distance Education*. Oxford: Pergamon Press.

Milligan, C. (2000) Virtual learning environments in the online delivery of staff development: delivering staff and professional development using virtual learning environments. Online at: http://www.jisc.ac.uk/jtap/htm/jtap-044.html.

Morgan, A. (1985) What shall we do about independent learning?, *Teaching at a Distance*, 26: 38–45.

Musselbrook, K., McAteer, E., Crook, C. and Macleod, H. (2000) Learning networks and communication skills, *Association for Learning Technology Journal*, 8(1): 71–9.

Nipper, S. (1989) Third generation distance learning and computer conferencing, in R. Mason and A. Kaye (eds) *Mindweave: Communication, Computers and Distance Education*. Oxford: Pergamon Press.

Pask, G., Scott, B.C.E. and Kallikourdis, D. (1973) A theory of conversations and individuals, *International Journal of Man–Machine Studies*, 17–52.

Perraton, H. (2000) *Open and Distance Learning in the Developing World*. London: Routledge.

Perry, W.G. (1970) *Forms of Intellectual and Ethical Development in the College Years*. New York: Holt, Rinehart & Winston.

Resnick, L.B. (ed.) (1989) *Knowing, Learning and Instruction: Essays in Honor of Robert Glaser*. Hillsdale, NJ: Lawrence Erlbaum.

Tait, A. (1994) The end of innocence: critical approaches to open and distance learning, *Open Learning*, 9(3): 27–38.

Thorpe, M. (1998) Assessment and 'third generation' distance education, *Distance Education*, 19(2): 265–86.

Wenger, E. (1998) *Communities of Practice: Learning, Meaning and Identity*. Cambridge: Cambridge University Press.

Chapter 9

Learning as cultural practice

Charles Crook

Introduction

The psychologist Roger Saljo has remarked that, when he began his research on learning, he was struck by the fact that the strongest predictor of students' success was whether or not they read many books. This apparently common-place observation may be striking only to professional cognitive psychologists, for it confronts them with a sobering idea. It suggests that the theoretical struc-tures of their psychology may not be up to analysing what really makes a difference when it comes to successful learning. Accordingly, Saljo himself side-stepped the information-processing metaphors of cognitive psychology and concentrated instead on researching students' private conceptions of know-ledge and what it was to engage in learning. This work became an early land-mark in the now substantial literature on 'learning styles' (Marton and Saljo 1976).

Arguably, that tradition has fostered the idea of individual students possess-ing characteristics – rather like personality traits – that determine the approaches they adopt to studying. 'Style' of learning became especially associ-ated with the distinction between surface and deep approaches (Entwistle and Ramsden 1983). In the projects of many researchers, that distinction became a matter of measuring and correlating individual differences. However, as Ramsden has noted, this individualised conception misrepresents what was intended: 'An approach to learning is a description of a relation *between* a learner and a learning task – the description of an intention and an action. An approach is not something inside a student' (Ramsden 1987: 276). The signifi-cance of accepting this conception is that it must shift our attention from the taxonomony of individuals to the variety of settings in which learning is organ-ised. It is the texture that is found in a learning context which then encourages the idea of 'cultures of learning'. A prominent concern of this chapter is to characterise learning as a form of distinct cultural practice. In one important sense of 'learning', this is something we decide to *do*.

A second concern here arises from current preoccupations with developing more virtual forms of education, particularly in the sector of higher education. I take virtualisation to involve an agenda of 'de-schooling' (Illich 1973) higher education so as to make it possible to study within a less rigid schedule of time and place. Such study becomes loosened from the bricks-and-mortar world of institutional education. New information and communication technology

(ICT) is strongly implicated in the realisation of these new structures. The apparent impact of ICT in de-schooling study is the second major concern of this chapter. I wish to theorise such impacts in relation to learning as cultural practice.

There are many reasons to embrace more virtual forms of study. This virtualisation agenda promises to make educational opportunity available to a wider constituency of students. Such developments might also offer economies in the financial management of education. Finally, study in an ICT-intensive setting might provide a more powerful form of learning experience. In this chapter, I argue that appropriating ICT to virtualisation ambitions does not *ensure* any of these outcomes. There are choices as to exactly how the technology is used as a resource for learning and we need to debate those choices now. Some may lead to an empowering of de-schooled learners, some may serve to set them adrift. More particularly, I wish to suggest here a framing for the necessary debate: a framing that takes seriously the notion of learning as cultural practice. This invites us to understand better the current organisation of that practice. The reward should be a firmer basis for managing virtualisation and predicting its likely success.

I first make some observations that concern reactions to more virtual forms of teaching and learning as I have investigated them in a traditional university setting. Broadly speaking, these reactions are not encouraging for an easy transition to such new methods. The data suggest the conditions for electronically mediated learning demand some scrutiny. I believe it requires us to note the difference between informal and formal learning. That distinction is explored here by taking its expression in early childhood as a particularly accessible example. It is in relation to *formal* learning that the idea of cultural practice is developed. Moreover, tension between the informal and the formal bears on the important idea of 'communities of practice' in learning. Finally, some aspects of formal learning culture are exposed by documenting disturbances to an existing educational culture that are brought about by more virtual practices. In a sense, virtualisation is used here as a lever to access and note certain features of established institutional life.

Reactions to the virtual in higher education

Here I highlight some difficulties that seem to attend the virtualisation of university teaching and learning. Because what is claimed might suggest a somewhat negative and pessimistic attitude, it is important to preface these observations with some qualifying remarks that serve to recognise a degree of complexity in the situation.

There is no question that educational experiences based on distance teaching methods can be highly successful. The Open University in the UK is but one example of how readily students engage with learning methods that are not strongly tied to working at particular times or working in particular institutional spaces. Of course, the success of the Open University may depend on the fact that it does manage a particularly large and expensive infrastructure of support and communication. However, there are other emerging 'electronic universities' where the management of teaching and learning is more narrowly focused on computer networks. These modes of learning also claim success, yet it is important to keep in view the self-selected nature of the student constituency in each case. This is not necessarily a mode of study with universal appeal (Schlosser and Anderson 1994). Indeed, electronically mediated versions of distance courses have been shown to be particularly daunting for some (Hara and Kling 2000). Therefore, if society wishes to sustain the contiguity between secondary and higher education, it must be determined whether distance and virtual methods of learning will prove engaging to that large constituency of young people who currently dominate undergraduate campuses. They are not well represented in research celebrating the attractions and successes of distance methods.

Doubts about the comprehensive appeal of such methods to traditional undergraduates may be countered with examples of courses in current higher education that have successfully adopted computer networks as the central context for their teaching and learning. Yet these are necessarily self-contained case studies. Typically, they are research-led examples in which the virtual mode of delivery will be relatively insulated from a traditional curriculum experience students are otherwise receiving. It is one thing for traditional students to thrive on some isolated courses with a virtual flavour, but another to manage their whole degree in distance terms.

My own expectation is that wholesale transition to virtual higher education will meet with difficulties. This view arises from researching the impact on teaching and learning of computer networking in my own institution. Of course, it is not a virtual university. However, at present there is no such institution – at least, none that caters for an arbitrary sample of the young people drawn from the population and about we are making projections. However, the developments on this campus were sufficient to give some useful pointers to the problems and prospects for a larger scale appropriation of this technology. It was a campus institution, and an unusual proportion of students (over 50 per cent) lived within its boundaries. All of the associated study bedrooms have now been linked to local computer services as well as to the Internet, and students have generous access to network tools. Moreover, every taught module in the university has unlimited file space on a 'learn server'. This disk space is available to staff as a directory on their own office computers and can easily mount material accessible by web browsers. Training in the use and development of such material is widely available. In addition, a specialist unit in the university maintains a 'CAL server' offering what is claimed to be 'one of the UK's largest collections of fully-functional, networked LT [learning technology] materials' (http://www.lboro.ac.uk/service/fli/services/lt/matl/lt2.html). Elsewhere, I have described and interpreted use of these materials in greater detail (Crook 2001). Here, I merely summarise the main observations that concern staff and student use.

The learn server has been active for almost 3 years; yet, at the time of writing, more than 70 per cent of modules have no resources mounted. This is despite a demanding period of external teaching audit in which web-based resources might be regarded as a straightforward way to display innovative attitudes. Although the university has remained light-handed about prescribing such new methods, it has certainly been generous in the level of material encouragement provided. Despite this, it is clear that most staff are not persuaded that it is an important priority to publicise learning material in this networked arena.

The picture in relation to student use is somewhat different. A sample of 45 undergraduates (stratified by faculty affiliation) was recruited from doorstep invitations in residence halls. As response was good, these conversations represented an accurate cross-section of student reaction. Over half felt the university could make more use of ICT. The resource most in demand was lecturers' notes, which it was thought should be published as web pages (in fact, this was already the most common form of published material on the course sites that staff had developed). On the other hand, students had no particular enthusiasm for more CAL software, and our system logging of their own computers indicated this was rarely accessed by them. Neither was there any student appetite for the e-mail-based text conferencing facilities attached to each module on the learn server. In sum, these students were confident users of the technology but fairly pedestrian in their preferences and habits of use.

However, the most striking findings concerned students' perception of a virtual university as a mode of learning; these reactions are very relevant to the arguments developed here. Although there is much rhetoric concerning the importance of moving towards more virtual forms of higher education, there is scant consideration of what students themselves might want. The informants here are one small sample but their views are likely to be representative. After all, they were drawn from all academic disciplines and they had no inhibitions about using technology. We asked whether virtual universities were likely to happen, whether this was desirable and whether they would study within one. Students did differ as to whether they thought it was likely to happen: 52 per cent believed it was likely, many were unsure, and only 20 per cent gave a confident 'no'. On the other hand, when discussing whether it was desirable, they showed themselves to be fairly comfortable with the public arguments for pursuing this vision. In particular, they spoke of economies in delivery, flexibility in terms of when courses might be taken and the prospect of greater social inclusion. However, these were theoretical arguments: not one expressed a wish to study at a virtual university – despite a recognised reduction of present financial commitments. Many vigorously dismissed the whole virtualisation prospect.

The bases for their doubts were (1) the essentially social nature of learning, (2) reservations about the bandwidth of electronic media in terms of capacity to give a rich basis for study, (3) doubts regarding their own ability to sustain motivation in a more unstructured learning setting, (4) a need to protect the social and recreational life associated with full-time institutional study, and (5) attachment to the breadth of experience associated with the independence and variety of university living. Taken together, the various comments of all these students were broadly about two central issues. The first was a feeling that sustained and effective learning depended upon the opportunity for face-to-face interaction. The second was an understanding that what was acquired at university went beyond what was tested in Finals examinations.

Enthusiasts for virtual learning may argue that these student opinions are of little interest, as they are solicited from respondents with limited understanding of what new educational technologies will make possible. On the other hand, the precious features of university experience that were prioritised in these interviews will undoubtedly tax the versatility of new media. It is not as if students' doubts were about the adequacy of the possible learning resources – in relation to which enthusiasts may invoke all sorts of forthcoming wonders. Instead, students' concerns focused on matters that were essentially about the possibility of synchronous and well-grounded social interaction. Although there is a long tradition of paying scant attention to user opinion in the design of educational resources, it would be wise to evaluate the user appeal of changes as radical as virtual institutions. This must surely be the case insofar as society wishes to continue serious provision for young people of school-leaving age.

In anticipation that there might be *some* student resistance to virtual education, my aim here is to make sense of this through a certain strand of theorising over the nature of learning. Through conceptualising learning in terms of cultural practice, I believe we appreciate why appropriating virtual methods might be troublesome. It may be naive to imagine that some new educational technology is simply going to amplify the best of our existing education; or that it will helpfully brush aside any obstacles currently impeding energetic learning by students. However, the difficulties students experience in accommodating those new technologies may be useful in making more visible the important aspects of teaching and learning we may not recognise. Gaver puts this well:

> new technologies seldom simply support old working practices with additional efficiency of flexibility. Instead they tend to undermine existing practices and to demand new ones. In this disruption, subtleties of existing social behaviors and the affordances upon which they rely become apparent.
>
> (Gaver 1996: 112)

In the following section, some distinctions in relation to the meaning of 'learning' are made. This will lay the ground for recognising 'subtleties of existing social behaviors' that arise in the course of learning – and thus to consider consequences of their likely 'disruptions' by new technologies.

Learning: the formal and the informal

As a developmental psychologist by background, I am keenly aware of how much a child achieves in his or her first 4 years. In fact, my own introduction to developmental psychology was in the context of studying children's learning: researching its nature in the very earliest weeks of life. We approached this challenge as a matter of teaching rather than learning; that is, ingenious arrangements were constructed for presenting and recording stimuli and responses. Such management of contingencies was the accepted basis for exposing and studying the early plasticity of behaviour. It certainly needed to be pursued in the setting of a laboratory. What impressed me was that it was quite possible to demonstrate such learning in early life, but it was hard work. The arrangements were certainly ingenious, but the rate at which infants learned about them seemed slow; slower in fact than the pace at which they were learning about the rest of their world.

It is true that a lot of learning does take place very early in life, but, oddly, it seems to do so without the aid of teaching. Perhaps the decontextualised procedures of the psychological laboratory define the sort of contrivance infants find difficult to learn: an unusual encounter with just the kind of teaching that does not normally happen to them. Perhaps the point about early learning is that its progress does indeed depend on contingencies – orderly relations between infant and world – but, to make a difference, these contingencies need to be encountered in the natural flow of intentional action, and to be relevant to the infant's here-and-now concerns. The standard language of psychological description for these early achievements is significant. In my behavioural laboratory example above, the successful infant might be said to have 'acquired a response'. In the more contemporary climate of cognitive science, the infant might be said to 'acquire a representation'. The acquisition-into-container metaphor is natural, but it is not our only option here. It might be more helpful to claim not that the learning child has 'acquired' something, rather they have 'come to take part'. Thus what is achieved in the early years is a capacity for coordinated participation within the local cultural context.

This is possible in circumstances where sympathetic and experienced adults choose to orchestrate the world so as to encourage such participation. Fortunately, most infants will be surrounded by adults who are motivated to make such an investment. Note that this perspective on the first achievements of learning is rather different from that which has previously dominated the developmental psychology of early childhood: namely, the constructivist account associated with Piaget (e.g. Piaget 1953). The infant's agency as an active 'constructor' of knowledge has not been questioned; but what is now taken more seriously is the importance of other people for structuring a world in which such energy can be optimally exercised. What these adults seem to do so vigorously is anticipate, predict and interpret the child's momentary concerns. This species of adult social sensitivity and the resulting adult–child reciprocity has been well observed and documented (e.g. Schaffer 1992). Only recently has it been appreciated how far the young child's own motives for action are derived from the world of interpersonal events. The Piagetian infant is typically cast as experimenting on the *material* world (a putative physicist). The infant of contemporary developmental psychology (e.g. Dunn 1988) is more curious about the world of other people (a putative psychologist).

All this captures what might be termed 'informal learning' – in its earliest and therefore most vivid form. By age 4, the typical child will have command of considerable resources relating to communicating and manipulating both the social and material world; yet it is quite clear (if only from tragic cases of social neglect) that such achievements depend on opportunities for participation in that world that are coordinated by sympathetic others. These will usually be adults with the necessary long experience and interpersonal sensitivity – in addition to an emotional commitment to the responsibilities of enculturation. Indeed, human beings may be unique among species in respect of their motivation and capacity for instructing their young (Premack and Premack 1996). Yet the term 'instruction' sits uneasily in this description, because what is going on in these early years rarely resembles the kinds of activities we normally label 'instruction'. What is distinctive about the dramatic achievements of this early period is the indirectness of the underlying influences. What others do to effect an influence seems folded into the child's (the learner's) ongoing and spontaneous activities. Not, of course, that children are allowed unilateral control over their early social lives but, most likely, the richest opportunities for informal learning reside in situations that are both child-directed and readily precipitate a guided mutuality with others.

In many societies, enculturation is achieved solely through such informal experiences of learning; yet what is striking about our own culture is that we have evolved practices that capture, concentrate and re-locate the events of these early learning encounters. We thereby turn the experience of learning into something with a more recognisable *formal* structure, so, around the age of 4 or 5, most of us will go to school. This is not a seamless transition of experience, but it is abrupt in terms of offering a new basis for orchestrating action. Most central of the differences between the domestic and the scholastic are those that concern motivation and relevance. Many demands of schooled intelligence simply do not surface in the spontaneous world of childhood social relations – the world outside of school. Typically, the young schoolchild will initially have no strong appetite for the challenges of number, reading or writing; perhaps, therefore, the motives for engaging with such material have to be generated from within the contrived agendas of schooled life. This makes it important to investigate the *practice* of educational institutions. A further handicap suffered by the formal teacher over the informal adult (the parent, say) is a lack of intimate knowledge of individual children: their histories, vulnerabilities and tastes. Thus the anticipation and exploitation of optimal learning chances may be more difficult to achieve.

It is valuable to note how these constraints are dealt with, and involves constructing a circumscribed and ordered world: a design-for-living in which the locations, rituals, roles and agendas are carefully stage-managed in the interests of making curriculum material 'matter'. There is nothing particularly sinister about this. In fact, this difficult transformation of experience is generally handled with great sensitivity by the cast of characters involved. The metaphor of theatre is quite apt here. Children generally accept the terms of a schooled world much as any of us might adapt to the narrative and context of a dramatic production. Children agree to suspend their indifference to the demands of certain classroom tasks and engage with the relevant stage directions. A more difficult issue to assess – and one that I shall return to in the context of undergraduate learning – is whether or not what pupils end up doing is another species of 'taking part'. If it does mirror something of what we recognise as *participation* in the world of informal learning, the conditions of that schooled life have arguably achieved something significant.

The basis for achieving this difficult contract with the learner (a suspension of indifference and an active appropriation of the curricular agenda) is a certain decoupling from the informal world of out-of-school life. Thus, formal learning is institutionalised in that it takes place in specialised premises relatively insulated from the surrounding community. Moreover, the adults involved are typically not informed by out-of-school contact with their pupils; those adults may, for example, live outside of their own school's catchment area. This world is so decoupled that children may not seem to allow the two to cross-talk.

Parents often comment on how difficult it is to persuade young children to discuss the events of classroom life. This segregation of school and home experience is clear; less obvious is a form of activity segregation that is typical *within* school, namely the separation of the timetable into periods of classwork and of recreational play. From a very early point, the agenda of formal learning creates an eccentric pattern of relationships with peers. The same group of children are encountered as companions in two very different settings, with very different terms of engagement. Peers are companions in the unstructured and (largely) child-directed context of the playground and they are also companions in the more orchestrated and (largely) teacher-directed context of the classroom. What takes place between children in these two settings is often very different.

There is a further social feature of these 'dual worlds' of learning, and it highlights problems of interpenetration. The literature celebrating the potency of informal learning makes strong assumptions about learners' motivation – that willingness to be 'scaffolded' through social participations as those outlined above. Lucinda Kerewalla and myself are investigating children's use of ICT in their homes and their use of educational software in particular. We find that most children's experience of home computers tends to be solitary rather than collaborative. This is the case despite advertising images encouraging the idea of parents supporting children engaged in school-like ICT-based activities. One observation of a number of parents is that their children can be *resistant* to parental involvement with such activity. Our understanding of this reaction is that it concerns an unease about parents (or perhaps other people close to the child) acting in a tutorial role. This may be experienced where the mechanics of scaffolded tuition somehow become visible to the learner: where the teaching *role* is made explicit.

Comfortably maintaining the relationship between the worlds of formal and informal learning is of particular concern in this chapter, since it is argued that virtual technologies of learning may have a strong effect at this interface. Examples will be given below but, first, it is necessary to note some further conceptual distinctions that have been made in the interests of understanding the optimal management of the formal. In particular, I am interested in the notion of the formal harbouring 'communities of practice'.

Communities of practice

The above distinctions and arguments have been cast in terms of early child development. My wider interest here is in higher and continuing education, yet it is important to note the developmental roots of educational practice. This encourages consideration of how the separation of formal and informal evolves over the time-scale of human educational experiences.

It may be tempting to believe that the culture of educational practice in later years (say, in higher education) has taken on a character that is more in harmony with the student's informal world of learning. One hint of this is perceived in the promotional imagery that is associated with, say, universities. Pick up an undergraduate prospectus and consider the photographs illustrating departmental entries. David Barrowcliff and I have done this in a carefully sampled

(a)

(b)

Figure 9.1 Promotional images of university study.

(c)

Figure 9.1 continued

manner and have classified the contents of these images. The prospectus student is typically active, exploring, often out-of-doors and – most of all – social. In short, such students are portrayed doing things and often doing them in harmony with others. If that company includes a tutor, then their disposition is typically supportive and the setting is typically intimate, conversational or exploratory (Figure 9.1). In fact, the concerns of the prospectus student seldom require that they be in lectures or libraries, and it is unusual for them to be simply reading. Yet it is libraries, lectures and books that activity-diary studies show to occupy most of the 'real' student's time. These images are curiously discrepant in another sense: in terms of mood, the prospectus student is decidedly upbeat. There is no suggestion that study might ever be tiring, frustrating, tedious or lonely. Of course, to convey such messages to intending students would be perverse. The prospectus is about projecting an attractive image and, increasingly, universities embrace promotional methods to achieve this (Wernick 1991).

The important point here is not simply that these seductive images are dishonest – for some of the time at least, study may be constituted in the ways portrayed – but most of us would accept that being a student at university is often a demanding commitment. Learning is about *doing* things, and doing them well is not always easily motivated or achieved. What is interesting about the promotional imagery of higher education is that it actively suggests that there is no significant discontinuity between formal and informal learning. It suggests that what the prospective student will be doing as a learner looks and feels like only a modest transformation of the kind of fun they normally enjoy.

However, a gap between the formal and the informal continues to be visible well into this later period of education. Many of the students we interviewed (see above) were quite clear that their principal orientation was towards the social and recreational life of university. Study was coped with, sometimes enjoyed, but not strongly constitutive of their identity. Students also revealed this split in another way (which I shall return to below): they often partition their social relations into the curricular and the recreational, such that the concerns of each did not strongly overlap. Perhaps this echoes that earlier partitioning of social relations within a single peer group, namely into classroom and playground.

Many commentators have expressed concern at the failure of educational provision to close the gap discussed here; that is, to make the experience of formal education shift to resemble more the flavour of learning captured in promotional prospectuses. For example, Tharp and Gallimore (1988) propose the closing of this gap as a necessary educational goal: 'When true teaching is found in schools, it observes the same principles that good teaching exhibits in informal settings.' Central among these principles are methods of 'assisted performance'; that is, occasions (as discussed above) in which a child and an adult participate in joint activities scaffolded by the sensitivity and judgements of the more experienced partner. Tharp and Gallimore (1988: 41) conclude that: 'Even with the benefits of modern instructional practice, there is still too large a gap between the conditions of home and school. Most parents do not need to be trained to assist performance; most teachers do.'

Tharp and Gallimore acknowledge one reason why assisted performance is lacking in classrooms: a large group of pupils and one teacher does not allow such dedicated interaction. However, perhaps assisted performance should not be seen as the inevitable means to realise the goals of formal settings. It may be that this intimacy of social exchange actually becomes less well suited to what formal education strives to achieve. A possible limitation is the scope of what may be encountered in that format. Assisted performance is a close interaction between expert and novice (teacher and pupil, parent and child) in which the novice is coordinated into appropriating some cultural artefact, tool or practice. The skill of this coordinating empowers the novice to take part in an experience that is otherwise beyond their solitary capabilities. However, in complex social orders, much of what must be learned involves knowledge that is inherently distributed. The novice needs opportunities to participate in social coordinations that are less intimate in the sense that they require coordination among *groups* of people. Such possibilities shift attention from dyads as the unit of participative 'assistance' towards communities as the ideal context for learning.

Invoking the notion of community is characteristic of a general move in educational theorising from metaphors of 'acquisition' to metaphors of 'participation' (Sfard 1998); that is, learners are conceptualised less as containers into which knowledge is delivered and more as actors who are coordinated into 'taking part' in knowledge. This, in turn, reflects a contemporary interest among formal educators in the successes of learning as managed informally. So, in the reform of schooling, Tharp and Gallimore illustrate a hankering after the sort of tutorial intimacy that characterises the informal learning typical of Vygotsky's zone of proximal development. The notion of 'communities of practice' also represents a hankering for the potency of the informal; but it takes us beyond the tutorial dyad. It recognises a complexity that evolves for informal learning: a move towards modes of interaction and learning that are more socially dynamic, more distributed, more systemic. One consequence of this community emphasis is a greater interest in making educational experiences more authentic. This principle is central to theoretical arguments where education is urged to respect the 'situated' nature of cognition (Brown *et al.* 1989), or instruction is designed to be 'anchored' to disciplinary practice (Cognition and Technology Group at Vanderbilt 1990).

It is widely debated how far formal education should embrace communities of practice as a structural principle – perhaps so as to make learning resemble more the apprenticeship experience. There is no space here to add significantly to that particular debate. I am especially anxious not to promote stark dichotomies between, say, didactic methods of schooling and methods that are community- and practice-oriented. However, I am also uneasy about reinforcing too romantic a vision of education such as is often the connotation surrounding 'community of practice' – as if learning could and should always have the authentic and uplifting quality visible in undergraduate prospectuses. It is doubtless right that we should strive to ensure students do have a stronger sense of (communally) practising their discipline. Yet, certainly for the bureaucratic/scientific forms of practice so valued in western culture, it has to be recognised that legitimate 'practice' often involves activities very close to the formalisms of traditional schooling. The authentic practitioner who is, say, an accountant, a technician, a manager or a psychologist has to engage in activities that closely resemble those of deliberately planned learning. Documents are read, positions synthesised, calculations performed, and the expositions of experienced colleagues attended to, summarised and revisited. What is distinctive about the *schooled* experience of such activities is that they are intensively concentrated and, perhaps, too rarely linked to any natural motives of the learners. Yet in both traditional formal education and authentic communities of practice, we witness the same forms of intentional intellectual engagement: forms of activity people arrange to promote their own learning.

The types of activities being discussed – practices of deliberate study – are often demanding. They require us to relinquish our availability to the improvised flow of social life and make a commitment to what may be focused and socially insulated states of engagement. They will often involve struggle with representational formats that have been designed to optimise the summary and organisation of conceptual material (maps, diagrams, symbol systems, texts). Such 'struggle' perhaps involves disciplined private dialogues with this material, as it is interrogated for meaning. The challenging question is how we motivate and sustain such commitments – made in the interests of concentrating learning. One answer again invokes communities of practice, suggesting that we manage this by ensuring legitimate and relevant *purposes* for such activity. The problems served by it must be problems we want or need to solve. For learning practitioners this comes more easily, as study is bound into their identity as defined by the type of practice they have chosen to cultivate. For learners in education with perhaps a variety of parallel disciplinary obligations, it is more difficult to create convincing motives of that kind. Creating a stronger sense of 'community' within institutionalised learning is one route (and one that is usually underdeveloped). Otherwise, the challenge of motivating study is met by thoughtful design of the learning *environment*: creating a fertile ecology for sustaining that learning.

This analysis merely mirrors our undergraduate interviewees' comments (above). In part, they found the virtual university unattractive because it would deny them an organisation or design that was important to motivating their engagement as learners. If cut free from the familiar structuring of institutional education, many current students seriously doubted their capacity to manage the distractions of their extracurricular lives and balance this with the demands of study. Yet in one way I have tried to go beyond what traditional undergraduates have already warned us about: I have suggested that the demands of 'doing learning' are unlikely to be comprehensively dealt with by cultivating within educational settings communities of practice, even though this surely remains a worthwhile ambition. It is arguable how convincingly attempts to cultivate communities of practice can be undertaken where the breadth of the syllabus demands membership of multiple and parallel disciplinary communities. There are also limits arising from our ambitions in formal education to force an exposure to disciplinary tools that is particularly intense and concentrated. Finally, practitioners outside of school, in their authentic communities, will often themselves have to wrestle with demands of doing deliberate learning. Formal education offers experience in the personal management of such demands.

A declared concern of this chapter was to address possible difficulties associated with virtual learning methods as they might be applied to the principal constituency of students now in higher education. I have raised issues concerning how bricks-and-mortar institutions distinctively sustain the demanding activities of deliberate learning. However, in the final section, I address this issue of virtualisation more directly. The point will be to relate the problems discussed – of sustaining deliberate study – to structural features of virtual education.

Virtual disturbances to the cultural practice of learning

I have argued that formal learning is usefully recognised as a species of cultural practice; namely, learning comprises a set of cognitive activities involving distinctive coordinations with cultural resources. Such resources have evolved across a history in which prior human activity has fashioned them into their current form. This embedding in history gives the activities their status as 'cultural'. Naturally, formal learning must involve engagement with disciplinary material, but that engagement is structured by the formats and rituals of the institutional experience: expositions, texts, annotations, discourse genres, roles, social relations, and so on. Although the virtualisation agenda may share many of the ambitions of conventional education, it does promise to unpick much of the detail in a structure defining the cultural practice of learning. In some respects, we may welcome some redesign of this activity, yet, in others, we may be apprehensive. We may be concerned because it appears unlikely that individuals who are well encultured in the present system of learning practice will be able to adapt easily. Those who view learning as an abstract cognitive activity (perhaps a 'skill') that exists free from a cultural context may be more optimistic about unpicking the structure.

To illustrate (rather than analyse) the issue of virtual disturbance, I take three examples where virtualisation of higher educational practice is involved in order to note entrenched enculturation in the existing system that can thereby be revealed. One example is centred on the tutor, one on the peer and one on solitary study.

A consequence of virtualisation seems to be a much less prominent role for the teacher. One enthusiast for these developments asserts: 'Kids simply learn best when they teach themselves and each other . . . teachers have to stop teaching and get out of the way of student work; they have to stop thinking they're conveying information and, instead, focus on strategies to help students learn' (Twigg 1995). This rhetoric of 'learning autonomy' is seductive, as is the idea that such autonomy will be readily found outside of the institutional structure. Some commentators expect to find it is through the supplementary training that may be applied to learning-as-skill: 'Students will have to be taught how to manage their own learning processes to an unprecedented degree' (MacFarlane 1998: 83). However, it is also expected that, whatever processes of dialogue orchestrate students' present approach to learning materials (practices of selecting, monitoring, pacing, giving feedback, etc.), this would be designed into the presentational format of the new electronic materials. One public report on the future of ICT in higher education comments: 'self instructional materials are designed not only to present information, but also to encourage an active approach to learning through question "boxes" and built-in activities' (Committee of Scottish University Principals 1992: 8–9). Educational developers are confident about the opportunity here, and thus propose radical challenges to the status quo:

> Online self-learning packages fundamentally question the traditional role of the educator by giving students greater individual control. Effective learning can be realized by providing a student with a computer, loading the educational software and walking away.
>
> (Gell and Cochrane 1996: 252)

As it happens, this example returns us to a topic raised at the start of this chapter – namely, learning styles. In an effort to turn surface learners into deep learners, some researchers developed independent learning materials that did contain 'question boxes' and so on – in the hope of guiding surface learners into asking the same questions of themselves as would deep learners. As Ramsden (1987) noted, this often had the opposite effect to the one intended: the focus for study often narrowed to a preoccupation with answering these questions (a 'technification of the task'). This is not to challenge the enterprise of trying to design materials with a more effective dialogic quality. However, it does remind us that the management of, say, independent reading is, at present, much more subtly tied into an institutional structure (particularly involving tutors) than we acknowledge.

My second example concerns peers. In contemporary educational thinking, fellow students are significant for the role they play in furnishing chances for discourse and intellectual experimentation; openings for challenge and encouragement. On reviewing years of research, Astin (1993: 398) concluded that, for US college students, peers are 'the single most potent source of influence'; thus it is natural that virtual universities will endeavour to provide arenas of peer communication in what is otherwise a socially distributed constituency. Current solutions to this are dominated by asynchronous text conferencing. The success stories associated with this technology tend to be concentrated within non-traditional undergraduate populations, since the technology is less obviously attractive to mainstream undergraduates (Light *et al.* 2000). Perhaps future communication media will be more successful. The point is not to rule this out, but problems in re-mediating such communication do remind us of the fragile nature of existing practices and alert us against making too many strong assumptions about the ease with which important educational experiences will be reproduced electronically.

Our interviewed traditional students (above) were again informative. They reinforced the suspicion (cf. Crook 2000) that peer support did not typically occur as conversations in organised out-of-class gatherings, because students rarely convened in this way. However, what did occur was a persistent practice of short and serendipitous exchanges as students moved about the campus. These fleeting conversations often enabled students to evaluate how a course was developing; or they allowed the sharing of gripes; or they helped with the search for reassurance and benchmarks on personal progress. In a more abstract sense, such improvised campus exchanges also seemed to create a feeling of corporate activity which imparted a significant motivational dimension to the task of sustaining study. Given this pattern of communication in the background, it is not surprising that mainstream undergraduates make very little use of e-mail discussion boards but prefer quick and occasional e-mail exchanges or instant messaging (Crook 2001).

Finally, we consider the example of private, solitary study. Here there is a promise that:

> Technology can transform an individual's learning environment by presenting richly structured information to aid the assimilation, by providing highly-structured instantiated knowledge for easy and flexible interactive access, and by generating highly interactive simulations for experiential learning.
>
> (MacFarlane 1998: 83)

The liberational flavour of this promise surely arises from the hint that such rich material must be *inherently* attractive. It promises to cope with a problem I have identified above; namely, that intentional learning is often felt as demanding. Moreover, sustained private study (perhaps directed at material not of immediate interest) is one of the most demanding of activities. To cope with this, cultural practices of learning have evolved to optimise the circumstances for such activity: spaces, materials, schedules and various sorts of human support have been designed to nurture such focused private study effectively.

The implicit promise of MacFarlane and others is that the paraphernalia of electronic learning will release the student from the necessity of this institutional framework, yet we must not underestimate what such ambitions entail.

Observations of residential undergraduates making use of such rich ICT facilities suggest why this may be problematic. In a study of students' computer use in networked study bedrooms, we found that the interactive versatility of this technology created distractions as well as academic opportunities (Crook and Barrowcliff 2001). The context for studying occupied by these students is very much a transition point on a virtualisation path. Students continue to enjoy a structure (e.g. deadlines, private living space, full-time study) that supports independent learning; ICT facilities are merely superimposed upon this structure. However, the intrusion of such facilities reveals a delicate balance that has to be managed between the practices of formal learning and the rest of people's lives. In this case, ICT could possibly empower study and shift the balance of commitments towards investment in study. However, this single technology (the powerful PC networked to local and global resources) services both playful and learning motives. The interface between school and play is blurred at a single site for action. Our records of how students used the technology revealed a highly animated style of engagement, whereby activity frequently occurred between different multi-tasking applications: word processors, media players, e-mail, instant messaging, news tickers, games, and so on. In the end, these students spent no more time on private study than do their matched peers in study bedrooms with no PCs. Indeed, over half expressed real concern that they spent too much time on recreational computer use (Crook 2001).

Concluding remarks

Learning is pervasive to human experience: dramatic achievements observable in the early years of life alert us to this fact. Uniquely among species, however, *teaching* is also central to our nature. Those dramatic achievements of the early years do involve teaching, although the term is not commonly used to describe the participative coordinations that parents and others arrange for us. Beyond the early years, our culture offers ways of living that invite expertise or knowledge exceeding what may usually be provided in the arenas of informal learning. Formal education is designed to focus and accelerate experiences supporting the demands and values of that society into which the novice or learner is developing. An important question then becomes: how far should the methods of formal education echo experiences typical of informal learning? Schank and Cleary express such aspirations by quoting the novelist Walker Percy:

> A young Falkland Islander walking along a beach and spying a dead dogfish and going to work on it with his jackknife has, in a fashion wholly unprovided for in modern educational theory, a great advantage over the Scarsdale high school pupil who finds the dogfish on his laboratory desk.
>
> (Schank and Cleary 1995)

This certainly identifies a tension inherent in educational practice. We do expect the high school pupil to have a different quality of engagement to that of the Falkland Islander. There is much that could be done within formal education to regain some of the difference: the motive of spontaneous curiosity, and the goals of using and communicating discovery in an authentic manner. However, the high school pupil is challenged to achieve more than the skills of jackknife dissection and more than a working recognition of anatomical structures. Using these opportunities, the pupil must encounter material of a more cultural nature – diagrams, calculations, genres of description, and so on – all of which require the superimposition of other tasks at the 'laboratory desk' beyond the pupil's actions with a knife (record-keeping, certain sorts of controlled investigation, and so on). The persistent problem for educational design is to create a balance to learner experience. The balance concerns, on the one hand, imparting to students a sense of (disciplinary) identity and purpose (such as might be captured in a community of practice) and, on the other hand, designing materials, spaces and social relations that give students experience in managing the demands of deliberate and often de-contextualised learning.

The embedding of student activities in a structure of institutionalised design helps define learning as an expression of cultural practice, although exactly what form it takes may vary across the many cultural settings that support schooling. However, as participants in such a structure, people develop and change. One way they develop is to be more firmly encultured into the relevant practices, and thereby more autonomous (and more comfortable) in 'managing' the underlying cognitive engagements. Thus we might expect the effect of cutting learning loose from a bricks-and-mortar context would have different consequences for different students – according to their own cultural histories of experience. The older and continuing student does not confront learning opportunities in the same way as the school leaver. My argument here is fairly parochial: namely, that we must be wary of thinking that this de-schooling will be straightforward for the particular constituency of school-leaving undergraduates who make up the current population of higher education. Looking at virtualisation in progress can reveal some of these dependencies and their precarious nature. Then, if we are cautious and reflective in going about this re-mediation, there is every hope that new technology may be mobilised to further optimise the balances I am discussing here, rather than unhelpfully disturbing them.

References

Astin, A.W. (1993) *What Matters in College?* San Francisco, CA: Jossey-Bass.

Brown, J.S., Collins, A. and Duguid, P. (1989) Situated cognition and the culture of learning, *Educational Researcher*, 18: 32–42.

Cognition and Technology Group at Vanderbilt (1990) Anchored instruction and its relationship to situated cognition, *Educational Researcher*, 19: 2–10.

Committee of Scottish University Principals (1992) *Teaching and Learning in an Expanded Higher Education System*. Edinburgh: SCFC.

Crook, C.K. (2000) Motivation and the ecology of collaborative learning, in R. Joiner,

K. Littleton, D. Faulkner and D. Miell (eds) *Rethinking Collaborative Learning*. London: Free Association Press.

Crook, C.K. (2001) The campus experience of networked learning, in C. Steeples and C. Jones (eds) *Networked Learning: Perspectives and Issues*. London: Springer, 293–308.

Crook, C.K. and Barrowcliff, D. (2001) Ubiquitous computing on campus: patterns of engagement by university students, *International Journal of Human–Computer Interaction*, 13(2): 245–58.

Dunn, J. (1988) *The Beginnings of Social Understanding*. Oxford: Blackwell.

Entwistle, N. and Ramsden, P (1983) *Understanding Student Learning*. London: Croom Helm.

Gaver, W. (1996) Situating action II: affordances for interaction: the social is material for design. *Ecological Psychology*, 8: 111–30.

Gell, M. and Cochrane, P. (1996) Learning and education in an information society, in W. Dutton (ed.) *Information and Communication Technologies*. Oxford: Oxford University Press.

Hara, N. and Kling, R. (2000) Students distress with a web-based distance education course, *Information, Communication and Society*, 3.

Illich, I. (1973) *Deschooling Society*. Harmondsworth: Penguin.

Light, P., Nesbitt, E., Light, V. and White, S. (2000) Variety is the spice of life: student use of CMC in the context of campus based study, *Computers and Education*, 34: 257–67.

MacFarlane, A. (1998) Information, knowledge and learning, *Higher Education Quarterly*, 52: 77–92.

Marton, F. and Saljo, R. (1976) On qualitative differences in learning: I. Outcome and process, *British Journal of Educational Psychology*, 46: 4–11.

Piaget, J. (1953) *The Origins of Intelligence*. London: Routledge & Kegan Paul.

Premack, D. and Premack, J. (1996) Why animals lack pedagogy and some cultures have more of it than others, in D. Olson and N. Torrance (eds.) *The Handbook of Education and Human Development*. Oxford: Blackwell.

Ramsden, P. (1987) Improving teaching and learning in higher education: the case for a relational perspective, *Studies in Higher Education*, 12: 275–86.

Schaffer, H.R. (1992) Joint involvement episodes as context for development, in H. McGurk (ed.) *Childhood Social Development: Contemporary Perspectives*. Hove: Lawrence Earlbaum.

Schank, R.C. and Cleary, C. (1995) *Engines for Education*. Hillsdale, NJ: Lawrence Erlbaum.

Schlosser, C. and Anderson M. (1994) *Distance Education: Review of the Literature*. Washington, DC: Association for Educational Communications and Technology.

Sfard, A. (1998) On two metaphors for learning and the dangers of choosing just one, *Educational Researcher*, 27: 4–13.

Tharp, R.G. and Gallimore, R. (1988) A theory of teaching as assisted performance, in R. Tharp and R. Gallimore (eds) *Rousing Minds to Life*. Cambridge: Cambridge University Press.

Twigg, C. (1995) The future of technology in education, *Multimedia Today*, 3: 10–21.

Wernick, A. (1991) *Promotional Culture*. London: Sage.

Chapter 10

The university campus as a 'resourceful constraint'

Process and practice in the construction of the virtual university

James Cornford and Neil Pollock

The way forward is not to look ahead, but to look around.

(Brown and Duguid 2000: 8)

Introduction

It may appear strange to devote an entire chapter of a book on distributed learning to the subject of the university campus. Surely, one might suggest, the whole point of distributed learning – its appeal to students, its very rationale – is to extend learning opportunities beyond the confines of, perhaps even to transcend, the university campus. Furthermore, one might argue, the Open University (and many similar institutions around the world) has proved that higher education can do without the encumbrance of the campus, since communication between staff, students and administrators may be undertaken by telephone, post and e-mail.

Yet look closer and the campus refuses to disappear. The OU has both a significant campus of its own in Milton Keynes for staff, researchers and postgraduate students – what we might regard as 'the campus as back office' – and makes extensive use of the facilities of other universities for its summer schools. In this chapter, we explore the role of the campus in distance education. We show how the campus – or, more generally, the co-location of learners, teachers, labs, class-rooms, lecture theatres, libraries, and so on – refuses to lie down and die. More specifically, we want to show some of the subtle and powerful, if often taken-for-granted, ways in which the campus *works* to support higher education. This is not to say that a campus is necessary to effective education or that distributed education is in some sense inferior to a campus-based educational experience. They are simply different. What is important, however, is that those seeking to develop distributed education should understand the support a campus setting gives the education process and should be prepared for the necessity to find new ways of providing that support in a distributed education context.

The virtual university and the campus-as-constraint

Around the world, both new and existing higher educational institutions are seeking to harness the capacities of information and communications technologies (ICTs) to build 'virtual universities'. This signifies a seeming diminution in the importance of the traditional campus-based university since degree courses are increasingly being delivered and assessed over the Internet. Although the specific features of the various projects underway may vary widely, they share a core vision, a notion of distributed learning in which geographical distance is fetishised as that-which-is-to-be-overcome, a constraint that we may (now) transcend. Tom Abeles, for instance, is one of many authors who sees in ICTs the promise of freeing knowledge from the confines of the campus:

> knowledge, which was once captured in the cloistered halls and libraries of academia, in a wired world, is immediately made available. Similarly students who once travelled great distances to listen to lectures of scholars, can now access this knowledge via the world of the internet.
>
> (Abeles 1998: 606)

Here we have a description of the virtual university in terms of a disruption of the traditional understanding of how knowledge is positioned in space and time: knowledge once contained within the physical and temporal constraints of the university campus is now, as a result of the Internet, available anywhere and at any time.

Taking a slightly different perspective, consider the following summary of the virtual university from an Australian government report:

> Picture a future in which students never meet a lecturer face to face in a class room, never physically visit the on-campus library; in fact, never set foot on the campus or into an institutional lecture-room or learning centre. Such is the future proposed by the virtual university scenario.
>
> (Cunningham *et al.* 1998: 179)

Here the defining feature is principally an absence. The essence of the virtual university is thus how it presents a future characterised by the *lack* of physical co-presence ('never meet . . . never physically visit . . . never set foot on'). With the need for co-presence removed, it is often argued, so too is the need for the specialist site of co-presence, the conventional university campus with its class-rooms, library, lecture rooms and learning centres.

In the virtual university scenario there is still, of course, a kind of coming together of students, teachers and texts, but it is a 'virtual' coming together, mediated by modern digital communications networks rather than one facilitated by the concrete physical presence of the campus. With no face-to-face meetings and no need to access physical resources such as books, the physical context for such coming together of things and bodies becomes redundant. From the perspective of this vision of the virtual university, then, the conventional campus is seen as, at best, an anachronism, and at worst a constraint on the reach of the institution and a drain on its resources. The dominant spatial form of higher education as we have known it since the Middle Ages is transcended.

University-level or 'higher' education has seen a gradual geographical extension since its origins in Bologna and Paris in the Middle Ages. As it has become more widespread (or even perhaps distributed?), it has undergone several transformations (e.g. secularisation, extension of the curriculum beyond the liberal arts and professions to take in the sciences and technology, the incorporation of research as a core university mission, the admission of women). Most dramatically, perhaps, there has been the expansion in the number of institutions that call themselves 'universities' and, more recently, in the proportion of the population that, in the richer countries at least, will experience a 'university education' at some point in their lives. Through these many changes, both revolutionary and evolutionary, the dominant spatial form of the university – the campus – has been if not unchanging, a relative constant. Throughout its history, most people with a university education have 'gone to' a university and they have gone to it with others.

Let us be clear: there have certainly been institutions which have successfully laid claim to the title of 'university' and which have not relied, or not relied totally, on the traditional campus (the Open University to name but one), and we are well aware of the significant differences between campuses – in the UK, for example, from the collegiate sprawl of Oxford or Cambridge, through the compact city-centre redbricks of a Leeds, Sheffield or Manchester, to the secluded edge-of-city campuses of the 1960s such as Lancaster or Sussex. There are even 'multi-campus' universities (such as London or California). Nevertheless, all these manifestations still call themselves, and are recognised as, university campuses.

The virtual university vision of distributed higher education still has a spatial form, of course – the irreducibly physical components of the educational experience, the students and some form of shelter for them, the technologies required to display texts and images, the networks of wires, fibres and switches that connect them, still have to exist in some definite space (although they may be increasingly mobile). What is significant, however, is that these various elements are seen as being widely *distributed* in space, tied together by information technology. These elements cannot be quite anywhere – there are enough inequalities in the quality and costs of the necessary network infrastructures to ensure that, for much of the world population and in many places, this scenario is unfeasible. But for a large, and growing, portion of the world's population, there are no substantial *technical* barriers to such a vision.

However, let us examine this scenario more closely. To be able to distribute the elements of learning in this way requires the coordinating and communicating power of digital network technologies to enable texts, sounds and images – in short, information – to be communicated and shared in a timely fashion. The reliance on these technologies, and the kinds of information they handle, promotes a strong notion of the learning experience in terms of 'information', its creation or assembly, storage, transmission, sharing and processing. Higher education comes to be seen almost exclusively in terms of *information* (Pollock 2000).

The modern(ist) concept of information that lies at the heart of the vision of a virtual university carries with it an implicit (anti)geography. Theodore Porter, for example, writing on the role of information in social organisation, has highlighted the close link between information as a social category and questions of space and scale:

> the creation and use of information needs to be understood first of all as a problem of space and of scale, of getting beyond what is local, personal or intimate and creating knowledge that is, so far as possible, neutral and well standardized ... knowledge detached from the skills and close acquaintanceships that flourish in local sites.
>
> (Porter 1994: 217, 229)

'The ideal,' he suggests, 'is to go beyond perspective, to turn a view from somewhere into a "view from nowhere"' (ibid.). Note how closely this 'view from nowhere' mirrors the promise ICTs hold for the university of permitting an escape from ('getting beyond') the confines of the campus ('local sites') and entry into a global higher education market – the possibility of being present everywhere. However, Porter also contrasts 'a world of information', understood as 'a world of standardized objects and neutralized subjects', with a 'local site where skill and intimate familiarity with people and things provide the most promising route to success' (Porter 1994: 221; cf. Boden and Molotch 1994).

This contrast between an informational view of higher education, characteristic of the virtual university discourse, and other areas of knowledge more rooted in place, echoes many critiques of the virtual university. For example, Newman and Johnson identify the virtual university as being based on a 'naive sociology' that 'ignores the role of apprenticeship and implicit craft knowledge in the generation of technical progress and scientific discovery' (Newman and Johnson 1999: 80), the role of face-to-face interaction and group socialisation. Other writers reinforce these latter points, building on notions of 'the hidden curriculum' and the notion of a university education as being a 'rite of passage'. Krishan Kumar, for example, argues that:

> Nowhere else, and at no other time in their lives, irrespective of age, will students encounter each other with so much time and so many resources to do so much, unconstrained by the requirements of job or family. The university is indeed a *place*, a physical space with buildings and grounds that exist to facilitate the pursuits of students and teachers.
>
> (Kumar 1997: 32, emphasis in original)

The informational view of the university, then, has not gone unchallenged; the significance of place and co-presence for the wider higher educational experience has been asserted. In the next section, however, we delve deeper into how the campus, as the place of higher education *par excellence*, reasserts itself without recourse to these wider arguments. To do this, we need an analytical framework within which to view the process of development of distance education.

Creating distance education as the assemblage of actor networks

How can we think about distributed education in a new way? Here we attempt to borrow the notion of actor networks as one way of doing this. Actor network thinking has arisen primarily in the field of science and technology studies and is associated with the work of, among others, Bruno Latour (1987) and Michel Callon (1986) in France, and John Law (1994) and Steve Woolgar (1988) in Britain. Through studies of the construction of scientific knowledge and technological artefacts, actor network accounts have taught us to recognise more of the real work involved in the process of building 'facts', or the production of technological systems. Traditionally, we have understood the invention and diffusion of important and transformational scientific theories and technologies (e.g. the process of pasteurisation, the invention of the electric light or the telegraph) in narrow and simplistic terms. The result has been that the history of science and technology has been told in a certain way, often from the viewpoint of certain heroic human actors.

More recent work, however, has sought to challenge this view, seeing science and technology as a matter of 'network' or 'system' building, where various elements are brought together or 'enrolled' into an assemblage capable of 'acting as one' (see e.g. Bruno Latour's analysis of Pasteur in *The Pasteurization of France* (1988), or Thomas Hughes' description of Edison in *Networks of Power* (1983)). What the metaphor of the network allows is the foregrounding of all the work, processes, objects and actors that are essential in understanding how entities such as the campus endure but which typically remain invisible in conventional retrospective accounts.

Many conceptualisations of the virtual university are based on an implicit analysis of education as an informational process concerned with the movement of information from one place to another. This point of view is well illustrated by the widespread use of terms such as 'course delivery'. Using concepts from actor network theory, we attempt to move away from this narrow informational view of learning and theorise these attempts to build distance education as a form of 'heterogeneous engineering' (Law 1994) – the binding together of various elements (typically people, texts, objects and machines), all of which may be regarded, in different ways, as actors – entities that can act (or fail to act) to support the network as a whole. From this wider point of view, we turn our attention to the role of the campus – itself a complex assemblage of objects, people, texts and machines, brought within spatial scale of everyday life and coordinated in time – in higher education.

To exemplify what is meant here, we might start with Edward Thompson's (1980) classic book, *Writing by Candlelight*. Writing at the time of a miners' strike in the UK, Thompson describes how when we throw a switch to turn on an electric light we do not generally think about the work of those who laboured to dig out the coal, or pump the oil or gas – labour that is necessary to make the connection between throwing the switch and the light coming on actually work. From an actor network perspective, however, we would highlight not only the labouring bodies of the workers but also the huge network of wires, switches, fuses, transformers, power-stations, gas and oil-drilling rigs, tankers and lorries; the shadow control networks and monitoring systems; the customer billing systems and international commodity exchanges; the regulatory texts and bodies that control standards and prices; the huge volumes of technical and financial documentation necessary to run these systems; and finally, the disciplined consumers who both 'plug in' and pay for the benefits of doing so.

Of course, this huge network will only become visible to most when some part of it breaks down (i.e. when throwing the switch fails to turn on the light). In Thompson's example, the cause of the breakdown was the withdrawal of labour by the miners. However, from an actor network perspective, not only people, but any of the elements in the network might cause the breakdown – a blown fuse or light bulb, a power line that has blown down in a gale, and so on. In short, all these elements have to *work* together for the light to respond to the switch. Even though what it means to work is very different for a miner, a wire and a light bulb, they can all be seen as performing, or not performing, their role in the context of the network as a whole. In other words, no one element (human or non-human) is assumed, a priori, to be more important than any other; they all, methodologically at least, have equal status.

What is valuable for us about this perspective is that it enables us to move away from an analysis of learning solely in terms of its informational *content*, and thus to introduce a concern for the real effects the *forms* which that content takes have. Finally, it also enables us to rethink what a campus is, to extend the notion of the campus from an exclusive focus on the everyday time–space convergence of human actors and to treat seriously the physical nature of the campus, its buildings, labs, library, classrooms, quadrangles, halls of residence, and so on, and to acknowledge the work they perform (or fail to perform).

How does all of this relate to questions of distance education and the role of the campus in distance education? First, we can describe the construction of distance education courses in terms of the construction of an actor network – the painstaking piecing together of people (lecturers, authors, technicians, librarians, graphic artists, publishers, assessment experts, administrators, students, etc.), machines and other physical items (computers, telecommunications networks, offices, etc.), texts (textbooks, course lists, examination papers and assessment forms, etc.) and, of course, money (budgets, accounts, direct debits, etc.). Second, the virtual university aims to transcend the constraints of the campus. But, we ask, to what extent is the campus a constraint? If you want to know the role of the campus in the existing actor networks of the university, imagine the extra work necessary if that entity was not present. Once we begin to embrace the complexity of the actor network approach, we might think of the campus as other than a constraint, perhaps even as a resource.

The campus as a resourceful constraint

To work towards a better understanding, we step back from the notion of the actor network for a moment and draw on Etienne Wenger and Jean Lave's notion of a 'community of practice' (Wenger 1998) and contrast this with what we feel is the dominant process-oriented or flow-oriented view of distributed learning.

The current explosion of interest in, and experimentation with, distributed learning has occurred in a wider context strongly shaped by process-oriented views of socio-technical systems. The paradigmatic version of this view is the popular management notion of business process engineering (BPR). From a BPR perspective, an organisation may be broken down into, and is understood in terms of, its core value-adding processes. The aim of the organisation should be to make these processes as lean and efficient as possible. The stress in BPR, then, is on the *flow* of work, activities and documents through the organisation. Re-engineering is focused on making these pathways *through* the organisation as smooth and speedy as possible. The application of ICTs to the task of simplifying and speeding up these 'document flows', 'workflows' or 'act flows' has become a central component of the 're-engineering revolution' that has, in turn, shaped the thinking and practices of technology design companies (for a more general critique of BPR, see Knights and Willmott 2000).

In practice, then, the stress in BPR is on converting the outputs of one process quickly and effectively into the inputs for the next process. Far less attention, however, is given to how work is actually undertaken within each process, and workers are seen primarily in the context of the chain of processes in which they are involved, a 'longitudinal' view.

Wenger and Lave's notion of a community of practice stands in stark contrast to this process-oriented view. For Wenger, the process-oriented view, which sees the worker only in the context of the linkages running longitudinally through the organisation, misses out on important lateral relationships. In Wenger's classic study of clerks handling medical insurance claims forms, the managers of the insurance company saw the work of the clerks almost exclusively in terms of their insertion within the longitudinal business process. Their work and reward structures were constructed in terms of how effectively they processed the constant flow of medical claims forms that flowed into and out of the office (did they meet 'production'). Wenger's ethnographic research with these claims processors, by contrast, revealed the extent to which their work was supported and facilitated by 'lateral' interaction among the claims processors, interaction that was all but invisible to the managers. Jointly, the claims processors had developed a body of knowledge that enabled them to process the forms, drawing on shared knowledge, heuristics and precedents. Wenger goes on to theorise this lateral interaction in terms of the notion of a 'community of practice' (see Wenger 1998).

John Seely Brown and Paul Duguid's (2000) work has usefully developed Wenger's insight and helps us to challenge the view of the campus as *just* a constraint. This notion, we suggest, relies on a specific and partial perspective on (higher) education that privileges the kind of longitudinal-, process- or information-oriented understanding of universities, and fails to acknowledge adequately the importance of lateral linkages between individuals engaged in the same (kind of) task.

Brown and Duguid provide a useful example, drawn from the Xerox Corporation (for whom Brown works) of Xerox copier machine repair engineers. Xerox's management understood the work process of these engineers as being essentially concerned with the interpretation of the error messages produced by machines, the interrogation of technical manuals concerning each particular type of photocopier and the application of the recommended solution. The engineers were seen by management as primarily working in the context of these flows of information, each independently linked to the company's knowledge base via the (centrally determined) error messages and the (centrally produced) technical manuals. The view of the engineers' work was in the context of the officially prescribed *process*.

Following an ethnographic study of the engineers in one US city, it became apparent that this was far from the case. In *practice*, the engineers were meeting for breakfast before starting work, and swapping a vast store of practical knowledge about fixing photocopiers. In addition, particular engineers became acknowledged experts and were called upon by other engineers to help fix particularly difficult problems. Thus, far beyond the individualised relationship between the engineer and the corporation, mediated via the standardised error messages and technical manuals, there was an elaborate and continually reconstructed knowledge pool built up by the engineers and on which they all freely drew to get the job done. Only by closely examining the actual *practice* of the engineers was this knowledge pool revealed.

While Brown and Duguid's work is essentially concerned with these human or social linkages, by drawing on the points from actor network theory made above, we are able to extend this perspective to incorporate not only the lateral *social* networks – that is, networks of human beings – involved in learning but also to extend that concept of networks to incorporate other 'actors' (in the actor network sense) – buildings, spaces, texts, machines and objects – that act to facilitate and support the learning process. From this perspective, the role the campus undertakes for the university, the subtle ways whereby it supports the processes of learning and research, become apparent and its 'submerged resourcefulness' (Brown and Duguid 2000: 244) is revealed. We illustrate the argument drawing on fieldwork in a number of established UK universities.

The return of the repressed: the campus bites back

As a first example, we take the creation of an online course, based on an existing course taught in the conventional manner at one of the universities we have studied. The aim of the course development team is to provide a course that may be taken by students in other parts of the world, accessing materials and tutors via the web, e-mail and real-time conferencing. One of the many issues that arises during the process of course construction concerns the assessment and accreditation of the students. In the conventional mode of delivery of this course, students are assessed by an 'unseen', sit-down examination, undertaken simultaneously with other students in a large examination hall. This all appears natural and problem-free in the context of the university campus. The course team is keen to make as few changes in the course as possible, in part to save time and in part because substantial changes would require the course to be 're-validated', a difficult and time-consuming procedure.

In the distributed mode, however, problems arise. How are the students to be assessed? There is, of course, no problem in transferring the examination paper to the web, thus providing access to the students. This transfer can be delayed until a given moment so that the paper remains 'unseen' (although this raises problems for students in different parts of the world – is it fair if some students take the examination in the afternoon while others take it in the middle of the night?). More problematic, but still technically possible, the students' examination answers can be e-mailed or electronically transferred back to the tutors for marking (although time delays in the transfer of materials over the web or by e-mail mean that it is less easy to ensure that all students enjoy the same time to complete the examination). A further difficulty arises when the notion of the identity of the student emerges – how does the course team know that the student's responses are really those of the student and not of someone else? How can the team control for 'real-time plagiarism' in which a student copies model answers posted on the web? In the campus situation, there is relatively little direct checking of the student's identity in the examination hall; indeed, the staff undertaking the exam invigilation may not even be from the same faculty as the student. In practice, there is little to stop a student paying someone to sit their exam for them. Nevertheless, the physical co-location with other students from the course provides enough of an ordinary everyday level of surveillance to effectively discourage such behaviour. In the distributed scenario, without such peer surveillance, the course team is concerned that plagiarism or forms of 'cheating' based on impersonation will be unconstrained.

How can the checks on plagiarism and impersonation which the campus situation so elegantly and discreetly provides be replicated in cyberspace? The discussion takes several directions. One set of possibilities explored is essentially reliant on using more technology to plug the gap. Increasingly baroque potential technologies are invoked. Various forms of identification and authentication may be used from simple passwords to, at least in theory, biometrics (technologies for recognising unique biological features such as fingerprints and the iris patterns in the eye). All these add to the potential cost and complexity of the course, without essentially solving the problem. An alternative solution is to re-create the examination environment nearer the students. The university in question is working with a number of partner institutions in the countries where the course is to be marketed and these institutions could provide the examination halls and invigilation. Here the campus, as a physical setting for co-location of the examination candidates at least, has been re-created, but on a distributed basis. Again, the costs and complexity of the course look set to balloon as the team contemplates the task of booking examination space, distributing examination papers and ensuring that all students on this distributed course are able to travel to a suitable partner institution. Again, if the students have not been in contact before the examination, the peer surveillance that works so effectively in the residential campus setting cannot be relied on.

The final option, and the one eventually pursued, is to change the mode of assessment for the course. This, too, is time-consuming, given that the course may well need re-validation. Of course, there are many strong arguments for abandoning traditional 3-hour, unseen examinations sat in a large exam hall – and many were rehearsed above. However, these arguments are made *after* the decision to change the mode of assessment has been taken. While the shift to a distributed mode for the course certainly does open up some new possibilities, it is also important to note how it closes down other options – specifically, the traditional unseen 3-hour examination. What is being revealed here is how the campus, understood as the co-location of the students and staff in time and space, quietly and unobtrusively facilitates a particular form of assessment. With the shift to a distributed mode, this form of assessment, although still possible, become far more technically complex and costly.

A second example, drawn from another university, shows a further feature of how the campus works to underpin learning. In the previous example, the physical nature of the campus was invoked simply as a suitable 'container' for students to sit the exam together, and thus for lateral linkages (peer surveillance) between human beings. In this example, we show how the physical fabric of the campus can play a more active part in the lateral linkages that underpin higher education.

A course team is developing an online module taught entirely over the World Wide Web. The course is intended both for on-campus students and, given the entirely web-based mode of delivery, for distance learners who are expected to pay. All that is required to access the course materials on the web is the correct uniform resource locator (URL) and a user name and password. Technically, this is simply a matter of providing this information by means of an e-mail or a letter; yet at this point the course developers begin to get nervous. How, they ask themselves, will distance learners feel about receiving a few simple lines of text in return for their substantial fees? Will the on-campus students undervalue a course that is so virtual? Does a simple letter or e-mail containing the URL, user name and password adequately symbolise the course, the work that has gone into its creation and the status of the institution offering the course? The team decides that an e-mail or letter is not enough. The problem is, it seems, that the course is *too* virtual. The task is therefore to make it more concrete.

In subsequent discussions, the team attempts to create a more concrete manifestation of the course, a token that it is felt adequately symbolises the standing of the course and will, it is hoped, be seen as fair exchange for the fees handed over by the proposed distance learners. Instead of a letter or e-mail, the team decides that the password and URL should be accessed from a floppy disk, a more concrete object which the intended students will receive in return for their fees. Over the weeks, a significant amount of time is spent in discussion within the team and with a graphic designer on what this disk should look like, the design of the label, the packaging for the disk, even how the packaging should be sealed. Elements of the packaging, such as the positioning and prominence of the university logo, are extensively discussed.

Much of this considerable volume of effort was undertaken for the benefit of the distance learners, while less concern was shown for the on-campus students. For them, the weight of the institution was literally concretised in the form of the campus buildings, and the bustle of staff and students within and around them. For them, the university was understood to be self-evidently there, although similar concerns about the extent to which they might undervalue the work that had gone into the development of the course meant that, for them too, the course packaging was used. For the distance learners, not only the work of course production but also the institution itself had to be symbolised with a disk, labels, paper and logos. Unable to rely on the sheer physical presence of the campus to symbolise the university to the distance learners, elaborate substitutes had to be constructed.

Conclusion

Why did the distance learning course developers so often encounter the kinds of situations described above? Using these two examples, we have attempted to show some of the work that the campus performs in conventional education – the role of mutual surveillance and the symbolic role of the campus – and to outline the additional work undertaken to replace these functions in the move to effective distributed education.

What we wish to draw out from the work of Wenger and of Brown and Duguid is this focus on the lateral interactions. In many of the examples of development of distributed education that we studied, the developers initially focused strongly on the process perspective, the (computer- and internet-supported) flow of documents, and interaction and work between teacher and learner. Much less thought was given to the possibility of lateral relationships between learners (or, indeed, between teachers). It is, we believe, primarily this kind of lateral relationship that the campus acts to support. For example, the mutual peer surveillance that makes traditional exams work is not dependent on any official flow of documents or communicative process, but rather on the simple lateral relationship of mutual recognition and non-recognition facilitated by the co-presence in the campus setting.

We have also tried to use the notion of actor network thinking to extend this focus on lateral links beyond the notion of human interaction, which is supported by the campus environment, and to take seriously the role of the physical campus as an *actor* which does *work* (of various kinds – in the example we gave, this was primarily the work of symbolising the university as an institution).

The literature on virtuality may easily be read as contrary to all things physical, such as the university campus. This is because for some, the campus denotes a constraint on the reach of the university and a drain on its resources. It is therefore, to this way of thinking, a limitation that needs to be transcended. Moreover, if we view education in terms of the creation, assembling, storing, transmission and processing of information (as does much of the literature on virtual universities, and distributed education more generally), then the transcending of the campus is both possible and appropriate.

However, what we have discovered from our research and tried to convey here is how university-type education seems to resist such treatment – it demands to be seen as other (or more) than information. Thus the university campus can equally be seen as discretely providing a wide range of educational resources. For instance, within conventional university life, it would be difficult, although not impossible, to schedule a seminar before 9 a.m. or on a weekend, since this would have ramifications throughout the institution (opening buildings, turning on heating, providing catering, computer and lab support, never mind the question of whether colleagues and students would turn up – see Becker's (1982) discussion of a similar set of constraints in his book *Art Worlds*). Such temporal limitation may be contrasted unfavourably with the 24 hours a day, 7 days a week, 365 days a year time frame of the Internet.

Yet most of us live quite happily with, and indeed put to use, the constraints of traditional campuses. It is only when everyone has gone home and the university is closed, for example, that many of us find time for research or writing. In this sense, the campus is best thought of not simply as a constraint but, to borrow Brown and Duguid's phrase, as a 'resourceful constraint' (Brown and Duguid 2000: 246), one it would be premature to write off and which those developing distributed learning need to take seriously.

Acknowledgement

This chapter draws on a number of research projects, primarily 'Space, Place and the Virtual University', funded under the UK Economic and Social Research Council's 'Virtual Society?' Programme (http://www.virtualsociety.org.uk/) . We would like to acknowledge the support of our collaborators on that project, John Goddard, Kevin Robins, Frank Webster and David Charles.

References

Abeles, T. (1998) The academy in a wired world, *Futures*, 30(7): 603–14.

Becker, H.S. (1982) *Art Worlds*. Berkeley, CA: University of California Press.

Boden, D. and Molotch, H.L. (1994) The compulsion of proximity, in R. Friedland and D. Boden (eds) *No(w)here: Space, Time and Modernity*. Berkeley, CA: University of California Press.

Brown, J.S. and Duguid, P. (2000) *The Social Life of Information*. Boston, MA: Harvard Business School Press.

Callon, M. (1986) Some elements of a sociology of translation: the domestication of the scallops and the fishermen of St Brieuc Bay, in J. Law (ed.) *Power, Action, Belief: A New Sociology of Knowledge*. London: Routledge & Kegan Paul.

Cunningham, S., Tapsall, S., Ryan, Y., Stedman, L., Bagdon, K. and Flew, T. (1998) *New Media and Borderless Education: A Review of the Convergence between Global Media Networks and Higher Education Provision*. Canberra: Department of Employment, Education, Training and Youth Affairs, Evaluations and Investigations Programme, Higher Education Division.

Hughes, T.P. (1983) *Networks of Power: Electrification in Western Society, 1880–1930*. Baltimore, MD: Johns Hopkins University Press.

Knights, D. and Willmott, H. (eds) (2000) *The Re-engineering Revolution? Critical Studies of Corporate Change*. London: Sage.

Kumar, K. (1997) The need for place, in A. Smith and F. Webster (eds) *The Postmodern University*. Milton Keynes: Open University Press/SRHE.

Latour, B. (1987) *Science in Action: How to Follow Scientists and Engineers Through Society*. Harvard, MA: Harvard University Press.

Latour, B. (1988) *The Pasteurization of France*. London : Harvard University Press.

Law, J. (1994) *Organising Modernity*. Oxford: Blackwell.

Newman, R. and Johnson, F. (1999) Sites of power and knowledge? Towards a critique of the virtual university, *British Journal of Sociology of Education*, 20(1): 79–88.

Pollock, N. (2000) The virtual university as 'timely and accurate information', *Information, Communication and Society*, 3(3): 1–17.

Porter, T.M. (1994) Information, power and the view from nowhere, in L. Bud-Frieman (ed.) *Information Acumen: The Understanding and Use of Knowledge in Modern Business*. London: Routledge.

Thompson, E. (1980) *Writing by Candlelight*. London: Merlin.

Wenger, E. (1998) *Communities of Practice*. Cambridge: Cambridge University Press.

Woolgar, S. (1988) *Science: The Very Idea*. London: Routledge.

Chapter 11

Identity, community and distributed learning

Gill Kirkup

Introduction

In this chapter I explore a particular model of learning (Lave and Wenger 1991; Wenger 1998) that stresses the importance of the construction of meaning and identity in the context of communities of learning. This social model of learning has become increasingly popular as a theoretical justification for information and communication technology (ICT)-based distributed learning. I discuss how well the key concepts of identity and community, in particular, carry over to Internet-based distributed learning.

Identity and learning are inseparable. Identity is a person's source of meaning and experience (Castells 1997). Identity is a product and a process of learning (Wenger 1998). Learning enables new ways of being and understanding: it is transformative. Meaning, learning and identity are all constructed socially within the various communities to which we belong: 'One needs an identity of participation in order to learn, yet needs to learn in order to acquire an identity of participation' (Wenger 1998: 277).

Whether the focus is on collective or individual identity, formal educational activity is a part (and only a part) of any 'learning community'. In a 'networked society' (Castells 1996), information technologies have changed the nature of information access and distribution, and communication technologies have offered new and faster ways of human communication. These technologies have an impact on learning communities and how they function. One of the drivers of distributed learning has been the belief that, in a networked society, ICT-based distributed learning is a better way of supporting learning communities, and providing resources for the individual students in them, than traditional face-to-face campus universities or print-based open and distance learning.

I begin with an examination of the idea of communities of learning and communities of practice (Lave and Wenger 1991; Wenger 1998); this is a social model of learning in which individuals and collectivities are seen to create/perform their identities through their learning. In the process of discussing identity and learning communities, I introduce debates about virtual community and virtual learning to raise questions about the nature of identity and learning as it might be performed in electronic networks. I have tried to avoid aligning myself with either technophobes or technophiles, since I aim to raise questions for those involved in distributed learning about how learning communities may be supported, and the potential limitations of 'e-learning'.

Social learning

Wenger's (1998) model of social learning involves four components (Figure 11.1):

1   *Community* (communities) to which the learner belongs, where the process of belonging is one of learning.
2   *Identity*, which is a negotiated experience and one that Wenger describes as a trajectory, with a history and direction. It is produced through learning.
3   *Meaning*, which is also an outcome of negotiation in the community. The community makes meaning and this comes out of the experience of its members as well as helping construct that experience.
4   *Practice*, which is the engagement with a community in a joint enterprise or activity.

Wenger's approach comes from a focus on work-related learning: the learning the people do to carry out their job in cooperation with others. Much of our teaching in any education system is not directly involved with work practices. This has not stopped educators exploring Wenger's model, as I do here. In educational communities, students are modelled as apprentice practitioners within their discipline or field of study. This is obviously the case with vocational subjects such as dentistry, journalism and accountancy, but also with many other subjects such as the 'applied' sciences. However, this implies that their community of practice may not be within the educational institution. I do not have space here to explore this issue; instead, I focus on three components of Figure 11.1 within the educational institution: identity, meaning and *learning* community.

On the surface, this model of learning is not clearly distinguished from other theories of learning, in particular constructivist theories based on psychology. However, Wenger distinguishes his theory by identifying it as primarily a social theory, and which he claims has roots in sociology back to Durkheim, Marx

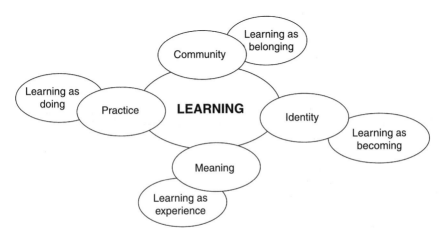

Figure 11.1 Components of a social theory of learning (from Wenger 1998: 5).

and Plato (Giddens 1971). Other perspectives, he argues, are not necessarily incompatible with his, but they have a different objective. For example, his model focuses on the processes of community participation and identity, and he contrasts this with constructivist theory which concentrates on the learner's mental structures and is concerned with task-oriented activity (Piaget 1954). Wenger also contrasts his model with other social theories, such as functionalist socialisation theory and activity theory (see Russell, Chapter 4 and Billett, Chapter 5). In his model of learning the focus on the individual in relationship to the community, both engaged in creating meaning and identity, is its distinguishing characteristic.

Identity and learning

For Wenger, identity is a social process involving:

- an experience negotiated with others;
- community membership;
- a learning trajectory;
- a point of intersection of many forms of membership;
- a relationship between the local and the global.

Identity evolves both through our participation and our non-participation in all the communities with which we interact. All the experiences we have with these communities contribute to our learning, but the problem in education is that this is often not the learning explicitly intended. Students may learn erroneous things – misconceptions that stay with them for life – as well as learning the messages of the hidden curriculum, for example, about appropriate values and behaviour, which may run counter to the explicit curriculum. Wenger describes our relationship with any community as being of three possible kinds:

1   active engagement in the community;
2   imaginative engagement with the community or its ideas;
3   alignment with the aims of the community.

   He models how these three 'modes of belonging' contribute to membership of a community and the kind of learning that takes place. I have modified Wenger's original figure, which was generic, to illustrate the possible activities regarding a learner's relationship with an explicit learning community, for example, a university (see Figure 11.2). Figure 11. 2 demonstrates both the impact of non-participation and the fact that a sense of belonging to a learning community, and having ownership of the meaning produced by that community, does not necessarily depend on the experience of active social engagement in the community.
   The traditional elitist learning institutions, in particular, universities, have attempted to provide students with all the possible identities of participation mapped by Wenger. To provide identification with a community (left-hand side of Figure 11.2), students were provided with residential collegiate living, common set texts and common collegiate ideals. To provide the opportunity for

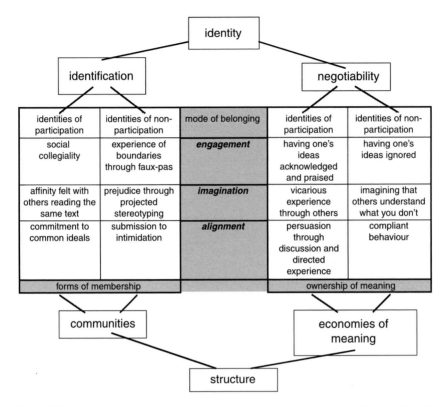

Figure 11.2 Social ecology of identity with respect to learning communities (modified from Wenger 1998: fig. 9.1).

negotiated meaning (right-hand side of Figure 11.2), students had the opportunity to enter specialist discourse, guided by experts and with the vicarious experience of learning through listening to these experts. But the expansion of post-school education and the consequent reduction in resources and widening the knowledge base included in university programmes has made many of these identities of participation unavailable to students, and changed the experience of many into one of non-participation rather than participation.

Identity and meaning

A key component in Wenger's model, together with identity and community, is meaning. Meaning is negotiated through participation and reification. Participation in the community is discussed at length below. Reification is what happens when meaning is projected or solidified through the production of an object such as a book, a set of rules, a code of practice, a procedure, a tool. All these things 'congeal' meaning/knowledge into a fixed form. In educational communities, meaning has usually been fixed in texts, in print. But the construction of meaning is negotiated around these texts: by the students as they read the book and reflect on it against their experience outside the text; and by the groups of students and scholars who discuss the texts, produce annotations, interpretations and ultimately new reifications – new texts.

Reification is as necessary as participation and negotiation in the construction of meaning and in learning. It allows meaning to be consolidated, to be transmitted across time and space, and to be built on. As Lankshear *et al.* discuss in Chapter 1, the knowledge medium changes the nature of knowledge content. Wenger argues that knowledge is negotiated through the community, and without negotiation it degrades into information or even data, which *can* exist without meaning. Knowledge, as Brown and Duguid (2000) remind us, needs a knower, and the knower is a community as well as an individual.

Communities and networks

Wenger's interest is in a particular kind of community, what he calls 'the community of practice' (see Lave and Wenger, Chapter 3, for their early work on this idea). All communities of practice, he asserts, are learning communities, but I believe some learning communities have a more explicit goal of learning than do others. It is these that I am interested in, so for the remainder of this chapter I focus on explicit learning communities – those which have learning as their *raison d'être*. Learning communities may be recognised through their way of working. They are engaged in 'meaningful activities and interactions, the productions of shareable artefacts and community building conversations and in the negotiation of new situations' (Wenger 1998: 184).

How, then, do we define a community? This is one of the central problems both in understanding learning communities and what constitutes a learning community and, an even more heated issue, what constitutes a 'virtual community'. Wenger uses an example (which is interesting for our purposes) to illustrate what is not a community of practice. He describes what he calls a community of interest: a 'community' of TV soap opera fans, who all view the same programme at the same time but have no contact with each other. His use of 'community' to describe what others might call an 'audience' or even a 'market' suggests that his concept is very broad. He argues that the shared activity of these fans is simply the result of the distribution of the hardware and the TV broadcast; that there is no shared practice. But he does not discuss whether it is a learning community, since learning is obviously taking place during the viewing of the soap opera. Although it is clearly debatable whether this is regarded as a community – especially I imagine by 'soap' fans and cultural studies theorists – it leaves us with a question of whether this community would become a learning community for its members if they engaged in soap-related discussion. Can a learning community exist if there is no communication among its members? Is the possibility of communication alone enough to turn a community of interest into a learning community?

Wellman and Gulia (1999) describe the extensive search for an understanding among social theorists of what constitutes a community, and how it changes over time and is affected by social and technological change. The problem with the term is that it comes with symbolic baggage: it carries with it a pastoral myth, a pre-lapsarian notion of some human organisation that was once better, closer, more supportive of human needs. 'Where is your sense of community?', we might say to challenge someone, and we would be unprepared for the answer, 'On my laptop when I log onto the Net'. But social scientists now define community in terms of social networks rather than spatial location, and the strength of community is in the strength of relationships regardless of the geographic distance between members.

Brown and Duguid (2000) distinguish between networks and communities. Networks link people together who do not know each other, but who are engaged in similar practices. Thus if the soap opera fans are linked, would they then constitute a network rather than a community? Networks are described by Brown and Duguid as being wide-reaching but having little reciprocity. Communities, on the other hand, are seen as having strong reciprocity and members are actively engaged in the negotiation of meaning.

But do learning communities need a spatial location? Wenger implies that either they or the individuals in them have to be 'somewhere', because identity is located:

> Viewed as an experience of identity, learning entails both a process and a place. It entails a process of transforming knowledge as well as a context in which to define an identity of participation. As a consequence, to support learning is not only to support the process of acquiring knowledge, but also to offer a place where new ways of knowing can be realised in the form of such an identity . . . The transformative practice of a learning community offers an ideal context for developing new understandings because the community sustains change as part of an identity of participation.
>
> (Wenger 1998: 215)

But if a learning community is a social network, where does that leave the question of the location of identity? Is it, too, located within social networks, rather than spatially? In the past, European networks/communities of scholars have been sustained through handwritten letters. These allowed the expression and exchange of ideas. Meaning was negotiated and reified; however, each scholar's identity was firmly located in a particular material context. The spatial location of the identity, the process of becoming, is most obviously the body, but not only the body. For example, texts of all sorts may be seen as locations for identity, from the obvious ones of personal letters and diaries to the public ones of monuments, paintings, symphonies, even constructed landscapes. (Living near the great gardens of Stowe in Buckinghamshire, I see the landscape there as a text expressing the identity of the Temple-Granville family.) It is this complicated relationship of mind–identity–embodiment that has been the focus of philosophical speculation for centuries, and the possibility of virtual identities has revived this discussion.

This leads me to the issue of virtual communities and learner identity, but first I would like to review an incarnation of learning community which historically pre-dates distributed learning and ICTs, and one that is important to take account of in understanding these more recent developments.

Distance learning and the learning community

Most of my working life has been spent in a major international institution for what has been known, since the 1970s, as 'open and distance learning', although we might now refer to such a context as 'distributed learning' (see Introduction, p. 2, for further discussion on this point). The Open University (UK), for example, was born as an institution with an explicitly radical progressive mission, part of a post-war UK socialist government's attempt to create Britain as a meritocracy, with the route to success through educational opportunity. The educational community of 1960s Britain was viewed as being a closed community. The inaugural address of the first Chancellor in 1969 expounded the meaning of 'Open' in the University's name, placing the human dimension first: 'We are open, first, as to people.' This was followed by a paragraph stressing the 'outreach' ambitions of the University: 'We are open as to places.' The technologies of teaching and learning made it to the third place: 'We are open as to methods.' The fourth and final aspect of openness was rather more vague: 'We are open, finally, as to ideas.' To refer this back to Wenger's four components of learning, what were being challenged were the community and who belonged to it, the practices of that community and the meanings it constructed.

The open and distance teaching technologies of the second half of the twentieth century allowed a particular kind of participation and reification. The teaching methods were reified into the teaching media and content, and students and academics could interpret and negotiate them. But little community negotiation was possible between students, since they were largely engaged in the individualised activity of working with the text. There was indeed often serious misunderstanding outside the UO about the process of open and distance learning. This led on the one hand to people believing that all teaching was delivered via television broadcasting, teaching as transmission (literally broadcast) of reified knowledge; and, on the other, to a picture of the UO teaching through a Socratic face-to-face teacher–student dialogue, teaching as negotiation of meaning between expert and apprentice. *Educating Rita* (1983) by Willy Russell (a play made into a film) casts the Open University as the force which transforms the lives of the main characters. Despite its misrepresentation of methods, the film could be described as representing Wenger's description of the learning process, where:

> learning transforms who we are and what we can do, it is an experience of identity. It is not just an accumulation of skills and information, but a process of becoming – to become a certain person, or, conversely, to avoid becoming a certain person.
>
> (Wenger 1998: 215)

Open and distance universities have always used a variety of media to communicate with students and to enable them to communicate with each other, and with teaching and other institutional staff. Although in the twentieth century they relied on industrial mass technologies – print, the postal services and broadcast media – it would be wrong to categorise them as only distributors of information, in the model of the audience for soap operas described earlier.

Learning texts in all media may be seen as examples of 'congealed meaning', but they were also designed using interactive and conversational models of learning such as those of Park (1976); (see Thorpe, Chapter 8). They applied constructivist models of learning in a way that positioned students as active agents in their own learning, in the construction of their own knowledge. The importance of a learning community – contact with other students, subject experts and educational counsellors (tutors) who facilitated learning rather than provided it – was also part of the model.

Printed study guides in institutions like the Open University were interactive, more so in some cases than courses now being 'delivered' over the web. Although a number of more recent Internet-based e-courses use this technology as a delivery system for electronic reified knowledge, there is little attempt at interactivity beyond electronic 'page turning'. These sites treat their student community very much as if they were an audience of soap opera viewers. The strength of the new media is its capacity for intelligent delivery of content. To see it as a process of community building and design is both more difficult and more open to, at least partial, failure. Nevertheless, technologies that appear to extend the capacity to provide 'support' and increase the geographic and temporal range of the 'learning community' are welcomed. However, this returns us to the question, 'What is the nature of the learning community and what role does ICT-based distributed learning play in it?'

The virtual learning community

In the early 1990s, Howard Rheingold named the social interactions that he saw on the Internet 'virtual communities'. His book began a decade of debate about the nature and significance of virtual communities. Unfortunately, Rheingold encouraged the transfer of the pastoral myth of community by subtitling his book *Homesteading on the Electronic Frontier* (Rheingold 1993). But, in the revised edition of his book, Rheingold had second thoughts:

> If I had . . . learned about social network analysis when I first wrote about cyberspace cultures, I could have saved us all a decade of debate by calling them 'online social networks' instead of 'virtual communities'.
>
> (Rheingold 2000: 359)

However as I discussed earlier, there is a significant distinction to be made between networks and communities. His book might have had much less impact without the 'c' word.

Several critics (see Wellman and Gulia 1999) have argued that online interactions are antipathetic to community. Dreyfus, who has long been a philosophical critic of ICTs (Dreyfus 1972), argues that overall, the Internet discourages the commitment necessary for significant learning or personal growth (Dreyfus 1999). His description of the Internet is of a large, undifferentiated stew of information, where users poke about without any sense of responsibility or commitment, picking out bits that look interesting, and dropping in morsels from their own tables regardless of what the mixture is already:

Since expertise can only be acquired through involved engagement with actual situations, the possibility of acquiring expertise is lost in the disengaged discussion and deracinated knowledge acquisition characteristic of the Net . . . one can only care about one's performance and so develop skills if one has a strong identity based on a serious, long-lasting commitment.

(Dreyfus 1999: 18, 19)

His view of e-learning resembles that of online delivery of pick-and-mix components described earlier. Although his is a description of the Internet *en masse* and not of educational programmes in particular, it resonates with the criticisms made by Brown and Duguid of some kinds of Internet-based distributed learning systems:

Certainly the word *community* crops up all over the Web sites of distance courses. But it often refers to groups that are communities in little more than the sense that eBay is a community. More generally, the Net can give the appearance of membership or access that it does not provide in any meaningful way.

(Brown and Duguid 2000: 225–6)

Brown and Duguid are also critical of what they call the 'unplug and play' model of distributed learning, where learning is recognised only when it is reified into learning objects which students can download and 'run'. For proponents of the educational power of the Internet, they are surprisingly supportive of a traditional model of campus education where, they argue, some of the most important aspects of learning took place outside the formal curriculum; for example, where students use university resources for activities that are not part of the formal curriculum, such as Bill Gates' first serious forays into programming and making money.

Identity and the virtual learner

For Wenger, community and identity are mutually constituted. Although, as indicated above, there is some concern about whether it is possible to have a community online, there is even more debate about whether it is possible to create an identity online, and what relationship this online identity might have with any other, embodied or textual. In the early language of the Internet, the term 'cyberspace' came from the fiction world of William Gibson (1984). It carried with it a notion of the separation of the material body from the identity, which could exist in its 'pure' disembodied form in 'cyberspace'. When one was in cyberspace, one transcended the limitations of the physical body, in the same way that 'cyberspace' transcended the limitations of physical space and produced a boundless equivalent in another dimension. This notion of identity fits well with those stemming in particular from theorists like Lyotard (1984; see Lankshear *et al.* Chapter 1) and Butler (1993), who view identity as a product of performance – an idea similar to that expressed by Wenger where identity is a product of practice and learning.

There are two ways of understanding performativity of identity; one is simpler and one is much harder to grasp with revolutionary implications for our understanding of ourselves. The simpler notion is identity in the theatrical sense, where an identity is assumed, acted out, as a role on a stage. But the presumption is that the act – being the only thing present – is the reality, thus being someone is a performance. It is as if only the characters on stage had reality; the actors did not exist outside the characters. The other is a linguistic meaning, that identity is performed in a linguistic sense, 'a speech act that constitutes its referent' (Warhol 1999). We create identity through speech and texts: this equates identity with meaning. Online identities may be seen as theatrical performances, especially in those realms of fantasy where people act out games, but what people describe in computer-mediated communication may be readily identifiable as a set of texts and so, in that sense, identity is constructed through these texts. The question is: What connection, if any, does this textual identity have with an embodied identity?

If the online identity passes the Turing test[1] of seeming to be real to those who interact with it, then for all intents and purposes it is real – at least in cyberspace. The most famous example of virtual identity is 'Eliza', sometimes known as the 'computer therapist' (http://www.manifestation.com/neurotoys/eliza.php3). 'Eliza' was the brainchild of Joseph Weizenbaum who, in 1966, argued for a computer application that could mimic natural language process and so continue a conversation. 'Eliza' is still being produced by more recent and advanced programming techniques, to be faster and more sophisticated (http://ecceliza.cjb.net/). 'She' has no information, simply a set of procedures that allow her to form responses from any questions given to her by using the content of those questions. Other intelligent agents like 'Julia' do gather information in response to requests by users made in the form of natural language questions (see the work of Lenny Foner[2]). There is a significant question here about what functions these kinds of artificial agents play in educational systems, but such discussions are outside the brief of this chapter.

A further important question for education about online community and online identity is: What is the relationship between the learner identity online and the embodied learner? This is less of a problem for institutions where the students are physically present for some of the activities and online for others. A correspondence is presumed between the identities performed in these different environments. The community created online is an aspect or subset of the other institutional communities to which the members belong. However, there is a real problem for distributed e-learning, where the community only exists online, and the identities of students and perhaps teachers are performed solely online. At its most simplistic, this gives rise to administrative issues such as proving the identity of the author of an assessment submitted from a 'never-met-in-the-flesh' student (see Cornford and Pollock, Chapter 10). Here there is a concept of fraud. There is also the widely held belief that the Internet enables students to plagiarise materials and to fraudulently present work that others have written as their own. There is a presumption in the 'material' world – in the e-commerce material – that false identities (and credit ratings) are fraudulent, while proponents of Internet identity see the performance of identities different from those lived in the 'real' world as a positive way of experimenting with identities that are unavailable to them in embodied situations (Turkle 1997).

Apart from 'intelligent agents' like 'Eliza' and 'Julia', who exist only as online entities, there are several ways in which an identity on the Internet can correspond to the embodiment of the entity creating the identity. Donath (1999) lists three:

1   Category deceptions, in which a person adopts an aspect of identity that does not correspond to their material/social embodiment; for example, changing their age, gender, occupation.
2   Impersonation of someone else.
3   Concealing a real-world identity behind a 'fantasy' identity or avatar.

She notes that it is not easy to make clear boundaries between these:

> It is useful to distinguish between pseudonymity and pure anonymity. In the virtual world, many degrees of identification are possible. Full anonymity is one extreme of a continuum that runs from the totally anonymous to the thoroughly named. A pseudonym, though it may be untraceable to a real-world person, may have a well established reputation in the virtual domain.
>
> (Donath 1999: 53)

Is this kind of authoritative online persona the equivalent of an author's penname? Lankshear *et al.* (Chapter 1) discuss how our recognition of authoritative knowledge has altered with changing media. The wide circulation of false rumours on the Internet suggests that people are having problems in assessing the authority of any source of Internet information. One way of authenticating statements has been through trusting the reliability of the source; that reliability is attached to accountability. How are pseudonymous people accountable?

There has been much discussion about identity deception online and the impact of disclosure, when it happens, on those who had 'trusted' the identity presented (Turkle 1997). Although trust is obviously an issue in online learning communities, there is also a question about the validity of the knowledge created by that community where there is ambiguity or even deception about members' identities. Wenger's argument about the relationship between knowledge and identity implies that the knowledge developed by a learning community depends for its authority on the participation of the individuals in that community, and at the same time the grounds of *their* identity depend on the knowledge produced by the community. However, if online identities are 'fictive' – that is, they have no location in the material world – this raises questions about the knowledge produced by the community of which these identities are members, and also about authenticity of the identities developing in these communities. In Wenger's model, identity and meaning are inextricably entwined. Post-modernists like Wenger do not presume that identity is monolithic, stable over time and space. He understands that people inhabit/perform a number of identities, constantly resolving the tensions between them.

For most people, '(Re)embodying the self in a disembodied realm is an exercise in textual production' (O'Brien 1999: 87), and it is easier to do this by falling back on stereotypes where familiar images and situations can be compressed into a few signs. It should be remembered that text-based computer-mediated communication is 'low bandwidth': it contains few of the signals present in other kinds of communications. It has been argued that this facilitates communication in some situations, but in an educational environment skilled writers and expert practitioners may be better able to manipulate this low bandwidth (as did eighteenth-century European scholars) than apprentice learners.

Donath (1999) found three reasons why people participate in online communities: (1) to exchange information, (2) to provide affiliation and support, and (3) to gain recognition. However, she describes voluntary members of online communities rather than students who may be required to join as evidence of their studying. Many students do find online group communication productive, but the high rates of non-participation in Open University online courses suggest that many others find it difficult or unrewarding, since they cannot access enough information, support or recognition to motivate them to continue their participation in a learning community in this way. For many, this is not part of their learning community.

The potential for ICT-based distributed education to support the virtual community

After 10 years of research on Internet communication, Wellman and Gulia state quite reasonably:

> we suspect that as online communication becomes more widely used and routinely accepted, the current fascination with it will decline sharply. It will be seen much as telephone contact is now and letter writing was in Jane Austen's time: a reasonable way to maintain strong and weak ties between people who are not in a position to have a face-to-face encounter at that moment.
>
> (Wellman and Gulia 1999: 182)

Their research positions technically mediated communication as a less preferred alternative to face-to-face communication, and one generally used between people who often meet face-to-face. Brown and Duguid occupy a similar position. They see the web as enhancing local communities that already have a basis of reciprocal relationships and activities. Globally, they feel its lack of potential for reciprocity means it is good at providing information networks but not at producing communities. They believe that any educational provider needs to offer three things: (1) access to authentic communities of learning, (2) resources for knowledge creation, and (3) accreditation. These they believe are best offered through institutions which mix face-to-face activities with other kinds of media. They worry that solely Internet-based education of the 'plug-and-play' model will provide the less wealthy with their only access to information. Economic drivers, which have not been touched on here, make this a possibility for some populations. An understanding of the relationship between community, meaning and identity in learning may help to produce sophisticated designs for distributed learning systems that have a more grounded understanding of the role of the community in learning and are better able to choose media on the basis of their strengths.

In this chapter I have examined how well a social model of learning, where individuals and collectivities are seen to create/perform their identities though their learning, may be implemented through electronic networks. I have asked: What is the nature of a virtual learning community and, in particular, what complexities arise if those interactions within the virtual community are *only* available electronically? Referring back to Figure 11.2, which maps the identities of participation in any community, it appears that virtual learning communities (when compared with an *ideal* learning community in which all forms of inter-action are possible) may provide only limited kinds of participation. There is even a question of how appropriate it is to describe the networking that hap-pens online as a community at all, but I have also suggested that social learning online should not be seen simply as a deficit version of face-to-face learning. It is certain to be a valuable component of any multiple-media distributed learning system, most valuable when there is a clearer understanding of its strengths and weaknesses. Finally, there is also significant work yet to be done on understanding the nature of online identity – of students and, more radically, of teachers.

Notes

1 The Turing test is named after the mathematician Alan Turing, who invented the notion of artificial intelligence. If questions are 'posted' into a 'black box' and answers are returned that are in all ways indistinguishable from those a human being might give, then the thing producing them is exhibiting 'intelligence'. If the answers also suggest the presence of a human identity, then we could say it has passed a Turing test of identity.
2 http://foner.www.media.mit.edu/people/foner/short-takes.html#julia.

References

Brown, J.S. and Duguid, P. (2000) *The Social Life of Information*. Boston, MA: Harvard Business School Press.

Butler, J. (1993) *Bodies that Matter: On the Discursive Limits of 'Sex'*. London: Routledge.

Castells, M. (1996) *The Information Age: Economy, Society and Culture. Vol. I. Rise of the Networked Society*. Oxford: Blackwell.

Castells, M. (1997) *The Information Age: Economy, Society and Culture. Vol. II. The Power of Identity*. Oxford: Blackwell.

Donath, J.S. (1999) Identity and deception in the virtual community, in M.A. Smith and P. Kollock (eds) *Communities in Cyberspace*. London: Routledge.

Dreyfus, H.L. (1972) *What Computers Can't Do: A Critique of Artificial Reason*. New York: Harper & Row.

Dreyfus, H.L. (1999) Anonymity versus commitment: the dangers of education on the Internet, *Ethics and Information Technology*, 1: 15–21.

Gibson, W. (1984) *Neuromancer*. New York: Ace Books.

Giddens, A. (1971) *Capitalism and Modern Social Theory: An Analysis of the Writings of Marx, Durkheim and Max Weber*. Cambridge: Cambridge University Press.

Lave, J. and Wenger, E. (1991) *Situated Learning: Legitimate Peripheral Participation*. Cambridge: Cambridge University Press.

Lyotard, J.F. (1984) *The Postmodern Condition: A Report on Knowledge*. Minneapolis, MN: University of Minnesota Press.

O'Brien, J. (1999) Writing in the body: gender (re)production in online interaction, in M.A. Smith and P. Kollock (eds) *Communities in Cyberspace*. London: Routledge.

Park, G. (1976) *Conversation Theory: Application in Education and Epistemology*. Amsterdam: Elsevier.

Piaget, J. (1954) *The Construction of Reality in the Child*. New York: Basic Books.

Rheingold, H. (1993) *The Virtual Community: Homesteading on the Electronic Frontier*. Reading, MA: Addison-Wesley.

Rheingold, H. (2000) *The Virtual Community: Homesteading on the Electronic Frontier, revised edition*. Cambridge, MA: MIT Press.

Turkle, S. (1997) *Life on the Screen: Identity in the Age of the Internet*. New York: Touchstone Press.

Warhol, R.R. (1999) The inevitable virtuality of gender: performing femininity on an electronic bulletin board for soap opera fans, in M.A. O'Farrell and L. Vallone (eds) *Virtual Gender: Fantasies of Subjectivity and Embodiment*. Ann Arbor, MI: University of Michigan Press.

Wellman, B. and Gulia, M. (1999) Virtual communities as communities, in M.A. Smith and P. Kollock (eds) *Communities in Cyberspace*. London: Routledge.

Wenger, E. (1998) *Communities of Practice: Learning, Meaning and Identity*. Cambridge: Cambridge University Press.

Chapter 12

Flexible literacies

Distributed learning and changing educational spaces

Richard Edwards, Kathy Nicoll and Alison Lee

We need more generative, challenging frameworks and more rigorous, informed practical theories, in negotiating the complexities of the new literacies and new forms of knowledge and identity that characterise, increasingly, educational practice today and tomorrow.

(Green 1999: 45)

Introduction

Universities are increasingly subjected to policy pressure from the state to serve better the needs of a globalised economy; yet they are also subjected to public-sector funding constraints. Increasingly, international organisations such as the Organisation of Economic Cooperation and Development (OECD) influence policy developments in higher education. Driven by such global policy transfer, by funding needs and by the cultural and economic logic of globalisation, educational institutions are developing international markets, with the education export industry growing rapidly. Global alliances and partnerships between universities are emerging. Worldwide the spread of English as a medium for curriculum seems inexorable, at the same time as linguistic and cultural differences assert themselves in the particular local sites of engagement and exchange between and within institutions (see Mayor and Swann, Chapter 7). Within this context, the development of more flexible forms for the provision of learning has been significant in recent years, as universities seek to become more responsive in a market-like environment and provide more learning opportunities to individuals and groups spread across time and distance. Forms of workplace learning, distance learning and the provision of opportunities to international markets, all increasingly mediated through information and communications technologies, have been symptomatic of this search for flexibility.

Moves towards greater flexibility in the provision of learning opportunities may be located in the context of broader educational, economic and social changes. Flexibility, as a contemporary idea, may be understood as a 'governing metaphor' in many societies (Nicoll 1997), to the extent that Coffield (1999) has argued that policy aims not so much to produce a 'learning society' as a 'flexible society'. Flexibility is a characteristic demanded of workplaces, organisations, whole economies and, indeed, contemporary forms of identity – flexible workers and learners (Usher 2000). As we see it, the principal features associated with more flexible forms of learning – the heightened access to post-school education of increasingly diverse cohorts of learners, the 'opening' of boundaries between education and work, the growing use of information and communication technologies (ICT) – also raise crucial questions for literacy. Flexibility, in particular that associated with ICT, has created changed literacy practices that are not always noted (Bruce 1997; Green 1999), even while the materiality of literate practices is rendered hugely complex by the increasingly diverse forms of reading and writing through which learning is mediated. Knowledge and information and its interpretation and communication have become more central to many workplaces. In response to the changing demands of education and work, the question of literacy in university education should loom large. Lea and Stierer (2000) indicate, however, that the changing forms of textual and electronically mediated literate practices are in play in curriculum and pedagogy without any explicit attention. In general, literacy is struggling to arrive on the mainstream agenda in higher education research and policy. Lankshear's (1998: 356) identification of the 'elevation' of literacy, from being 'a marker of marginal spaces, used mainly in relation to "marginal people" ("illiterates") to becoming a lofty mainstream educational ideal', has yet to be felt in higher education. Changes in employment and education associated with the notion of flexibility therefore seem to be important issues to explore from the perspective of literacy.

This chapter arises from conversations between us which drew upon our differing experiences of working in higher education. Specifically, we were interested in the reconfiguration of courses within the University of Technology, Sydney that occurred in the late 1990s. This reconfiguration had been embarked upon with the aim of improving access to courses by increasing their flexibility. Within this context, we were individually considering the new demands upon teachers and students of changed provision. However, in conversation, it became apparent that the discourses we drew upon to discuss flexibility and flexible learning were quite different. Drawing upon our different research interests, we each contributed to these conversations in ways we considered to be significant, but we also recognised how academic dialogue in related areas often takes place in parallel, without much overlap or interchange. In particular, we became interested in how the recent research in academic literacy did not seem to be influencing those developing flexible learning provision, or those providing staff development for academics who were having to teach through flexible learning. We were also interested in how flexible learning related to wider changes in the economy and workplaces, in which flexibility and lifelong learning have become significant goals. The discussion of flexible workplaces, flexible learning and academic literacy was operating in parallel universes rather than interacting with each other in any significant way.

It appeared that this phenomenon had been produced in part by the relative insularity of the domains of academic practice and research journals from which our particular discourses emerged. In our conversations, we drew on the literature on open and distance learning, literacy and academic literacies, staff development, educational technology, and those that discussed broader changes in the economy, society and lifelong learning. We shared a concern that these different branches of educational practice and research do not always speak to each other or, when they do, they fail to communicate effectively. Thus, the spaces opened up for thought by recent work on academic literacies on higher education, or on flexibility within the contemporary economy and society, are hardly drawn upon in the discussion of flexible learning. We were interested in finding interpretive spaces through which to introduce research and debate from certain areas of education into others. In this particular case, we were interested in opening up a heuristic space through which to explore the possible significance of contemporary debates about literacies for our understanding of flexible and distributed learning.

Central to the exploration in this chapter is the notion of flexibility, which we take to be a central characteristic of distributed learning, and the consequences of this notion for the conception of literacies with which we work. We believe the space we are opening up in this chapter may be of wider interest and not simply to those involved in university education, since trends towards flexibility and distribution are occurring quite broadly within institutions of post-compulsory education in Australia, as they are elsewhere around the globe. We believe the demands for flexibility through distributed learning require different forms of literacy practice from learners and academics and that this is becoming prevalent in many areas of educational practice.

In this chapter, we introduce a notion of flexible literacies in an exploration of the literate demands on learners within the domains and practices of flexible and distributed forms of learning. The latter is understood both as a symptomatic policy-driven change in post-school education and as a site for the exploration of the increasing salience of flexibility as a metaphor for trends in many contemporary economies and societies. Our task is two-fold. First, we seek to locate the moves towards more flexible forms of learning, and their requirements and practices within the wider demands for 'flexibility' and 'reflexivity' in the contemporary worlds of learning, work and social life in general (Edwards 1997). We are concerned to explore the literacy learning of new workplaces, given the growing textualisation of such spaces (Lee *et al.* 1999). Our second task is to ask more specifically what it might mean to talk of being or becoming flexibly literate. What new sites for literate practices are opened up, what changes in forms and modes of symbolic exchange? What specific literate capacities and dispositions are required within the increasingly distributed environments of post-school education and work? In the second part of the chapter, therefore, we outline how some current discussions of literacies might be supplemented within this specific domain by the possibilities and problematics associated with notions of flexibility.

Locating moves towards flexible learning

Flexible learning is one policy-driven response to the changes confronting higher education. Flexible learning generally involves the removal of barriers to accessing higher education, the creation of new student markets, the customisation of products, increased efficiency of delivery and, perhaps most saliently, the use of ICT for the delivery of curriculum and the practice of learning. These developments have resulted in the expansion into new forms of provision – distributed, open, distance – by a wide range of institutions. These are largely framed within discourses of efficiency, competitive edge, access and 'choice' for lifelong learners, as well as those of information technology itself (Kirkpatrick 1997). The dispersal and flexibilisation of learning has itself resulted from the development of notions of distributed cognition and learning. At the same time, it is becoming clear that some of the effects of pedagogical practices using information technology, such as web-based delivery, can blur distinctions between courses and between information and knowledge. In addition, the increased emphasis on computer-mediated learning creates considerable changes in curriculum and pedagogy, with attendant new forms of textual context and practices and, with that, changing literacies (Lea 2001). Moreover, the relatively firmly located, campus-based 'students' of traditional conceptions of universities begin to mutate into 'deterritorialised "learners"' within the new, more flexible environment (Edwards and Usher 1997: 262).

Moves towards more flexible forms of learning and their demands and practices may be located within the wider discourses that demand 'flexibility' and 'reflexivity' in the contemporary world of learning, work and social life. The contemporary period has been widely analysed as one in which there is a significant reconfiguration of economic and social relationships and practices. There are many characterisations of these trends, including late modernity, globalisation, post-industrialism, postmodernisation, post-Fordism, the information society, the knowledge age, the learning society. What lies at the heart of many of these characterisations, however, is the transformation of the global economy, the workplace and culture, made possible at least in part by the development of ICT and the de-regulation of markets. The goal is greater flexibility and, associated with this, insecurity, risk and reflexivity. As a result, the need for the provision of flexible lifelong learning opportunities and for people to become flexible lifelong learners has become increasingly important in educational policy. We will briefly outline some of the main contributors to the position we are drawing upon in opening up this space for discussion and debate, in particular the work of the British sociologist Anthony Giddens and the German sociologist Ulrich Beck.

Giddens (1990, 1991) has argued that central to modern societies is a constant search for the new. He refers to this drive for innovation as a 'juggernaut': it is this that drives change. Giddens argues that modernity is a process of constantly breaking with tradition through a reflexive monitoring in an onward drive to develop 'the new'. In this process of self-constitution, modern societies and the modern nation state produce more information about themselves as a condition for their ongoing development. This is not only true for societies and nation states, but also for individuals. For Giddens, therefore, modernity itself signifies the loss of tradition at a personal as well as a social level, where 'in the context of a post-traditional order, the self becomes a reflexive project' (Giddens 1991: 32). In other words, who we are becomes something we experience as a question to be answered, and about which we seek information and knowledge, rather than the answers resting in a pre-given order of things. Self-identity becomes conditional upon decisions about lifestyles and lifestyle choices. This makes life planning an integral component of late modern existence. Giddens (1991: 21) argues that this situation is 'existentially troubling', since the very uncertainty and reflexivity upon which modernity is grounded means that the decisions confronting people are ambiguous and insecure.

Within contemporary changes there is an increased reflexivity, wherein societies, organisations and individuals are required to change, to learn to change and change to learn. Lifelong learning has become central to education and economic policy, with an increased emphasis on individuals, workplaces and providers of learning opportunities becoming more flexible. Reflexivity signifies the enhanced options available and the necessity of decision-making, even as the implications of those decisions become less certain. Previously structured choices and opportunity structures are no longer held to be as determining of auto/biographies as once was the case (Alheit 1999). People need to become more flexible to negotiate this uncertainty and complexity.

For Beck (1992), reflexive modernisation is linked to his concept of a 'risk society' wherein the limits of modernisation become available for challenge. For him, modernisation is the process whereby certain agrarian social formations were transformed into industrial ones. Beck argues that the processes of modernisation, governed by scientific knowledge and industrialisation, have resulted in risks that are no longer limited by time or space, since the potential for catastrophe can now be global in scale (e.g. global warming). Risk is spread globally and unequally, but, importantly, it is not always apparent who is responsible for causing the risk. At one level, reflexive modernisation refers to the forms of critique of the risks being generated by modernisation, offered by such groups as the Green Movement. It refers to the modernisation of industrial society, and the attempts to challenge the structuring assumptions and consequences of modernisation. In the industrial society, the principal concern was with the production and distribution of wealth. For Beck, in the risk society, it is the administration and distribution of risk that is the principal concern. As well as new issues of self-identity, therefore, significant new forms of social and political engagement are being produced.

Although they differ in significant ways, the views of Giddens and Beck stress reflexivity as a central aspect of contemporary change. Jansen and Van Der Veen (1992), following Beck, argue that central to a critical engagement with these processes is the need for lifelong learning with a focus on the challenges raised by the risk society. However, Giddens' notion of the reflexive monitoring of the self also suggests that lifelong learning can involve personal developmental opportunities. Underpinning each analysis is the notion of flexibility. Nowhere is this more apparent than in relation to changes in the economy, workplace and labour market. Thus:

> In the current and coming waves of automation this [industrial] system of standardised full employment is beginning to soften and fray at the margins into flexibilisations of its three supporting pillars: labour law, work site and working hours . . . Flexible, pluralised forms of underemployment are spreading.

> (Beck 1992: 142)

For Harvey, this signifies an era of capitalist flexible accumulation that

> rests on flexibility with respect to labour processes, labour markets, products and patterns of consumption . . . These enhanced powers of flexibility

and mobility have allowed employers to exert stronger pressures of labour control on a workforce in any case weakened by two savage bouts of deflation, that saw unemployment rise to unprecedented post-war levels in advanced capitalist countries.

(Harvey 1991: 147)

Here, flexibility is an attempt to resolve the problems of capital accumulation as capital becomes more internationalised and national economies more integrated into global market mechanisms. Rather than regulating the market, many governments have intervened to make their countries or regions more attractive to investment markets, in particular by creating a highly skilled, flexible workforce (Reich 1993). To be competitive in an uncertain and risk-laden environment, organisations need to respond reflexively and flexibly to market changes. This requires workers to be both flexible *within* the workplace, transferring from one task to another, and flexible *between* workplaces, transferring from one job to another. Increasingly, flexibility is promoted through the deployment of ICTs in the workplace, with symbolic analysts – those who produce, interpret and communicate information (i.e. engage in textual practices) – becoming a significant part of the workforce (Gee et al. 1996). Flexibility involves a constitution of the self as a lifelong learner, a reflexive and flexible self, committed to a constant cycle of 'innovation' and 'continual improvement'. Here the self, like the workplace, becomes more 'enterprising' (Rose 1996). It also needs to be more enmeshed in literate practices.

For providers of learning opportunities, these new forms of economic organisation, and the new forms of subjectivity they require and produce, force massive and rapid changes at every level of operation. Post-school education has felt keenly the effects of increasing globalisation of economic, social and political systems. The projected graduates of the contemporary university, for example, are required to be lifelong learners, to learn, work and communicate in many different professional, corporate, social, cultural and geographical locations, distributed across space and time. They increasingly require capacities of critique, high-order problem-solving, team-working and flexibility (Lankshear 1998) and, with this, the symbolic-analytic literacies associated with the capacity to access, interpret and communicate information.

Existing educational discourses have produced a range of embodied subjectivities, including 'the self-actualising, self-directing subject of humanistic psychology or the adaptive, information-processing subject of cognitive psychology' (Usher 1993: 18). Active subjects who regulate themselves through the principles of autonomy and self-reflection are expressed in and through notions, such as that of the 'lifelong learner'. The self-forming project of 'learning' becomes far more complex through flexible forms of learning, with, for example, modularisation, credit accumulation and transfer, the negotiation of learning contracts, and the potential for assessment processes to be distributed across contexts and undertaken by different people (Nicoll and Edwards 1997). As provision becomes more flexible and distributed across space and time, therefore, learners may not be bound by the arrangements within a single institution, or that of a single discipline. Multi-, inter- and trans-disciplinarity are characteristic of flexible forms of learning. Learners may engage with a range of knowledge in a variety of ways and be subject to several different norms. It may not be mere coincidence, therefore, that considerable policy interest has emerged in the cross-curricular outcomes of university education and the question of generic graduate capabilities – what a graduate can *do* – as conventional notions of disciplinarity have been challenged. Here the criteria for evaluating knowledge become less one of truth and more one of perform-ance and performativity (Lankshear *et al.*, Chapter 1). Within the discourse of flexibility, the learner requires transferable practices more centrally than conventional disciplinary expertise. As Gibbons *et al.* note:

> Formerly, secondary, largely multidisciplinary, competencies were added on to primary, largely disciplinary identities. This pattern will have to be abandoned. A portfolio of identities and competencies will have to be managed, none of which need to be preeminent.
>
> (Gibbons *et al.* 1994: 165)

To manage such a portfolio, the lifelong learner needs to develop the capacity to negotiate flexibly among many different discourses and text forms, across cul-tural and organisationally diverse sites, including via technologically mediated forms of exchange. They will require, in the words of *Australia's Language* (DEET 1991), 'purposeful, flexible and dynamic' literacies to project, interpret and mediate difference and change.

Although flexible learning is understood to concern the removal of barriers to accessing higher education, such initiatives raise quite different issues when located within discourses of the wider demands for flexibility and reflexivity in contemporary worlds of learning, work and social life. Here the goal is greater flexibility within the economy and society, associated with a requirement for an identity as a reflexive project. Reflexivity signifies increasing uncertainty in rela-tion to what can be learned and career possibilities, and so an increasing need for decision-making. Processes of individualisation increasingly place the onus of responsibility on the individual for negotiating such choices and decisions, as consumer, worker and lifelong learner. To negotiate this requires symbolic-analytic literacies – the interpretation, analysis and communication of informa-tion – as well as capacities of critique, problem-solving, flexibility, teamwork, communication and self-direction. Flexible learning produces these capacities, and frames the flexible subject in their role of contributing to a competent workforce within globalised economies.

Flexible learning initiatives concern 'production, distribution and interactiv-ity in education, along with a consequent shift towards the globalisation of education' (Kirkpatrick 1997: 162). Arguably, then, practices of flexibility in learning emerge from and result in a 'new learner', a 'flexible subject', who 'drives the direction and demand for knowledge according to their perceived needs, with legitimation of knowledge becoming largely a factor of its demand' (Kirkpatrick 1997: 163), and who is not confined within the 'spaces of enclosure' (Lankshear *et al.* 1996) of traditional forms of educational provision. The flexible subject is also to be found in the practices of the 'new academic', for whom the demands of the discipline are enfolded by those of the institution and learners, as well as external demands (Nicoll 1999). In this sense, flexibility attempts to 'produce' flexible learners and academics, and to distribute them in different, more flexible, pedagogic spaces.

By and large, contemporary understandings of learning and teaching in higher education do not consider questions raised by locating them within wider discourses of flexibility and broader contemporary change. Lea and Street (1998) suggest that mainstream accounts deriving from psychology, including constructivist educational theory, and anthropology stress the need to socialise students into the 'culture' of education. Of concern may be students' interpretations of learning tasks and their general orientations to learning, for example, 'deep', 'surface' or 'strategic'. Increasingly central to understandings of learning within many domains are those of the 'self-directed' and 'reflective' practitioner. These emerge from the work of, among others, Kolb (1984) and Schon (1983, 1987). Both emphasise the central role of the autonomous individual and, as Thorpe (2000) discusses, appear extensively within the accounts of practitioners of forms of distributed learning. What is lacking in such framings of learning is a concern for the wider context and significance of educational practices, and the forms of subjectivity and literacies they produce and require.

What might it mean to become flexibly literate?

We have argued for the centrality of notions of flexibility to the changes taking place in the economy, society and education, and how moves to develop more flexible and distributed forms of learning require and produce flexible lifelong learners. Central to these developments is the increased diversification of the media through which learning occurs and the pedagogic practices associated with them. These require a diverse range of literacy practices, what we term 'flexible literacies'. This notion can itself be set within the context of contemporary debates about academic literacies.

Street (1996) makes a distinction between work in the New Literacy Studies and work on multi-literacies (New London Group 1995). The New Literacy Studies sees literacies as social practices that are always contextualised. In his earlier work, Street (1984) made the useful distinction between 'autonomous' and 'ideological' models of literacy. The 'autonomous' model, as the dominant model in education, sees literacy as a thing, a decontextualised skill to be taught and learned. In contrast, Street's 'ideological' model recognises the diversity of literacy practices and how such practices can be understood only in terms of the specific contexts within which they exist. Any use of literacy and the meanings created around reading and writing are always embedded in relationships of power and authority. What we write and how we write are not skills that we learn free of context, but are the result of struggles over meanings in particular settings. Recently, work in higher education in general and distance education in particular has taken the New Literacy Studies as its theoretical frame (Lillis 1997; Lea 1998; Lea and Street 1998; Lea and Stierer 2000). Street (1996) suggests that the term 'multi-literacies' might be aligned with an 'autonomous' model of literacy because it prompts a close relationship between particular channels for literacy practices and particular types of literacy. He suggests that this is misleading since, for example, computer literacy is not a new single literacy but involves different uses of literacy in different contexts. The association of the word 'literacies' with another – for example, electronic literacies, digital literacies – has recently gained common currency in post-compulsory settings. Although we recognise, following Street (1996), that such use might suggest that certain literacies have a one-to-one relationship with 'other' categories – for example, specific technologies – they still seem to us to embed a notion of literacy practices as primarily socially situated and specific. It is this idea that we draw upon in this chapter. At the same time, literacy, particularly within discourses of policy, has become a code word for perceptions of successive crises in education and problems in the delivery of a competent workforce. Furthermore, the word literacy has been closely associated with the acquisition and exercise of many forms of social practice – from computers to the emotions, for example. This trend, in turn, has been critiqued for metaphorising and diluting the concrete, material and, for many, the intractable literalness of learning to read and write.

Whatever permutations literacy is subjected to, however, central to most informed current discussion within literacy studies is both the plurality and situatedness of literate practices in the contemporary world (Barton *et al.* 2000). Moreover, the proliferation of forms and modes of codification, textualisation and mediation in all domains of social life and the growing significance of symbolic exchange (Waters 1995) mean that more forms of social practice are being construed as literate practices. Globally, the spread of ICT requires increased engagement by more people – in learning, work and communal activity of all kinds – in the flow and exchange of information in codified and textualised forms. To be able to engage with this diversification requires a certain amount of flexibility, what we have termed 'flexible literacy'.

What is required to supplement existing accounts of learning in higher education that will address questions of flexibility and the role of literacy in all this? Contemporary understandings of learning in higher education do not generally factor questions of language or of literacy into the picture. This work has been critiqued on various grounds pertinent to our concerns here (cf. Lea and Street 1998). First, there is the implicit assumption in much of the work that the culture of the university is relatively homogeneous. Thus, despite some attention to disciplinary differences, there is a lack of attention to processes of change and the exercise of power, such as we explored above. Second, there is a general lack of attention to questions of literacy. Where the focus is on such issues as student writing, there has been a tendency (Lea and Street 1998: 139) to treat writing as 'a transparent medium of representation' that fails to address the complex literacy issues involved in the discursive-institutional production, and representation and exchange, of meaning in curriculum and pedagogy.

For many forms of distributed learning, teaching is itself embodied in texts and mediated through textual practices, whether print-based, electronic or hybrid, and integrated modalities (see Morgan *et al.*, Chapter 2). The body of the learner and the scene of learning are increasingly located in places other than the university classroom or lecture hall. The increasing flexibility of learning and its dispersal mark such moves. What takes place pedagogically, therefore, between learners and teachers occurs increasingly through literate exchanges, rather than, or in addition to, the transactions of physical bodies in space. There appears, then, an urgent need to interrogate the texts and textual practices, the modes of exchange within sites of flexible and distributed forms of learning.

What should be noted in such a task, however, is the already literate scene of higher education. Traditionally within the university, pedagogical practices are embedded within bounded literate systems of, for example, report- and essay-writing, appraisal and marking of attainment; the formal timetable; the schedule for handing in assignments; the movement and placing of bodies within the walls of the university; checking assignments received from students; the organisation of teaching space; determining work and learning goals; and, of course, the criteria for assessment of work. To attend to such literate systems is to see the university as saturated with literacies, perhaps nowhere more charged than in the consistent requirement of students that they write (Lea and Stierer 2000).

It is also worth noting that the various demands on students in traditional modes of higher education pedagogy already require considerable flexibility. As long as knowledge is divided along disciplinary and other lines, 'packaged' in subjects in structured curricula and 'taught' and assessed largely by individuals behind closed doors, learners must move from 'cell to cell' with little regard for how a learner might learn to 'code switch' or indeed 'translate' from one literate event to another. Lea and Street (1998: 161) introduce the concept of 'course switching', which they suggest 'can be paralleled with linguistic code switching . . . In the case of "course switching" students are having to interpret the writing requirements of different levels of academic activity.' Here we only have to look at the differences in the forms of writing required of students within differing 'packages' or 'cells' of learning to see the code switching or translations being made. Different assumptions about the nature of writing, different epistemological assumptions about the nature of academic knowledge, inform teaching and assessment practices across and even within disciplines and fields of study (Lea and Street 1998). The curriculum is mobilised in different ways and represented through different literature practices (Nespor 1994). From a student's point of view, therefore, as Lea and Street (1998) argue, a dominant feature of the literacy practices in the university is the requirement to switch codes and practices between one setting and another, to deploy a repertoire of linguistic practices appropriate to each setting, and to handle the social meanings and identities each invokes. It is against these enduring features of learning and literacy in higher education that contemporary changes must be factored. In this sense, the flexible literacies required by students may not be new, but intensified, diversified and distributed.

Attempts to conceptualise the increasing diversity of literacy demands associated with globalising processes have emerged in recent years. The term 'multi-literacies' was coined by the New London Group (1995) to refer both to the plurality of texts that circulate within culturally and linguistically diverse globalising societies and cultures, and to the growth and diversification of text forms associated with information and media technologies. Multi-literacies capture, then, the sense of specificity and situatedness, as well as proliferation, diversification and spread of literacies, rendering the materiality of literate practices hugely complex and making broad engagement with this complexity urgent. Addressing the consequences for pedagogy and learning, the New

London Group (1995: 69) wrote that 'the most important skill students need to learn is to negotiate dialect differences, register differences, code switching, inter languages and hybrid cross-cultural discourses'. Multi-literacies, therefore, express the condition of possibility for productive learning in a global society. This may be regarded as a form of social imaginary, of how things should or might be. We believe the notion of multi-literacies captures the diversification of literacy practices well, but not the flexibility that is central to negotiating this diversity, its relationship to wider debates about changes in the economy and society, or the empirical lived practices of learners. We therefore feel that the concept of flexible literacies provides a more productive heuristic space through which to examine the diversification and distribution of literate practices and bring together people engaged in different, if related, educational practices to discuss the issues raised in this chapter.

In his analysis of the policy texts of recent educational reform, Lankshear (1998) identifies four different constructions of literacy that appear to be of direct relevance to our exploration of literacies in flexible environments. The first of these, the seemingly familiar 'lingering basics', refers to 'the mastery of fundamentals of encoding and decoding print texts (including elementary math operations)' (p. 357). While it is often assumed that the basic 'building blocks' of 'generalisable techniques and concepts' (p. 358) are in place in the populations of higher education, empirical study suggests not only that this requires examination within existing university learning environments, but also that such a concept of literacy does not go very far in specifying what a 'basic' competence might look like in specific settings. At the very least, such generalisable basic capacities, whatever they are, will be put under renewed stress in circumstances where the various forms of the written word do more of the work of pedagogic exchange.

A second construction of literacy is identified by Lankshear (1998) as 'new basics', by which he means the literacies accompanying the shifts in social practices associated with late modernity (p. 358). This is very much in tune with the analyses of Giddens, Beck and Reich outlined above. These shifts require and produce more sophisticated 'abstract, symbolic-logical capacities'. These are associated with 'metalevel' capacities, often referred to as 'higher order skills', such as problem-solving or 'critical thinking' (pp. 358–9). These are the capacities put concretely to work in the 'new' workplaces of post-industrial capitalism, with their requirements for teamwork, communication skills and self-direction (p. 359). As we have noted, in these environments flexibility involves a constitution of the self as a lifelong learner, a reflexive and flexible self, committed to a constant cycle of 'continual improvement'. Distributed learning arrangements, such as forms of work-based learning where work itself becomes the curriculum (Solomon 1999), require the capacities of reflexivity, problem-solving and critical thinking. To some extent, they become formalised through the reading and writing required both to systematise and demonstrate learning and to achieve employment-related work outcomes. These literacies are hybrid, emerging forms of textual practice, invoking new relationships among participants – academics, workplace supervisors, fellow workers – new forms of addressivity and new selves, constituted through the textual-curricular practices of the representations of work, workplaces and the problems being addressed. New pedagogical relationships have to be negotiated across organisational boundaries, calling for different and reflexive practices of representation.

Globalisation has motivated and escalated the third and fourth characterisations of literacy discussed by Lankshear. The 'elite literacies', specified as 'higher order scientific, technological and symbolic literacies, imply advanced control over disciplinary knowledges, understood in terms of their "literatures" or "languages"' (Lankshear 1998: 360). These are, in contemporary policy terms, the literacies required for 'high-impact' innovation within de-regulated globally competitive economies. The fourth characteristic, foreign language literacy, similarly and increasingly involves proficiency in global dealings in policy terms.

This typology is useful, but seems to mix a hierarchical understanding – basics, new basics, elite – with a specific area of proficiency in literacy. Admittedly, this may reflect the characterisations of literacy in policy texts, but we believe it needs a more consistent analytical framework for their significance to be fully appreciated. Once again, we feel the notion of flexible literacies opens up a useful interpretive space, even if it has yet to be empirically grounded. In the context of the forms of flexibility discussed earlier, different inequalities are inscribed through these, positioning some as multi-literate and engaging in elite literacies, while peripheralising others as yet to obtain the basics. Literacy practices are therefore themselves always distributed unequally. Flexibility, however, produces and requires differentiated forms of literacy, even as elite literacies are formulated as a norm within policy. Distributed learning also distributes literacy practices in flexible and uneven ways.

Conclusion

In conclusion, it is perhaps necessary to consider some questions of the implicit teleology within narratives of flexibility – the view that flexibility is an inherently worthwhile end to be achieved. In many discourses, flexibility is assumed to have a positive value; it is difficult to oppose it. Flexibility enters into a binary relation with its other – inflexibility – where the former is viewed as positive, while the latter is assigned a negative value. This conceals some of the workings of power, wherein flexibility becomes a 'norm' whereby we may come to judge those who are inflexible as deficient. Flexibility as an idea, however, might be thought of as being ambivalent and containing multiple meanings. Like 'quality' (and literacy too), the term may encompass many meanings and be located and indeed colonise many discourses. Notions of 'flexible workers' and the risks of a 'flexilife' for the casualised and underemployed are examples of how to deconstruct what may be at stake here with specific regard to a notion of flexible literacies. When the terms 'flexible' and 'literacy' are brought together, the ideas generated tend to assert themselves as an unproblematic good, and we need to ask ourselves 'what is this concealing'? We need to think about the power relations that may be reconfigured in the literacy practices within flexible and distributed learning; for instance, the exchanges among the learners, and between the university and the workplace in work-based learning. We believe that the notion of flexible literacies provides a space in which to think through such issues, but also it provides a space to bring together a wider group of educational practitioners and researchers.

References

Alheit, P. (1999) On a contradictory way to a learning society: a critical approach, *Studies in the Education of Adults*, 31(1): 66–82.

Barton, D., Hamilton, M. and Ivanic, R. (eds) (2000) *Situated Literacies: Reading and Writing in Context*. London: Routledge.

Beck, U. (1992) *Risk Society: Towards a New Modernity*. London: Sage.

Bruce, B.C. (1997) Literacy technologies? What stance should we take?, *Journal of Literacy Research*, 29(2) 289–309.

Coffield, F. (1999) Breaking the consensus: lifelong learning as social control, *British Educational Research Journal*, 25(4): 479–99.

Department of Employment, Education and Training (1991) *Australia's Language: The Australian Language and Literacy Policy*. Canberra: AGPS.

Edwards, R. (1997) *Changing Places? Flexibility, Lifelong Learning and a Learning Society*. London: Routledge.

Edwards, R. and Usher, R. (1997) Final frontiers? Globalisation, pedagogy and (dis) location, *Curriculum Studies*, 5(3): 253–67.

Gee, J.P., Hull, G. and Lankshear, C. (1996) *The New Work Order: Behind the Language of the New Capitalism*. Sydney: Allen & Unwin.

Gibbons, M., Limoges, C., Nowotny, H., Schwartzman, S., Scott, P. and Trow, M. (1994) *The Production of Knowledge: The Dynamic of Science and Research in Contemporary Societies*. London: Sage.

Giddens, A. (1990) *The Consequences of Modernity*. Cambridge: Polity Press.

Giddens, A. (1991) *Modernity and Self-identity: Self and Society in the Late Modern Age*. Cambridge: Polity Press.

Green, B. (1999) The new literacy challenge?, *Literacy Learning: Secondary Thoughts*, 7(1) 36–45.

Harvey, D. (1991) *The Condition of Postmodernity*. Oxford: Blackwell.

Jansen, T. and Van Der Veen, R. (1992) Reflexive modernity, self-reflexive biographies: adult education in the light of the risk society, *International Journal of Lifelong Education*, 11(4): 275–86.

Kirkpatrick, D. (1997) Becoming flexible: contested territory, *Studies in Continuing Education*, 19(2): 158–68.

Kolb, D. (1984) *Experiential Learning: Turning Experience into Learning*. Englewood Cliffs, NJ: Prentice-Hall.

Lankshear, C. (1998) Meanings of literacy in contemporary educational reform proposals, *Educational Theory*, 48(3): 351–72.

Lankshear, C., Peters, M. and Knobel, M. (1996) Critical pedagogy and cyberspace, in H. Giroux, C. Lankshear, P. McLaren and M. Peters (eds) *Counternarratives: Cultural Studies and Critical Pedagogies in Postmodern Times*. New York: Routledge.

Lea, M. (1998) Academic literacies and learning in higher education: constructing knowledge through texts and experience', *Studies in the Education of Adults*, 30(2): 156–71.

Lea, M. (2001) Computer conferencing and assessment: new ways of writing in higher education, *Studies in Higher Education*, 26(2): 165–83.

Lea, M. and Stierer, B. (eds) (2000) *Student Writing in Higher Education: New Contexts*. Buckingham: Open University Press.

Lea, M. and Street, B. (1998) Student writing in higher education: an academic literacies approach, *Studies in Higher Education*, 23(2): 157–72.

Lee, A., Green, B. and Brennan, M. (1999) Organisational knowledge, professional practice and doctoral education: the professional doctorate at work, paper presented at the *BERA Annual Conference*, University of Sussex, September.

Lillis, T. (1997) New voices in academia? The regulative nature of academic writing conventions, *Language and Education*, 11(3): 182–99.

Nespor, J. (1994) *Knowledge in Motion: Space, Time and Curriculum in Undergraduate Physics and Management*. London: Falmer Press.

New London Group (1995) *A Pedagogy of Multiliteracies: Designing Social Futures*, NLLIA Occasional Paper No. 1. Sydney: New London Group.

Nicoll, K. (1997) Flexible learning – unsettling practices, *Studies in Continuing Education*, 19(2): 100–11.

Nicoll, K. (1999) The moving intellectual: globalisation and the flexible academic, paper presented to the *AARE/NZARE Conference*, Melbourne, December.

Nicoll, K. and Edwards, R. (1997) Open learning and the demise of discipline?, *Open Learning*, 12(3): 14–24.

Reich, R. (1993) *The Work of Nations*. London: Simon & Schuster.

Rose, N. (1996) *Inventing Ourselves*. Oxford: Blackwell.

Schon, D. (1983) *The Reflective Practitioner: How Professionals Think in Action*. London: Temple Smith.

Schon, D. (1987) *Educating the Professional Practitioner: Towards a New Design for Teaching and Learning in the Professions*. San Francisco, CA: Jossey-Bass.

Solomon, N. (1999) New partnerships, new knowledges, paper presented at the *British Educational Research Association Annual Conference*, University of Sussex, Brighton, September.

Street, B. (1984) *Literacy in Theory and Practice*. Cambridge: Cambridge University Press.

Street, B. (1996) Multiple literacies and multi-literacies, keynote address to *Domains of Literacy Conference*, Institute of Education, London, September.

Thorpe, M. (2000) New technology and lifelong learning, in *Support Lifelong Learning: A Global Internet Colloquium*. Online at: http://www.open.ac.uk/lifelonglearning.

Usher, R. (1993) Re-examining the place of disciplines in adult education, *Studies in Continuing Education*, 15(1): 15–25.

Usher, R. (2000) Flexible learning, postmodernity and the contemporary workplace, in V. Jakupec and J. Garrick (eds) *Flexible Learning, Human Resource and Oganisational Development: Putting Theory to Work*. London: Routledge.

Waters, M. (1995) *Globalisation*. London: Routledge.

Index